With My Bes
Margaret Sher
July, 1996

The Way of My World

An East Anglian Autobiography

Margaret Sherry Podgorska

Courtworth Publications
Colchester

Other Books by the Same Author

The Golden Garland
(A Venetian Romance)

A Timeless Fascination
(A Bicentenary Study of Byron)

Published by
Courtworth Publications
31 Maldon Road,
Colchester, Essex CO3 3AQ

Typeset and Printed by Technique,
Colchester, Essex CO1 1HP

ISBN 0 9512960 1 9

Front cover picture. Taken in the garden at St. Margarets 1951.

The Way of My World

AN EAST ANGLIAN AUTOBIOGRAPHY

Introductory Note

Part One of this book, covering the years 1922 – 1970 and bearing the same title as the present volume, was first published in 1971 and became a regional best-seller.

Now it appears again here in omnibus form with Part Two which covers the years 1971 – 1995 and is being published for the first time. In the preparation of this much-extended autobiography some additions have been made to Part One, but no alterations from present to past tense of certain passages relevant at the time the book was written.

Contents

Book One 1922 – 1970

Book Two 1971 – 1995

The Way of My World

Book One

1922 – 1970

To My Son with Love

Alas, that Spring should vanish with the Rose!
That Youth's sweet-scented manuscript should close!

FROM THE RUBAYYAT OF OMAR KHAYYAM

Give us Courage and Gaiety and the Quiet Mind.

R.L.S.

I shall go, I shall go on, from the zone I know I shall go.
I shall go to China and beyond China, further on I shall go.
I shall go and from the Hadjis of the journey ask to know –
'Is this the end of the road or is there further to go?'

FROM THE PERSIAN

CHAPTER ONE

A DOUGHTY BREED

I HAVE ALWAYS counted myself lucky being born an East Anglian. My deep attachment to this part of England stems not only from ties of blood but also from a gladly consenting bondage of the spirit. When I stand beside a ripening upland cornfield overlooking Kersey or stroll across the water meadows at Flatford in high summer or walk the ancient cobbles of Thaxted and Saffron Walden in the shadow of soaring spires, I know the truth of this.

I have travelled widely and seen some of the most beautiful and glamorous places on earth, but in my mind's eye my ideal home has always been a cottage with a living Constable landscape somewhere along the Essex-Suffolk border. Many of the best things that have happened in my life had their beginnings in East Anglia, and many of the people who have influenced me most have been East Anglians.

My birthplace was Colchester where two generations of my mother's family had already made their notable mark. Henry Nunn, my maternal great-grandfather, was the most talented and dynamic of three remarkably versatile brothers who owned the Theatre Royal, Colchester, between 1878 and 1889. During those eleven years they raised the standard of theatre-going in the town to a quality it had never known before and some of the greatest names* of the day brought their genius to a stage which had previously seen few things better than seedy melodrama. Shakespeare, pantomime and the D'Oyly Carte Opera Company came regularly to Colchester during the Nunn Brothers' administration and gained them an immortal place in East Anglian theatre history. My great-grandfather threw himself whole-heartedly into the venture, painting scenery, devising ingenious stage effects, writing librettos and appearing in costume himself.

A prodigiously sociable, generous and restless man, he entertained lavishly and, for that reason, installed his wife Eliza and numerous children in a succession of impressive-looking houses in various parts of Colchester. Abbeygate House, which overlooks St. John's Green, was the scene of his most spectacular parties.

Unfortunately the brothers' zest for living was not matched by any business acumen. Elaborate improvements to the theatre, too many free tickets and their taste for high living all took their toll. By 1889 they had run through a fortune and had to sell out. Eliza, a tiny rosy-cheeked country girl from Copford who in her old age ruled over the family as a lace-capped matriarch, regarded the Theatre Royal ever afterwards as a symbol of ruin and rejoiced when she watched it being

* My great-aunt Daisy, now in her ninety-first year, remembers sitting on Ellen Terry's lap.

burnt to the ground many years later. Henry, however, was much more philosophical about the whole affair and one suspects that, although the enterprise ended disastrously, it had brought him much artistic fulfilment. He had a military tailoring business to return to and lived to be 85. Photographs of him in old age show a still-handsome face surmounted by a jaunty velvet smoking cap. A touch of the laughing-eyed dandy and cavalier still lingered about him even then and it is easy to see why he had once moved so congenially in the company of actors. I clearly inherited my own passion for the theatre from him and probably my unquenchably cheerful disposition as well.

All Henry's sons were men of charm and ability in their various ways and one at least – my grandfather Arthur – also possessed to a marked degree the shrewd business sense his father so conspicuously lacked. In the early 1900's he established a highly successful chemist's and optician's business at 57 Crouch Street, Colchester.

My grandfather was a man of remarkably wide interests: a well-known lecturer, a strict but inspiring teacher, author of an admirable book on botany, an artist of above-average ability, a chorister, a keen carpenter and a breeder of budgerigars, as well as being outstanding in his chosen profession. His kind, clever face with white moustache and thick white hair made him an ideal Father Christmas at children's parties.

Above all, however, he was a dedicated town councillor who stood out fearlessly against any issue he did not approve of even when it made him unpopular with his fellow Tories. I shall never forget the tremendous rejoicing in our family circle when he came top of the poll in the Colchester elections of 1933. Unquestionably it was one of the proudest moments of his life when he stood on the Town Hall balcony acknowledging the cheers of the crowd, and his joy was in no way lessened by the sharp reprimand he got from a Tory colleague for chatting cordially to his Labour opponent and old friend Commander Digby.

Fanny Maria*, my grandmother, was a dark, stately, handsome woman very elegant in her amber necklaces, lace bodices and buckled shoes. In her youth she was known as *The Rose of Colchester* on account of her striking good looks and superb taste in dress. She used to tell me wonderful stories about a haunted house and was also very fond of quoting the famous lines in Byron's *Childe Harold* about the ball held in Brussels on the eve of Waterloo. 'There was a sound of revelry by night . . .'

Their elder daughter Effie Lilian was my mother. A vivacious brunette with fine eyes and a very sweet speaking voice, she inherited her father's interest in chemistry and became a dispenser. Her first meeting with my father took place in decidedly unromantic surround-

* Fanny Maria was very proud of her family connections with the Cheveleys who lived at Mashbury Hall near Chelmsford in the 18th and 19th centuries.

ings – the dispensary of a large London hospital – when he was on 'demob' leave. She had in fact taken over his job there during World War I.

No wonder she fell in love, for photographs of him in cavalry officer's uniform confirm how dashing and handsome he was at that time. He wined and dined her and squired her to theatres and they were married in October 1921. I was born in October the following year at the nursing home run by Nurse Horwood in Winnock Road, Colchester.

There was always a great bond of affection between my father and maternal grandfather, and they went into very happy partnership in 1925 as Nunn & Sherry. Christened Archie Reginald Paisley Sherry, but always known to my mother's family as 'Reg', my father was a small, neatly made man who had been *victor ludorum* of his school in Devonshire and could still vault a five-bar gate easily when he was forty. Remarkably agile well into middle age, he taught me many acrobatic tricks.

A gentle-natured man with a gift for getting along with all sorts of people, he excelled at his profession and customers had great faith in his prescriptions. From his own original recipes he made **a** much-sought-after hand lotion and a magically effective eczema balm. Nunn & Sherry's counted all the leading citizens of Colchester and most of the gentry from the surrounding countryside among their clientele.

My father was also clever with his hands and once made me a marvellous gold balalaika for a Russian song and dance I did in garrison theatre shows when I was in the A.T.S. during World War II.

I was also greatly attached to my mother's younger sister, my Aunt Audrey, who was the kind of aunt any youngster would feel lucky to have. In the early 1930's she was a typical modish bachelor girl of the period with her bangles, earphone hairdo, kimono dressing gowns and silk lounging pyjamas. Convinced from childhood that she was an ugly duckling, she was nevertheless proud of her very pretty legs and had a spirited, fascinating way with her. She was brainy enough to qualify as a doctor to please my grandfather who had set his heart on one of his children entering the medical profession. But it was a calling to which she was utterly unsuited by temperament. Animals and art were her true interests. She taught me to swim and play tennis and dance to music from *Hit The Deck* and *No, No Nanette.*

In 1933 Auntie Audrey married Arthur Churchyard, a young optician from Hadleigh. A direct descendant of the artist Thomas Churchyard, he was extremely proud of the connection. My uncle bore a striking facial resemblance to Thomas. 'Churchie', as he was always known to the family, had the look and manner of a benevolent country squire, a robust Rabelaisian sense of humour and a hearty laugh. He painted as a hobby – though not particularly well – and was inordinately proud of a head and shoulders portrait in oils which he had done of his father. It hung on the wall of the dining room at their home in Surrey and although my Aunt heartily disliked it, *Churchie* refused to take it down. So they came to an unusual compromise. When my uncle was absent Auntie Audrey would cover the portrait with a large yellow duster and when 'Churchie' came into the room at meal-times he would whip aside the offending cloth before sitting down at table. I remember being secretly amused by this regular procedure when I went to stay with them. It is a pity more newly married couples cannot solve minor disagreements in an equally simple way. 'Churchie' adored Auntie Audrey and admirably filled for me the role of jovial, generous uncle which I would otherwise have been denied as my father's two brothers lived far away in Devonshire.

I seldom saw my paternal grandparents down in the West Country though I spent several memorable childhood holidays with them at their splendid Georgian house, *Rosemount*, in Topsham Road, Exeter. Good-looking, eccentric and well-to-do, they were by nature very different from my Colchester grandparents. Money meant a great deal to them, culture very little. Of their four children three sons and a daughter – my father was the only one who really made much of his life distinguishing himself alike at school, in the Army, and in his profession.

My earliest memory of *Rosemount* is the sweet, full-bodied smell of ripening apples. As I lay at night in a huge mahogany bed with acorns carved on its posts, the delicious smell of fruit wafted down to me from the top floor where they were stored. I particularly remember two items in my bedroom: a wardrobe containing Grandma Sherry's old but much-prized sealskin coat, and tall, willow-patterned vases filled with fancy grasses.

This room opened immediately on to a dark twisting staircase leading down to a stone-flagged hall. Dominating the hall, and reflecting both my grandparents' strong political beliefs, was a painting of Disraeli looking extremely pale and wan. To the left of the corridor was the breakfast room, crammed with what would now be regarded as choice Victoriana and cast into perpetual gloom by heavy draperies across the windows. There was a piano with candlesticks fixed to the silk-embellished fretwork front. When one lifted the lid with the idea of coaxing a tune from stiff, discoloured keys, one found them covered many layers deep with family papers dating back 50 years or more. The whole house had about it rather the air of the cobweb-festooned residence of Miss Havisham in *Great Expectations – though not* for the same reasons.

My grandmother Caroline (or 'Carrie' as she was known to the family) outlived her husband by 23 years and died at the great age of 96. She was an astonishing woman in several ways. The daughter of a Scottish engineer who had travelled to Russia and back, she had been married as a ready-tongued pertly-pretty eighteen-year old to William, a curly headed young rebel who was regarded as the handsomest man in the district. All her life she remained a petite quicksilver bundle of garrulous vitality, and all her life she cared much more about her flowers, vegetables and hens than about housework. She would never employ a maid on account of the money hidden about the house.

'Carrie' certainly had green fingers and, as a result of regular waterings with the contents of a chamber pot, her raspberries flourished exceedingly. These, when in season, she served as dessert with generous dollops of Devonshire cream which my father and I thought delicious. But my poor mother stopped in horror, all relish gone, with her first spoonful halfway to her mouth when grandma casually mentioned the chamber-pot treatment.

In one respect 'Carrie' was a tremendous snob. She would not visit anyone who did not live in a double-fronted house. She also had an uncommonly original taste in clothes. Many were the blouses she ran up from sugar bags and dyed a startling heliotrope. I once saw her go for a drive in the great olive-green family car wearing her youngest son's tweed cap stitched round with lace. Still being a dashing looker even at 70 she could get away with it! Another of her pet economies was using fruit wrappers as toilet paper.

But there was absolutely no need for such penny-pinching habits for in addition to having a flourishing business, my grandfather owned considerable property and also a very pretty ship called *The Foam Queen*.

One of my Devonshire grandparents' greatest delights was having meals in the open air at some point commanding a magnificent view (an enjoyment I have abundantly inherited from them). They had brought the preparation of picnics to a fine art and I shared several feasts with them on the moors or by the sea. Every Christmas my grandfather sent an exciting hamper to our home at Colchester. I shall always remember what fun it was delving into the straw-filled tea chest to pull out gifts of all descriptions.

So East Anglian, Devonian and Celtic blood mingled in my veins and bequeathed to me tremendous vitality, a spirit of adventure and a deep love of nature.

But my childhood memories are coloured most by recollections of my Colchester relations on the Nunn side. In the 1920's and 1930's an unpretentious house known as 8, Lion Walk stood in a quiet cul-de-sac in the shadow of the soaring church spire. Now part of Boots large store covers the spot where it stood.

No. 8 was the home of my great-aunts Daisy and Eva and it was a cosy haven of Victorian-flavoured hospitality. The large table in the small dining room seemed to be permanently spread with a crisp, freshly-laundered cloth and laden with delicious home-made fare. When the black kettle rattled its lid on the fireside hob at teatime currant scones and carraway seed cake would be brought in, followed by coconut pyramids and cherry-topped madeleines.

A bottle of sherry was always at hand in the sideboard cupboard. By the window was a horsehair sofa and on a bamboo side table stood an elaborate grotto scene fashioned entirely from shells.

Auntie Daisy was one of the best-loved landladies in Colchester because of her cheerful personality and excellent cooking. Eva worked in the haberdashery department at Percy King's in Crouch Street. She was a small brisk figure in neat nigger brown with very bright eyes and an eager-to-please manner. When I knew Auntie Daisy she was middle-aged, but still retained her sense of fun, gentle sunny presence and the sweet, slightly lisping voice that was characteristic of so many Nunn girls.

Three of the Nunn brothers who lived locally used to call in regularly at No. 8. Jack, a dynamic reporter on the *Essex Telegraph*, would arrive on the threshold flashing a merry greeting with his one good eye. He was a close friend of Harold Watkin, Headmaster of the Boys' High School. They often took part in musical soirées together and founded a group of Glee Singers who were noted for their robust rendering of *Billy Boy* and *Trumpeter, what are you sounding now.*

Reg, of the lean Latin looks and nimble dancer's feet, worked at a men's outfitters on Queen Street corner and played the organ at Rowhedge Church on Sundays. Like all the Nunn boys he was a popular entertainer and was also regarded as the best waltzer in town.

Arthur, my grandfather, used to drop in at Lion Walk on his way home from the Council Chamber – sometimes to cool off after a fiery debate, He would always give Daisy some money before leaving, because he was by far the most affluent member of the family and cared deeply about his sisters' welfare.

Another frequent visitor at No. 8 was my great-aunt Ellen. One of the eldest of the family of sixteen, she had been born while my debonair theatre-manager great-grandfather Henry was prosperous, and received an excellent education. This had enabled her to become governess to the children of a high-ranking official in the Bank of England.

With her distinguished looks, genteel manners and aristocratic voice, Auntie Ellen had moved with ease in well-to-do circles and won the heart of Oscar Lay, son and heir of a rich local family. It is good to know they enjoyed some halcyon summer days together aboard his yacht at Mersea during their brief engagement. But Oscar's domineering mother strongly disapproved of the match and adroitly steered her son into the arms of another girl. I remember being told by my mother on more than one occasion that Auntie Ellen always chose the best cake on the plate because she had been crossed in love. In fact this was a sad little "aside" whispered by several members of the family.

Being situated in the heart of town No. 8 was a frequent rendezvous for me as a child. I remember lunching there on Auntie Daisy's succulent steak and kidney pie and bread-and-butter pudding.

It was in the parlour there that I first unwrapped my favourite party dress having just collected it from the dressmaker in Pelham's Lane. She was a chic, voluble French woman named Madame Rogers and the dress was pink chiffon with delicately plaited pale green trimming. It was a nice change from the fawn button-up gaiters and deep-crowned velour hats (both purchased from Polley's in Crouch Street) which figured among the more practical items in my wardrobe at that time.

One Christmas Eve, Auntie Daisy treated me to a new celluloid Cross for my school Bible. These gilded, floral-patterned bookmarks were much prized by the girls in my class. Then she bought some sugar lanterns with net lattice-work at a market stall in the High Street before taking me back to Lion Walk for my first-ever taste of Yuletide wine. I remember sitting entranced while she sang ballads with which her long-dead sweetheart Tom had once serenaded her, and she gave me one of the paper lace Valentines he had sent her. It was at No. 8, Lion Walk from this gracious little lady that I received my earliest and best lessons about hospitality and contentment.

CHAPTER TWO

PAVING STONES OF CHILDHOOD

COLCHESTER DURING THE 1930'S was a delightful town in which to grow up. Company shops had not yet gained a stranglehold on commerce and private enterprise flourished. There was about the whole town a colour and vitality which seems sadly lacking today and there were far more picturesque characters to be seen in the streets.

I have particularly affectionate memories of several shops in the West End of Colchester during this period. Three were in Maldon Road. Mr. Bays, a gentle-voiced, military-looking man, kept a sweet shop there. His halfpenny bags of assorted confectionery oddments were a tremendously popular sales line among youngsters. Nearby was Mr. Weaver the greengrocer, as round, rosy and agreeable as the excellent produce he sold. And up by Crouch Street corner was Ernie Sheppard, a most unlikely looking fishmonger who wore pince-nez and fondled the wares on his slab so affectionately that one felt he was reluctant to part with them.

Up Balkerne Lane, a stone's-throw from St. Mary's steps, was a quaint little shop known as Parker's Stores. In the Dickensian-style window was an endearing hotch-potch of sweet cartons containing 'black jacks' (at four a penny), 'gobstoppers' and 'chews' to beguile the palates of passing schoolboys. Chocolate-powdered 'coconut shag' which cost a halfpenny a packet was another quick-selling line. Inside the shop the topsy-turvy array of domestic goods included some of the tastiest cheese in town.

Church Street South had two shops as delightful as their names. There was The Kerry Cow, a high-class dairy that also sold art pottery and rustic handicrafts, and a flower shop called *Lilac Time* with an appropriately decorated front. The highly successful partnership of Neal & Robarts, which later moved to bigger premises in the High Street, started at this time with a tiny homemade cake shop in Church Street South (now known as Church Walk). Smith & Scott's in Head Street was generally regarded as the premier fashion house in town and was certainly the most expensive.

The advent of mobile shops and supermarkets was still a long way off during the '30's, but Mr. Wyncoll, a ruddy complexioned, athletic-looking man of very pleasing personality, was employed by Oliver & Parker's, the grocers at the top of North Hill, to travel round the district on his motor-cycle and write down orders at customer's houses. In the Manor Road area Mr. Byford, the greengrocer, was a familiar figure with his horse and cart. So was Mr. Austin, a weather-beaten fisherman from Brightlingsea who was noted for his shrimps.

When Robert Digby and Beatrice Radley founded the Colchester Repertory Company in 1937, one of their earliest members was a very youthful Trevor Howard. I still remember the tremendous impact he made as Rupert Cadell in Patrick Hamilton's thriller *Rope*. Even at that early date he already showed the star quality which has since made him an international name in the cinema.

The garden of our family home at *St. Margaret's,* Manor Road, Colchester, figures prominently in my happiest memories of childhood. It had originally been the garden of No. 55 Crouch Street, a splendid Georgian-fronted house owned by my grandfather, and was very romantic and old-world looking with its mossy sundial, greenhouses and singularly pretty summerhouse. The erection of our house in the late 1920's did little to impair its charms. Our rear windows looked across a rose-fringed lawn to the back of the gracious old mansion which dated back to Jacobean times.

At the bottom of our garden an age-worn wrought iron gateway led down a flight of steps to the flagstoned courtyard behind No. 55. Just within our territory at one side of the gateway was a fine hawthorn tree in the shade of which I scribbled my first stories and dreamed of becoming a writer when I grew up. A swing was set up by a lilac tree. At the foot of a strangely lopsided holly tree (which nevertheless bore a wonderful crop of berries every Christmas) a shallow pond was introduced.

In the summer a gaudily painted hammock was slung between the lilac and holly trees and surprisingly comfortable it was. But what I remember most about our garden is the abundance of roses and lavender and the spacious lawn where we played croquet and badminton.

We were delighted to learn that John Constable had once sketched in our garden. When we saw his study of the tower of *St. Mary's-at-the-Wall* we could actually pinpoint the spot where he must have sat at his easel.

At 11 I was a thorough tomboy and my hero was Buck Jones. At the *Hippodrome* on Saturdays (sucking a 'snowfrute' to cool my blood) I watched gallant Buck and his horse 'Silver' gallop through heart-pounding adventures in the Wild West. Then I would go home and re-enact them myself. The pond became Great Bear Lake, the summerhouse a ranch, and I learnt to shin up the holly tree on its unprickled side to look out for approaching Indians. Wooden crates from my grandfather's warehouse provided me with the material to build a whole cowboy shanty town at the bottom of the garden. My two constant companions in these joyful pursuits were Nigel Le Ball, who lived next door, and Terry Critchley from the greengrocer's further up Crouch Street.

In July 1931 my twin brothers John and Peter were born. I felt no pangs of jealousy at all, but rejoiced wholeheartedly at the news. Great-grandma Eliza Nunn had had twins and so had my grandmother Fanny Maria, so there was no particular surprise when my mother repeated the pattern. Our family was now happily complete.

My mother filled *St. Margaret's* with books on art, music and literature which greatly influenced my tastes as I grew up. I inherited her enthusiasm for foreign languages, travel and the theatre. She was an ardent upholder of all traditional occasions – even the lesser ones. On St. Valentine's Day I would receive a lace-trimmed card suitably inscribed in heavily disguised writing. She always made chocolate fudge cake for family birthdays and our customary Sunday tea was scrambled egg on toast followed by cream-filled jam sponge.

Our garden was connected with the rear of Nunn & Sherry's Pharmacy by a green gate, and I often went over to the shop. Remedies of some antiquity were stocked in the dispensary including – I vividly recall – a jar of leeches. Being masters of their profession my father and grandfather always had apprentices training at the shop, and the young men who passed through their hands invariably did well.

I remember being present when Carl Bebb, a brash, good looking extrovert from Clacton, was caught playing his ukulele to the other lads in the dispensary. Although my grandfather was a strict teacher he also had a keen sense of humour and he told the blushing apprentice to complete his performance while he listened with the rest of the audience. To Bebb's credit he finished his act with considerable *élan*.

I started my education in September, 1927, at the New Church School in Maldon Road. It was an admirable little school where educational foundations for five to eight year olds were exceptionally strong. My teacher there was Muriel Gill, daughter of the pioneer photographer William Gill. She was a tall, auburn-haired woman whose somewhat austere appearance completely belied her warmth, humour and enthusiasm. The pastor at that time was Victor Gladish, a gentle and shy American with a large family. The school took pupils of all religious persuasions (I was Church of England).

From 1930 to 1939 I was at the Colchester County High School where the Headmistress was Ruth King a dark, handsome eagle of a woman. History was always one of my favourite subjects, thanks largely to the fascinating way it was taught by Miss Shillitoe. Pert, petite and plump, with golden hair plaited in a halo, she reminded me of a pocket-sized Saxon princess. She had a seductive wiggle when she walked and several masters at the boys' Grammar School were very keen on her. Miss Shillitoe had a way of bringing history vividly to life and delighted her pupils by recounting various royal scandals in colourful detail.

Our Music mistress Margaret Gordon organised regular Wednesday afternoon concerts in the school hall. Because she had prestigious links with the musical world we were treated to visits from great names like Sir Richard Terry, of sea shanty fame, Sir Walford Davies and Stuart Robertson, a handsome baritone, who was Anna Neagle's brother.

My interest in writing first became apparent in the summer of 1931, when I was eight. All the girls in my form had to write stories on the set subject of *The Fairy Who Lives in Greyfriars Garden.* Greyfriars on East Hill was at that time the preparatory department of the C.C.H.S., and the singularly beautiful garden certainly lent itself to flights of fancy. I spun a bit of whimsy about an Autumn fairy, hollow trees and birch bark petticoats, won the prize and saw myself in print for the very first time.

After that I had regular successes in the school magazine and received encouragement from my English mistresses – especially Mary Mark, whose memory I revere. Looking back now I realise that the embryo journalist in me started observing and making mental notes for future use at a very early age.

When I was about 14 I started compiling a museum in my bedroom. The first exhibits were fragments of Roman pottery gathered in our garden. At any time, but particularly after rain, it was possible to look round our flower beds and find pieces of pottery lying on the surface soil. They spanned all periods of the Roman occupation and many bore interesting patterns.

I took the pottery to the Holly Trees Museum where it was dated for me by Eric Rudsdale. He was an immensely charming and enthusiastic character, tousle-haired and Shelleyesque in appearance, and an authority on the Civil War period in Colchester. He encouraged me in my museum project and dated many subsequent items for me. In the process he inevitably became one of my schoolgirl crushes.

The contents of my museum increased rapidly. My grandmother gave me an 18th century shopping journal written by a well-to-do housewife in Sudbury, together with a christening gown, sewing basket and fan from the same family. Coins, jewellery, snuff boxes and samplers were given me by other relations and friends. Our family G.P., Dr. Penry Rowland, whose surgery in Wellesley Road was filled with curios, gave me a collection of lace bobbins.

I bought many other items of genuine interest for a few pence each at an antique shop in Queen Street which was selling up all its stock prior to closing down. My purchases included a carved ebony locket, Georgian patch box and buckles, Regency scent bottle, filigree chatelaines and a punch ladle.

I must confess that now and then my judgment went a little awry – as when I bought a stuffed wild boar's head for 2s. 6d. at Partner's in Eld Lane. I had it delivered and I shall never forget my mother's face when she answered the door and had it thrust into her arms. But it found a place in my collection, and having such a grotesque room-mate never caused me any sleepless nights.

Of equal significance in my life during the years when I was assembling this museum was great literary activity. I fell ardently under the combined heady influences of Charlotte Brontiê and Lord Byron, and inevitably this brought flowing from my adolescent pen a stream of lurid stories about blighted, brooding heroes in storm-swept Gothic mansions, and also several exercise books of unmentionably bad poetry (called *Moments of Inspiration*, Vols. I, II and III).

In the case of Byron, what started as a teenage infatuation triggered off in the first instance by reading *Mazeppa* for school homework, was destined to become an enthusiastic life-long study of the man and his work. Later I was to accumulate a valuable collection of Byroniana and make a memorable pilgrimage to Missologhi in Western Greece where the poet died. As I grew up my passion for Byron was tempered somewhat by contemporary heroes and a career I adored, but when I was 16 and the Byron fever was at its height, my remarkably tolerant mother had to endure my life-size murals of the noble bard drawn in coloured chalks on my bedroom wall, and my rather Heath Robinson-like efforts to transform my common-or-garden white-painted bedstead into a canopied four-poster resembling the one I had seen in Byron's bedroom at Newstead Abbey.

I well remember as a Fifth Former going along to Mr. Jarmin's large second-hand shop at 103-105 Crouch Street. He reminded me of an amiable hippo but was always most civil, and I bought several excellent bargains from him. For ninepence each I obtained several well-worn but by no means dilapidated volumes of celebrated early 19th century literary reviews which (as a crest inside the front cover disclosed) had originally graced the library of a Scottish nobleman. To this day they remain in my now extensive collection of Byroniana.

Dancing also added considerable colour to my childhood scene. Between the ages of five and 12 I attended the dancing academy run by Miss Amy Harley at 14 Beverley Road, Colchester. In the 1920's and 1930's Amy Harley was one of the town's best known and most dynamic personalities. She was an Irishwoman with buck teeth and a mop of hennaed hair. Although at the time I knew her she was already well into middle age, she still had remarkably elegant legs clad in best quality silk stockings. She always wore velvet jackets and smelt of tobacco, and her fingers were darkly stained with nicotine.

Her dancing studio had the customary mirrors, practice bars and, of course, a piano at which a black-haired woman thumped away mechanically at Schubert's *Moments Musicales* and *Marche Militaire* while we marched round ('toes first' as we were constantly reminded) to limber up before bar work began. In our black practice ballet shoes, by the way, for the pink ones were reserved for public appearances.

I used to arrive with a capacious velvet bag containing ballet shoes, bronze leather pumps with rosettes, black patent leather ankle strap tap-dancing shoes and a brush and comb. Velvet was the fashion for dancing class dresses then and my favourite one was a brilliant emerald green.

Our dancing year was marked by definite seasonal events. During the Spring we gave our annual public display at the local Hippodrome or Playhouse. In the summer we performed at garden fêtes on the lawns of various stately mansions. Sometimes on Saturdays in August we would go and do dancing practice by the sea at Walton-on-the-Naze wearing the very fetching blue and white gingham costumes we used in our main acrobatic number. Every Christmas we had a grand party in the ballroom of Colchester's Red Lion Hotel, the climax being a display of some of the year's best dance numbers.

A first-rate showman, Miss Harley insisted on her dancing displays being beautifully dressed. My mother shared her enthusiasm and took immense trouble to see that all my costumes were expertly made. My dressmaker was a gaunt, sad-looking woman who wore drab grey and had a Prussian blue velvet pin cushion strapped to her wrist. She was a skilful needlewoman with much creative talent. Her room in Canterbury Road, Colchester, was heated by an antiquated paraffin stove and the floor was covered with highly polished linoleum. There were dress-hangers, aspidistras and brown paper bags everywhere. Yet somehow the place was invested with an air of glamour and glitter. My outstanding memory is being fitted there for my first ballet dress of sugar pink satin and billowing net.

After I progressed to the status of a solo dancer Miss Harley dreamed up a routine for me called *Pan and the Woodland Folk*. I do not think I bore any marked resemblance to that goat-footed gent, but her choice was influenced by my short curly hair. I wore a Grecian tunic, a garland in my hair, was barefoot and brandished a penny whistle.

First I skipped down-stage left, played upon my flute and listened. Then I repeated the business down-stage right. I was supposed to be summoning woodland creatures to come and revel with me. The remaining choreography was devoted to a dance with imaginary squirrels and elves interspersed with occasional toots on my pipe.

I think the most provocative *pas de deux* of my dancing days was when I portrayed a parlourmaid being pursued by a lecherous page boy.

During the summer months many of our lessons were held on the lawn behind Miss Harley's house. These were primarily devoted to Greek dancing in rose silk tunics and bare feet. It entailed a good deal of up-on-your-toes and leaping-in-the-air, the rule at all times being to keep your eyes skywards. Since the lawn was scattered with excavated bones and other less desirable souvenirs of Miss Harley's portly, white terrier, our unprotected feet sometimes had a hard time of it!

We made a notable contribution to a Carnival Pageant which was staged on the lower meadow in Castle Park. In one scene we appeared as roses scattering petals at the wedding of King Constantine and Queen Helena. Later we enacted oysters in very effective costumes made from silvery muslin material and edged with cockle shells gathered on West Mersea beach. On our heads we had dark green linen bandeaux cut to resemble seaweed and stitched around with more shells.

And all my years of growing up were regularly punctuated by summer holidays at Clacton where we had a family hut called *Sea Shanty*. It was situated close to a shack that sold fizzy drinks, "Sno-Frutes" and yellow-packaged sherbert that was sucked out with a liquorice "straw".

Our hut had a veranda and inside a curtain divided the main part from the cooking area where a spirit stove brewed up tea. Brisket of beef sandwiches, hard-boiled eggs and crunchy Colchester-made Priory biscuits were often on the menu.

Even now my memories of *Sea Shanty* include the mingled aroma of methylated spirit, damp towels and bathing costumes drying. Beach wear in those days was light years away from the daring designs of the 1990's. All-in-one wool bathing suits had striped tops like liquorice all-sorts. Sun tan lotions and filter cream had not yet been invented and we warded off the boiled lobster look with coconut oil.

When the tide was coming in we would go bathing, while when it was ebbing we played cricket on the moist expanse of sand, took family photos and read books under lacquered sunshades. We were often joined by Grandpa and Grandma Nunn and by Auntie Audrey and her fiancé.

And far out beyond the shimmering, tranquil sea were hazy blue horizons that seemed to symbolise our happy contentment. At regular intervals pleasure steamers passed by. Only a few years later they were to be part of the valiant fleet of *'little ships'* that sailed to the rescue at Dunkirk.

When we wanted more lively entertainment we strolled along the seafront to Clacton Pier. Here special attractions were the Blue Lagoon Ballroom and the Ocean Theatre. At the latter I attended a revue with the grown ups. Topping the bill was *Macari and His Dutch Serenaders*, a colourful accordion band. One of the melodies featured in their act, against a background of windmills and tulip-fields, was *Where a little Dutch girl met a little Dutch boy*. I remember how disillusioned I was to see the Dutch Serenaders in costume eating fish and chips outside the stage door.

More to the taste of my brothers and myself was Clown Bertram's Children's Theatre at the top of the Pier near the steamer stop. In full clown's costume and make-up he was an extremely versatile entertainer who played to packed houses. At every performance there was a talent contest for youngsters from the audience. My brother John won a prize with his rendering of *Little Sir Echo*.

There were two other special attractions at the top of the Pier . . . a stall selling waffles with maple syrup and a hen-shaped machine that made clucking noises and 'laid' a metal egg containing a tiny gift when you inserted a coin.

Set in a sheltered position in the seafront gardens, the Bandstand was a favourite with folk of all ages. Whenever I hear 'oldies' like *Red Sails in the Sunset, Life is a Song* or *I'll Never say Never Again* I am transported in memory to a deck chair in the front row. Just across the road was a charming little tearoom called *The Geisha* on account of its willow-patterned china and beaded curtains.

In the other seasons, with my parents or grandparents, I made countless Sunday motor trips all over East Anglia getting to know it well and love it profoundly.

During my final year at school there was a discussion about future careers. My headmistress, who knew about my private museum, told me I should go in for a job connected with antiques, but I had firmly decided long before this that I wanted to be a journalist. If I had taken Miss King's advice I should probably have made much more money but had much less fun.

My special friend during my last years at school was Margaret Bettles whose father was steward on Lawford Hall Estate near Brantham. At that time Margaret had a passion for John Constable that was comparable to my own for Byron and her prize possession was a teapot that had once belonged to the artist's family.

A pair of dreamy romantics, we spent many happy hours boating at Flatford or roaming through the Suffolk countryside talking art and poetry. We cruised down the River Stour together for the last time on the day before World War II was declared. For us – as for millions of others – it was the end of an era. Our schooldays has ended in July. That Autumn Margaret was to become a student at Salisbury and I was to become a cub reporter at Clacton.

CHAPTER THREE

AN EXCITING APPRENTICESHIP

IN OCTOBER 1939, a fortnight before my seventeenth birthday, I became a cub reporter on the *East Essex Gazette* at Clacton, and that frequently bombed coastal town was destined to provide me with the most exciting and eventful apprenticeship a fledgling scribe could desire.

My entry into journalism was made possible through my great uncle John (Jack) Hutley Nunn, a popular and accomplished Colchester newspaperman. He was a friend of Captain Quick, the proprietor of the Clacton paper. A keen Liberal and a man of great charm socially, Uncle Jack had a humorous, Puckish face and an excellent tenor voice. Like my grandfather and several other great-uncles Jack was for many years a chorister at St. Mary's-at the-Wall Church (where I was christened). At Christmas-time over a long period he took part in the Grammar School carol concerts at the Moot Hall, singing the role of the monarch in 'Good King Wenceslas' while a schoolboy was the page. Another of my great-uncles, Stanley Nunn, was a prominent journalist up in County Durham. So in entering the profession I was carrying on quite a strong family tradition, and I loved it from the very first day.

To mark the occasion my parents gave me a portable typewriter and an admirable book by C.E. Montague called *A Writer's Notes on his Trade.* This contained the following memorable passage about words which I have kept by me ever since and quoted many times when I have lectured on Journalism: *'Out of these illustrious atoms all the world's wit was made, all the glow and intensity of its eloquence and the sweet poignancy of songs. All things in literature are born of them. Each word lies shiningly new at the hand of every boy or girl who opens eager eyes upon life; it is as ready to enter into new melodies now as the single notes that were marshalled by Bach'.*

From the autumn of 1939 till the following summer I lodged with two aged great-aunts, the Misses Ellen and Clara Nunn, in Rosemary Road, Clacton. They were gallant old girls and it took a major crisis like Dunkirk to drive them away from the coastal town they loved.

The *Gazette* office stood at that time in Jackson Road immediately opposite the Bus Station. Its windows were well protected against splintering from bomb blast. There was a tiny wooden cabin snack bar just across the road where we bought bowls of soup when we were working late. Just around the corner in Pier Avenue was our opposition, the *Graphic,* which was run virtually single-handed by a remarkably industrious and versatile man of mild, bespectacled appearance, named Shadbolt.

When I joined the *Gazette* the Editor was a dark, handsome, saturnine Scot named Eric MacHardy. The six other reporters included Sheila Grinter, daughter of the well-known Frinton cricketer. She was a memorably charming personality who did not let the results of polio stop her from being a very energetic and capable journalist. Captain Quick's daughter Elizabeth (later Mrs. Geoffrey Hirst) wrote the Children's page and Women's Features. She was a stylish brunette with Fleet Street experience.

My very first night I was assigned to cover a variety show at the Tivoli Theatre. A fortnight after I started work the Editor told me in his dour Scottish way that he thought I would make a 'bloody good reporter'. I thrilled with pride and wrote a joyful postcard to my parents.

As time passed all the male members of the editorial staff joined up and Sheila moved to Hertfordshire. The last one to leave for active service was my fellow cub reporter Leslie Hollings – a tall, gangling, immensely likeable lad from Frinton. He gave me driving lessons so that I could collect district news in the firm's van when he left. I am afraid I was a somewhat hair-raising pupil and nearly reversed into the pond at Weeley on one occasion!

A warm friendship sprang up between Leslie and myself and when he was posted with the R.A.F. to Egypt we corresponded regularly. He sent me several generous gifts which were typical of those bought by all servicemen in the Middle East for their girl friends . . . a trinket box with inlaid mosaic, a handbag with embossed desert scenes, a mother-of-pearl bracelet with Arab horsemen on it, and a locket with a bird of paradise. In return I sent various luxuries from home which were hard to come by in foreign parts, and he told me that my letters were eagerly read not only by himself but also by many other home-sick lads.

For the first few months of the war life in Clacton continued very much as usual. Many social clubs and societies that had hastily disbanded at the outbreak of hostilities quickly reformed their ranks. Christmas festivities were held as usual in local hotels. But at 10.15 on the morning of Wednesday, 8th February 1940, the town had its first direct and terrifying taste of war. To quote from the *East Essex Gazette: 'There was a flash of light followed by a terrific explosion which rocked the whole town, shattered many windows in hotels and houses along the front, slammed doors, blew out lights on gas stoves and threw a stream of water, smoke and debris high into the air'.* Carried landwards by a strong wind at high tide, a German mine had struck against the piles under the pier, blown an enormous hole in the planking immediately outside the lifeboat house and done serious structural damage to toilets and other buildings on the pier. Walter Harding and 84-year-old Tom Fairweather were in the lifeboat house at the time of the explosion but miraculously escaped serious injury. At *the* top of the pier a coastguard was on duty on the look-out for mines, but apart from having his cap blown off he too had a lucky escape. He had heard the tap-tapping of some floating object under the pier but had thought it was flotsam.

I was sitting in the Reporters' Room of the *Gazette* at the time of the explosion and it was immediately obvious that the noise had emanated from some point just off-shore. A telephone call to the Coastguard Station in the Martello Tower along the front confirmed that a mine had hit the pier. To my intense delight I was sent out to follow up the story. It was one of the greatest thrills of my early days as a cub reporter.

Coat collar pulled well up against the strong chill wind, I passed through the unmanned ticket barrier at the deserted pier entrance and strolled briskly up towards the lifeboat house. The sea was choppy and I could hear various tapping sounds among the piles beneath my feet, but I was much too excited about covering this sensational scoop to be frightened. I located Messrs. Harding and Fairweather in the debris-littered lifeboat house and interviewed them. After that I spoke to the Scottish coastguard who had been on lookout duty. Their stories made first-rate 'copy'.

Even after this incident hoteliers remained optimistic about their prospects for the coming season, but their hopes were to be completely shattered by the tragic events of the night of Tuesday, 30th April. A Nazi minelaying bomber lost its bearings and crashed at the junction of Skelmersdale Road and Victoria Road in the heart of a well-to-do residential area. Its deadly cargo was still on board and the resulting devastation was heart-rending and widespread. Houses in Holland Road and Albert Gardens were also severely damaged and several people suffered dangerous eye injuries from splintered glass. In addition to the bomber's crew two Clactonians were killed and 160 hurt. Two little girls, Ann and Jean McLeod, had a miraculous escape when their home in Victoria Road was almost completely destroyed. Their bed was strewn with debris but they were unhurt.

By the end of May the steady exodus from Clacton had begun as old folk moved further inland and children were evacuated – many to Wales. For the people who remained behind Clacton now became very much a town at war. Daylight enemy raiders often flew in from the sea strafing the streets with machine-gun fire and aiming particularly at the gun emplacements along the front. Within sight of land there were many desperate pitched battles between fishing boats and Dornier dive-bombers. From time to time landmines were dropped indiscriminately, causing death and destruction in civilian homes. Quite a number of enemy planes crashed out in the open countryside and on several occasions I attended the burial of German airmen in some quiet village churchyard where the only people present besides myself were the officiating priest and the undertakers.

Apart from the terrible happenings on that mild Spring night in April 1940, Clacton's most serious air raid took place by the light of a full moon on 17th May 1941. Bombs fell on the shopping centre, destroying a bank, estate agents, and a cafe, and half-demolishing the clock tower which had long been a celebrated landmark. By a chance in a thousand, a nearby tobacconist shop was set on fire by a piece of white-hot shrapnel. Several fire-watchers had narrow escapes but there were no serious casualties. Next day, watched by large crowds, the stricken clock tower had to be totally pulled down for safety reasons. Its passing was later referred to by Lord Haw Haw in one of his broadcasts. I bore home as souvenirs a fragment of the porcelain clock face and a small hand.

The scars suffered in this raid proved a powerful incentive to Clactonians when the town's War Weapons Week was launched the following month. The target they had set themselves to raise was £50,000, but when the Week ended they had more than doubled this amount, the final sum being £100,225. The scenes of civic pride and rejoicing which followed this historic achievement are never likely to be forgotten.

Captain Quick, who had played a major part in Clacton's development as a flourishing holiday resort, died in the summer of 1940 and, since his son Arnold was in the Army, the responsibility for running the *Gazette* fell on the able shoulders of his daughter Elizabeth. When all the other reporters had left to join the Forces Miss Quick and I quite literally wrote the whole paper each week with the valuable assistance of numerous village correspondents. This provided me with an exciting challenge and opportunity which seldom comes the way of a teenage cub reporter, and I made the most of the experience.

After Dunkirk, when the great-aunts with whom I had lodged left town, I used to travel down to Clacton from Colchester every day. With lunch and tea packed in an ancient wicker picnic basket (a relic, I believe, of outdoor banquets on Devonshire moors), I used to catch an early morning bus to the coast. Frating, as I recall, was the official checkpoint where Police boarded the bus and only those with special permits were allowed to travel on to Clacton.

Naturally much of the news I covered was very sad . . . local boys missing or killed, the deaths of well-known Clactonians in air raids in other parts of the country – as well as the regular bombing and machine-gunning incidents in and around Clacton. It was particularly poignant to write about the weddings and the funerals of various young servicemen within a tragically brief space of time. One of the early ordeals of being a fledgling reporter was visiting bereaved homes to gather information for an obituary, and I never ceased to admire the dignity and courtesy with which people in great grief received me on these occasions.

But I wrote on many happy subjects too, and one of my outstanding memories is interviewing the nurse in whose arms Queen Victoria died. She was a remarkably vivacious old lady of 80 when I spoke to her and her room was full of letters and little gifts she had received from various members of the Royal Family. Among the most interesting were some picture postcards and home-made greetings cards sent her by the Duke of Gloucester and King George VI when they were children.

One of the most impressive-looking characters in the district was the Rev. Max Wontner, Vicar of Little Clacton, who bore a striking resemblance to Augustus John. He was a massively built, bearded man with a deep booming voice who strode along the village street acknowledging his parishioners with a hearty wave of his walking stick. He appeared to be held in awe by the villagers and was regarded by some as a bigoted tyrant. The grounds of the church served as the cemetery for all denominations, but he adamantly insisted that all Methodist coffins should enter by the side gate. A cousin of the actor Arthur Wontner, he also had artistic leanings and had published a rumbustious Ruritanian-style novel. I personally found him anything but the ogre many thought him to be.

Every Thursday morning I broke my journey down to Clacton at Elmstead to spend an hour gathering news. Our correspondent was Mr. Ernest Norfolk the baker, a burly, genial, red-faced man. If my news gathering was of brief duration he always let me wait for the next Clacton bus in the parlour of his Regency house immediately adjoining the bakery. When the time came to leave it was his regular custom to present me with a bag of cakes and a miniature loaf he had baked specially.

Living in Church Road, Elmstead, at that time was a Mrs. Rapp, wife of the British Consul in Zagreb. She and her daughters Heather and Margaret – with whom I became good friends – had had a dramatic escape from war-torn Yugoslavia.

In the autumn of 1942 my apprenticeship with the *Gazette* ended, and my call-up papers arrived soon afterwards. Elizabeth Quick gave me a marvellous reference and asked me what book I would like as a parting gift. I chose Howard K. Smith's *Last Train From Berlin,* which was a notable best-seller at the time, and she wrote in it the following: *To Margaret Sherry, In appreciation of her loyal co-operation June 1940 – October 1942. Elizabeth Quick, "East Essex Gazette", Clacton-on-Sea.* That book still has a proud place on my bookshelves.

CHAPTER FOUR

INTERLUDE IN KHAKI

LIFE IN THE A.T.S. was really not my line at all, though like everybody else I was very keen to 'do my bit' towards the war effort. At the training centre at Queen Ethelburga's School on the outskirts of Harrogate, where I spent the first few months, I found the trivial restrictions and all-female community irksome and depressing after the freedom, excitement and congenial company I had known as a journalist. At Queen Ethelburga's there were Lesbian undertones and petty power complexes that made me rush off for solitary walks in the magnificent surrounding countryside whenever I got the chance. My favourite moments of light relief occurred on drill parades when we girls were put through our paces by an extremely ferocious male sergeant-major. 'I'll chase yer round the barrack square till yer shirt's wet' he used to roar at us.

Undoubtedly my happiest interlude at Queen Ethelburga's was being asked to produce a variety show. I threw myself wholeheartedly into writing sketches and lyrics and devising song and dance numbers. I had a very co-operative and enthusiastic cast and it was a resounding success. However, when I got a posting to Norwich in the early summer I could not depart fast enough. It meant relinquishing the two stripes I had somewhat surprisingly acquired during my short sojourn in Yorkshire, but this was a trifling price to pay for returning to East Anglia, and anyway, throughout my Army career I had little interest in promotion.

In Norwich I was attached to the R.A.S.C., and the A.T.S. platoon to which I belonged was billeted in a large house in Upper Newmarket Road. My job was recording the dispatch of military equipment along the railways of East Anglia. Our favourite evening pursuit was going to dances at the Samson & Hercules Ballroom down in the city, and our frequent rendezvous for off-duty meals was the ancient Curat House. Like all the girls I got to know quite a lot of American servicemen and, contrary to general opinion, I found that many of them were decent and honourable young men who could converse intelligently on a wide variety of subjects over a pleasant evening meal. One named 'Rosie', who was a musician in civilian life, dedicated a composition to me called 'The Castle Hill Concerto', because that spot in Norwich was where we frequently met.

While I was stationed in Norwich I wrote a thriller called *Vengeance Has Wings* which was about an underground newspaper in wartime Prague. All through the war years I followed with particular interest and admiration the exploits of underground fighters in Europe, little realising what a close link I was to have with some of these gallant people twenty years later.

But perhaps the most significant thing that happened to me while in Norwich was attending Saturday morning lectures on current affairs run by the Army Education Corps. This led me to discover for the first time that I had a natural flair for public speaking – an activity which was to play an important part in my future.

In the autumn of 1943 I made the happiest move of all my national service days to A.A. Command H.Q., Stanmore, Middlesex. During that winter I was one of a hardy band of Ats living in a Nissen hut in the grounds of Hartsbourne Grange, Bushey Heath. I worked in the Camp Commandant's office at Glenthorn, a large estate adjoining Bentley Priory where so many legendary R.A.F. exploits were planned.

It was a congenial job in a rural setting close to London. The Camp Commandant was a little Major with a rasping voice and brusque manner. One of his ears had the upper half missing, the result – so it was said – of being bitten by an irate mule. He was held in awe by many on account of his acid tongue, but he was a very considerate boss to the girls who worked for him. Jimmy Kennedy, composer of many popular songs during the immediate pre-war years, was a Major on the entertainments side at the camp, and Vivian Jenkins, sporting journalist, was another familiar figure. The distinguished orchestral conductor Norman Del Mar gave regular lectures on musical appreciation.

Twice I was given temporary leave from the Camp Commandant's office to go on courses that particularly interested me. The first was a physical training course at Hendon Police College (commandeered by the Army for the duration) from which I emerged as a fully qualified P.T. instructor. The other was a Domestic Science course at Guildford Technical College where I managed to get a First Class rating even though I singed my omelette rather badly during one of the practical tests!

A Garrison Theatre Show on the stage at Hendon Police College marked my first performance of an energetic Russian song and dance number to the music of *Black Eyes*. I had devised a very dashing black and gold costume and a Cossack hat that stuck firmly on my head even when I was doing cartwheels and authentic Russian steps. My father made me a wonderfully realistic looking black and gold balalaika. I styled myself *Maggiotchka the Meteor from Murmansk*. The turn proved an enormous success and I repeated it later at a cabaret at A.A. Command H.Q.

But without any doubt at all the happiest outcome of my days at Stanmore was forming one of the greatest friendships of my life.

Jennifer Clark was Corporal in charge of No. 1 and 2 Orders and catering in the Camp Commandant's office. A very tall, good looking girl of Junoesque build, sharp intelligence and sparkling wit, Jennifer was – and is – a woman of considerable character and spirit. There was an immediate 'rapport' between us when we first met. Her father was an Irishman, an ex-Major in the Indian Army, and her mother a classically beautiful woman of surpassing charm.

I became a frequent visitor to Jennifer's home, which was only a short bus journey from Bushey. She had a rumbustious earthy brand of humour and possessed at the same time the air of an aristocrat and a hoyden, which was a singularly engaging combination. She wrote verse of real quality and later published an internationally acclaimed volume of poetry. After the war she married a Greek businessman and went to live in Athens, and during the 1950's she was to be my hostess during two memorable visits to Greece.

Whenever we meet now we still roar with laughter over a minor, but to us highly amusing episode which happened while we were at Stanmore together. Two outstanding films of the war years were *The Seventh Veil* starring James Mason, and *Jane Eyre* starring Orson Welles. They were both intensely romantic films with the sort of blighted brooding heroes both of us went overboard for at that time, and we went to see them on several occasions. Jennifer, like myself, was very short-sighted and at one showing of *The Seventh Veil* she said to me during James Mason's biggest scene, 'Mags, do lend me your specs so that I can get his dear face into focus'.

In September 1944, while I was stationed at Stanmore, my brother John, whom I adored, died at the age of 13 after an ear operation. I was granted compassionate leave when he became ill and was at his hospital bedside throughout the last night of his life. This was the first tragedy I had ever known and my grief was very deep. One accepted the passing of grandparents and elderly relations as inevitable, but the death of this gay and vital little boy whose future held such promise was absolutely shattering.

My brother John during his short life became a very well-known junior citizen in Colchester on account of his zestful personality and chirpy gaiety. In appearance he was small, dark and Italian looking. Though never robust physically he was charged with tremendous nervous energy and always had some project on hand to which he gave himself wholeheartedly. Most notable of all his projects was the highly successful form magazine *The 2A Journal* which he founded and edited at the Royal Grammar School during the year immediately before his death. All the boys in his class contributed to it with enormous enthusiasm and its readership soon embraced the entire school.

Our parents bought him a proper duplicating set and every Wednesday evening he would lay out his equipment on the flat top of the Morrison air-raid shelter in the hall of our home and get to work. His editorials were always pithy and to the point and he usually signed off with his favourite catch-phrase 'Keep your peckers up'. Copies of the Journal which are lovingly preserved to this day in our family bear testimony to how lively and entertaining the contents were. He certainly made his mark on school life and *The Colcestrian* paid a wonderfully warm and moving tribute to him in the issue of December 1944.

Always a witty and amusing companion, full of merry quips and quaint sayings, John had a wide circle of friends – among them Tom Dale who is now a leading Liberal in the Colchester district. One of his favourite cycling excursions with his pals used to be to Dedham and Flatford. *En route* they would stop at a little cafe which used to stand half-way down Dedham Gun Hill for a bottle of pop and a packet of crisps. The 'Gang' also got up to a good deal of harmless mischief at the Army gym. in Mersea Road, Colchester, and in the yard behind the Headgate Hotel.

When I returned to Stanmore after my brother's funeral Jennifer was a tremendous comfort to me and I gradually slipped back into the normal routine of Army life. We all did our stint of firewatching after dark but I do not remember any really frightening incidents. Miraculously German bombers never did any serious damage to Glenthorn or Bentley Priory. I do remember, however, the many nights when turning over drowsily in bed I was vaguely aware of the muffled sounds of sustained bombardment in the distance, and knew that London was yet again facing a murderous onslaught.

In the Spring of 1945 I had a particularly virulent attack of 'flu and was granted sick leave for quite a long period. While I was convalescing Dr. Penry Rowland, who knew I was an ardent Byron fan, sent me a copy of D'Orsay's drawing of the poet in Italy, and accompanied it with this message: *'Dear Miss Sherry, If you still have a Poet's Corner in your broadening heart make a note that Byron's own copy of Canto III of "Don Juan" and his quill pen are in Wisbech Museum where Eric Rudsdale (recently 3rd curator here) is established. I hope your vile catarrh is quieting down. Sincerely, Penry W. Rowland'.*

The prospect of seeing Eric Rudsdale again delighted me and as soon as I was fit enough I made a day's excursion to the charming Fenland town which, although I did not know it then, was to be my home for nearly two years during the 1950's. Situated in a secluded square overlooking the fine old Parish Church, Wisbech Museum had a magnificent collection of china which had been inspected and much admired by Queen Mary. Its other special pride was Byron's own copy of *Hours of Idleness* which I was thrilled to be able to handle personally. Neither of the Byron items mentioned in Dr. Rowland's note appeared to be housed there, however.

Eric Rudsdale, whom I had not seen since I was a schoolgirl, gave me a very warm welcome, and after showing me round the museum invited me to stay for tea. He lived down in the museum basement in a characteristic state of happy chaos, for he cared little about creature comforts. There were a few threadbare carpets covering otherwise bare floorboards and piles of old books everywhere. Flannel, soap and a toothbrush stood on the mantelpiece amid an incongruous miscellany of other oddments. On an ancient table spread with one of those blanket-like Victorian covers plum cake and a jar of pickles stood cheek by jowl. But we had a merry meal together and the conversation sparkled. When he saw me off at Wisbech Station he paid me some pretty compliments. We corresponded afterwards and I received a last letter from him shortly before he died in the autumn of 1951. I had recently returned from Greece and was planning to go up to Wisbech to tell him about my visits to Olympia and other classical ruins when I heard that he was fatally ill. He was only in his early forties and had made a major contribution to East Anglian historical studies. I heard later that he had quickened the heartbeats of quite a few ladies in Wisbech, but that he much preferred to disappear for several days at a time on solitary excursions into the wilds of the Fen Country.

When I got back to Stanmore the final phase of the war had begun. Buzz bombs and later V2's were now a frequent menace every day, but everyone pursued their duties and their leisure pastimes with remarkable unconcern. With Jennifer and other friends I often went up to London in the evenings to dine either at the Salad Bowl at Lyon's Corner House or at one of the many Continental cafes we knew (one called *The Troika* was our favourite). On the evening of VE Day we were among the jubilant crowds celebrating in Piccadilly.

But although the war was over demobilisation was still one year away for me. On 5th November 1945, when large numbers of A.A. Command personnel were dispersed, I was posted to Chelsea and billeted in a very imposing house in Sloane Court West. It was a part of London I had always loved, close to the King's Road and within easy reach of my favourite eating place *The Blue Cockatoo* along the Embankment. Shortly after my arrival I was made a sergeant and started doing more interesting and varied work than at any time during my national service. In the mornings I conducted P.T. sessions in a local park (I remember a workman shouting 'Up the Dynamos', an allusion to the topically popular Russian football team, as my Amazonian company went through their athletic paces!). One afternoon each week I gave talks to A.T.S. personnel at the War Office on such subjects as *The History of Dancing, How to be a Good Hostess* and *Drama Through the Ages*. The rest of my working hours were largely spent in giving cooking and domestic science lessons in the spacious basement kitchen of an extremely swish residence in Wilton Crescent, Belgravia.

One morning while preparing equipment for a cooking lesson in this splendid kitchen, I was astonished to find a pair of khaki socks airing in the oven when I opened the cooker door. Almost immediately a diminutive Irishman (who must have come from some nearby billet) appeared on the scene, confessed the socks were his and said his old mother always dried them that way. I was much too amused to be cross on grounds of hygiene and, after all, the house was WD property for the duration, so he was not really trespassing.

I had a very pleasant office in a large house at the other end of Sloane Court from my billet. This I shared with the sergeant in charge of musical instruction. We got along very well together and I found it extremely agreeable doing my paper work against a background of music played on the grand piano in the hall.

Not all my paper work was strictly business, however, and one week not long before I was demobbed I spent a considerable amount of time writing a fan letter to Orson Welles who had really set my blood racing with his portrayal of Rochester in *Jane Eyre,* and also with his own remarkable film *Citizen Kane* which was re-issued during the latter war years. I penned a fan letter to end all fan letters and in addition I composed the following *Eulogy* in which every line rhymed either with 'Orson' or 'Welles'. The influence of Byron's humorous versifying is clearly apparent and the tremendous fun I had composing it (I quoted my latest lines to eager listeners in the Sergeants' Mess at supper-time) shines through too.

Oh! the rich, heart-tickling spells
Woven by that devil Welles!
The men I know should take a course on
How to look and act like Orson.

Almost ev'ry actor smells
When compared with wild-eyed Welles.
I'd gladly my intentions force on
Such a guy as tense-faced Orson.

Just one fiery glance from Welles
My decorum quite dispels.
I'd never slam my boudoir doors on
One with a technique like Orson.

There's some gossip-scribe who tells
Us Welles is very fond of Welles.
That doesn't quell the praise I pours on
To the noble brow of Orson.

They say he is the biggest poseur
In the whole of Hollywood.
Be that wrong or be that so sir,
He just don't do me no good!

For his saturnine attraction
Makes me clear my decks for action,
And those dark disdainful brows
All my earthy instincts rouse.
As I've told you once before, son,
If you'd win me – study Orson.

P.S. I wonder how he ever came
To have such a peculiar name?
Just about as full of glamour
As a kipper or a hammer.
But then – *he'd* give immortal glow
To such a name as Percy Poe!

As an additional novelty I also enclosed a reply card with the following phrases asking him to 'cross out the ones that don't apply':

(1) Intercepted and destroyed by the Secretary-in-Chief.

(2) Received but not read. Have no time for fans.

(3) Away on location waiting for the right sky which will probably be quite some time.

(4) Received, perused, mildly amused.

(5) Received, not amused, libel action pending.

On the large envelope in which I posted the epic I painted a picture of *Mercury* in a rainbow-hued cloak standing on a cloud holding the *Torch of Drama* in his hand. The motif was *Mercury* because Welles's own first theatre venture was named after the messenger of the gods. When I posted it off to Hollywood at Chelsea Post Office the clerk behind the counter did not bat an eyelid!

I doubt if I really expected any answer – or at best perhaps a rubber stamp affair – so the great actor's response to my effusions exceeded my wildest dreams. As it happened his reply reached England after I had been 'demobbed' and the cream envelope with 'Orson Welles, Beverly Hills, California' printed in scarlet letters on the back was forwarded from Chelsea to my home address. I shall never forget my mother's excitement as she hurried upstairs to my bedroom with the letter in her hand.

It was a delightful acknowledgement from Orson Welles personally and read "This is to convey my very warmest thanks for your wonderful letter, for the provoking eulogy and the ingenious panted* son of Zeus. With all best wishes, Sincerely, ORSON WELLES." The reply card had also been duly attended to in his own handwriting. The phrase he selected was No. 4 Received, perused . . . and he had crossed out 'mildly amused' and 'inserted deeply appreciated.'

These direct links with one of the greatest film-makers of all time hang framed on my lounge wall and I prize them highly.

* I had given my Mercury a discreet cover-up.

CHAPTER FIVE

NEWS WAS MY BUSINESS

I WAS 'DEMOBBED' on 27th June 1946, and my Release Leave Certificate stated that I 'was an enthusiastic and persevering instructor, keen and cheerful with plenty of initiative'. I suppose this was proof that I had achieved something during my Army years but, nevertheless, I was more delighted than words can express to be back in Civvy Street.

After a holiday in Devonshire I joined the editorial staff of the *Bedfordshire Times* and spent three superlatively happy years there. It was widely acclaimed as one of the best weekly newspapers in Britain and I certainly count Bill (W. J.) Janes, the Editor at that period, and 'Clarrie' Carter, the Chief Sub-Editor, among the literary mentors to whom I owe most. Both men of outstanding ability in their profession, they were complete opposites in appearance and personality.

'W.J.' was a thin, sharp-featured man who seemed to be composed entirely of off-whites and clerical greys. He was the author of an admirable textbook on journalism and a brilliant leader writer with an elegant though austere style. Strictly T.T. and utterly faithful to his one and only wife, he was a perfectionist who would not allow one misplaced comma to pass his notice. I remember once in my expenses account writing 'bike' instead of 'bicycle', and when I got it back he had ringed the offending colloquialism and branded it with an outraged question mark. On the other hand he was equally swift to bestow praise where it was deserved, and more than once after I had written some special feature (the sort of work I enjoyed doing most) I found a note from 'W.J.' slipped in my typewriter saying, 'Much enjoyed your feature' on such-and-such-a-thing. 'Good work'. From a journalist of his calibre this really meant something.

'Clarrie' Carter was a large, lovable, bear-like man with a broad, rosy face, several mistresses (so it was said), an unlimited capacity for beer and a liking for bar-room ballads. He specialised in a weekly column on local history and had a rich, glowing way with words that I admired tremendously. He had, I remember, a severe impediment in his speech and I liked to think that Nature had compensated him by giving him this superb gift with the written word.

My colleagues in the reporters' room were a congenial and enthusiastic crowd presided over by Frank Knight, a dark, portly, unflappable character with a delightful Hampshire burr in his speech. The Office Social Club was a particularly lively one and we had lots of fun out of working hours. Shortly after I arrived a 'Welcome Back from the Forces' dinner and dance was held and volunteers were required to provide acts for the cabaret. In the first half I did my Russian song and dance and in the second half I did an acrobatic dance to the music of *If I had a Wishing Ring* dressed in black lace and white feathers.

My first 'digs' in Bedford were with a young couple in Harewood Road in an outlying suburb Elstow way. They had a little girl of seven and a little boy aged six months. The husband, an earthy, virile South African, was a garage mechanic who used to declare, much to my amusement, 'I have only got to hang up my trousers on the bedrail to get my wife in the family way'. Fry-ups predominated in the menu and I often dined within nose-shot of nappies being changed, but they were pleasant enough folk and I was comfortable there, well satisfied to bide my time till I could find a flat. This I succeeded in doing a few months later when I moved into a place of my own at 31 Conduit Road.

I liked Bedford as a town. The river and the gardens bordering it were beautiful. So was the market place in the shadow of the splendid church of St. Paul's. The Bridge was considered the premier hotel and the Dujon Restaurant and ballroom was the hub of social life. Culturally it was a go-ahead town too. Bedford School by St. Peter's Green was of public school status. In the late 1940's there was a live Repertory Theatre of quite high standard where Wilfrid Lawson made a guest appearance one week as the grim papa in *The Barretts of Wimpole Street.*

Robert Garrett was the leading actor-producer locally in the sphere of amateur drama and another one of note was Philip Barker who ran *The Oak Players*. An amply-built young man with a good profile, he seems to have been a somewhat complex character. On Sundays he played the big drum in the Salvation Army Band, but, according to gossip, he also lived in a *menage a trois* with wife and mistress. Both as actor and producer he certainly had an excellent sense of theatre.

My good friend Mary Clark was one of the founders of the Bedford Literary Institute which I addressed on *Byron – the Man at His Best.*

Scenically the Bedfordshire countryside was nothing special but there were several notably pretty villages like Biddenham, Sharnbrook, Pavenham and Elstow. The latter, besides its close associations with Bunyan, was noted during the 1940's for the lavish May Day Festival staged on the green every year by the children of the village school. The celebrations lovingly followed traditional lines and included the crowning of the May Queen and Maypole dancing. People came from miles around to see it. I believe the festivals were the idea of the then headmaster of Elstow School and were discontinued after he retired.

During my three years in Bedford I wrote on an astonishing variety of subjects ranging from folk dancing, the opening of the Cecil Higgins Museum and other similarly 'arty' occasions at one end of the scale to sewage disposal and brick-making at the other. I was one of a party of

Press folk taken up on a flight in a Halifax bomber from Cardington aerodrome. I attended school speech days and carol concerts, County Shows and Harvest Homes, garden fêtes and mayoral receptions, council meetings and police courts beyond counting. Perhaps the most dramatic story I ever covered was the mid-air collision of two aeroplanes which afterwards crashed in flames beside the railway line. Because Bedford was predominantly a rural area it was assignments with an historical flavour or to do with old country customs that appealed to me most.

In the course of my work I came into contact with many colourful figures. The late Jack Tanner, celebrated name in the Amalgamated Engineering Union, persistently tried to date me after we had met when I reported on a dinner and dance held by the Bedford branch of the Union at the Dujon. In the lush surroundings of the Bridge Hotel over afternoon tea I interviewed Vera Brittain when she came to Bedford to write her book *In the Steps of Bunyan*.

When Christopher Soames was prospective Parliamentary candidate for Bedford I accompanied him on a tour of the constituency which was at that time represented by a Labour M.P., Tom Skeffington-Lodge. The impression I gained of Mr. Soames at that period was of an amiable but by no means dynamic character with no great talents as a spontaneous orator, and certainly in no way indicating the ability which has distinguished his career since. I met his wife Mary Churchill too, a pretty, fresh-faced woman with considerably more presence and charm as a public speaker than her husband.

One of the most glamorous men in town (and abundantly aware of the fact) was Donald Harris, the remarkably youthful Archdeacon of Bedford. A very good-looking bachelor with a scintillating personality and immense charm, he was also an ultra-extrovert who thought nothing of standing on his head at garden fêtes. With singular skill he managed to elude the clutches of all the adoring females in his parish. I heard later that he had moved to St. James's, Piccadilly, a sophisticated and affluent parish where he must have been a great social success.

I was often assigned to do theatre, music and art critiques, and on one occasion (with what seemed outrageous presumption) it fell to my lot to review an exhibition of paintings by the distinguished veteran artist H. Sylvester Stannard. He was at that time 79 years old, the scion of a family of artists who originally had close ties with *Old Crome*. His bluebell woods and country cottages were constantly being reproduced on calendars and greeting cards. He was a small, wiry man who resembled Thomas Hardy very much in looks, and though nearly 80 he retained the same eternal vigour physically as his brushwork did on canvas. His skies and trees had much of the spirit of Constable about them which was not surprising as he idolised the Old Master's memory.

Sylvester Stannard had had several wives and no doubt a Bohemian quota of mistresses as well. At the time I met him his permanent home was at Flitwick, but as a studio and den he had a caravan parked just off the Bromham Road in Bedford. Inevitably my write-up about his paintings was warmly enthusiastic and devoted largely to describing in detail some of the pictures that appealed to me most. Anyway, what I wrote caught his fancy to such an extent that he invited me out to lunch at the Dujon and also round to tea at his caravan. Knowing that my father was a Devonian he gave me a splendid water-colour he had done of a thatched cottage in a lane near Powderham Castle. At Christmas that year he sent me a card on which with a few magic strokes of his brush, he had sketched an exquisite miniature landscape of the river and water meadows at Flitwick.

An equally delightful and memorable character was Professor A. E. Richardson, artist and architect of great international distinction, close friend of Sir Alfred Munnings, and shortly before his death President of the Royal Academy. I first met him when he opened an art exhibition in the Harpur Library at Bedford. It was 1948 and, rebelling extravagantly against the austerity of wartime, skirts were long and full and shoes all fanciful ankle straps and platform soles. In the course of his opening remarks the Professor expressed his approval of these current fashion trends saying that they reminded him of 18th century costumes in Venice. Some time later 1 went to his splendid Georgian house at Ampthill to interview him about a new memorial lectern he was designing for Westminster Abbey.

Stepping across his threshold was exactly like returning in one stride to the 18th century. This was the period he adored and his home was furnished in superb Georgian style down to the last detail. There was no electric light or television set. A telephone was permitted but only for strictly business needs in the office adjoining the house. Several very fine originals by Gainsborough and Romney adorned the walls.

The Professor often used to dress in Georgian costume to receive guests, smoked a long white clay pipe and drove out in an authentic carriage of the period. Queen Mary visited his house and was accorded a taste of this full dress 18th century pageantry. The evening I spoke to him he was wearing crumpled but expensive contemporary tweeds, yet even in modern dress there was a decided aura of Georgian England about his appearance and manner – a touch of Charles James Fox . . . warm, voluble and expansive.

I met him once more at a magnificent dinner held to mark the opening of *The Porch* at Shefford as a very exclusive period restaurant. Professor Richardson had supervised the extensive work which had been done to restore the rare Richard III house to much of its original beauty. During this work pre-Reformation paintings and texts had been uncovered on the walls of an upper room and tiny Plantagenet windows that had panes of horn instead of glass. Regarded as one of the finest surviving pieces of early 15th century architecture in Britain, *The Porch* was once a welcome landmark to travelling merchants, and to pilgrims on their way to Walsingham. Here they enjoyed the hospitality of Gilbertine monks.

Another unforgettable personality who had made his mark with rare distinction was Sir Fred Messer, M.P. for Tottenham and Chairman during the late 1940's of the North-Eastern Metropolitan Hospital Board. I met him when he opened a splendid new home for old folk at Oakington near Bedford.

Sir Fred Messer was a dwarf, so badly deformed that he could only move around with difficulty. Here was a man who might well have felt that he did not owe the world a thing. Instead, however, he had carved a fine career for himself in politics and public affairs generally, and been awarded a knighthood for his outstanding services to social welfare work. And I have never seen a merrier pair of eyes in any man.

Two members of the local nobility stand out in my memory. There was the exceedingly handsome and debonair Lord Luke of Pavenham who often presented rosettes at gymkhanas, and the Hon. Romola Russell, a kinswoman of the Duke of Bedford, who sat on many charitable committees. She was a rather austere looking but very kind elderly lady with pince-nez spectacles and dark, broad-brimmed hats closely resembling those worn by rich merchants in 17th century Dutch paintings.

A couple of memorable holidays belong to my Bedford period – one in Eire and the other in Scotland. I loved picturesque, easygoing Dublin with its green pillar-boxes and telephone kiosks, street names in Gaelic lettering and great general post office in O'Connell Street still bearing shrapnel scars from the Easter Rising of eternally bitter memory. Visits to the Abbey and Gate Theatres (where Orson Welles once played) had priority on my list of activities. I also saw a good deal of the lushly green surrounding countryside with its low, white-walled, thatched crofts, ancient burial grounds of Celtic crosses and misty, rain-washed valleys that are rich in legend. Above all there was Glendalough and Kevin's Seat, the lakeside cave home of a venerated monk-hermit long ago.

The Scottish holiday was even more to my liking as it took the form of a pilgrimage for painstaking research to the scenes of Byron's childhood in Aberdeenshire. Aberdeen – unquestionably one of Britain's most beautiful cities, has a passionately nationalistic air about it, and strongly anti-English slogans are to be seen scrawled on the pavement round the William Wallace memorial. I traced all the places in the city where Byron had lodged with his mother as an impecunious child with no idea of the rich and spectacular future which lay ahead of him, and I strolled through the woods leading to the surpassingly lovely *Brig o' Balgownie* which the Poet knew well. Later I travelled northwards to Banff, an enchanting little fishing town on the Firth of Moray, where Byron spent many holidays with his maternal great-grandmother in a house quaintly named *Little Fillacap*. Most exciting of all was my excursion in search of the remote ruins of Gight Castle, for centuries stronghold of the notoriously turbulent Gordon family of whom Byron's mother was the 13th and last Laird (her inheritance being squandered beyond recall by her reckless and dissolute husband). Some five miles from the hamlet of Fyvie in a wild and lonely setting that eminently befitted its stormy and romantic history, I found the crumbling fortress on a cliff overlooking the River Ythan. Nearby is a haunted glen containing an allegedly fathomless pool of extremely sinister repute.

I took this holiday in the summer of 1949 and that autumn I became keen to move from Bedford and get a job somewhere in the London area, though Fleet Street was *not* my goal. I left Bedford with a deep pride in my craft and plenty of self-confidence – tempered (I hope) by a lively enough sense of humour never to get insufferably cocky! On New Year's Day, 1950, I joined the *Croydon Advertiser*.

I lodged in Grange Road, Purley Hills, where my landlady was a kind, homely soul who loved reading and was philosophically resigned to the burdens set upon her by an erring and absent husband. Her rather tiresome son aged about thirty had religious texts all over the place, one of which read 'God first, self last'. The trouble was he did not place his poor old mum anywhere between and invariably put his own creature comforts before hers. Meals were brought up to my attractive blue and white bedroom which had a very pleasant view of suburban gardens and, as the rent was extremely reasonable, I was able to put a substantial sum in the bank each month.

The *Advertiser* Office stood in the heart of Croydon close to the Civic Hall and to a bustling market where one of the barrow boys was the well-known boxer Don Cockell. In my mind's eye the atmosphere of Croydon at that time was dominated by the rumble of trams, the aroma of fish and chips and roasting coffee. Beyond lay select residential areas like Sanderstead and Caterham, and beyond this again the lovely, richly wooded Surrey countryside . . . Dorking, 'Little

Switzerland', Godalming, Redhill, Reigate and Box Hill.

Working on a newspaper in metropolitan suburbia was a new experience for me and the stories I covered were, in the main, very different from those I had done as a reporter at semi-rural Bedford and Clacton. The activities of the militant Thornton Heath Chamber of Commerce, the building of the progressive and revolutionary Ashburton Secondary School with all its *de luxe* amenities, and an interview with the proprietress of a newly opened fashion modelling school were typical examples.

Unquestionably the most dynamic personality in Croydon in 1950 was the remarkably young Bishop Cuthbert Bardsley (who has since become Bishop of Coventry). A strikingly handsome man of splendid physical presence with powers of oratory to match, he caused a sensation which made front page news in the *Advertiser* when he condemned spiritualism as *stupid and dangerous.* I covered both the event at which the Bishop attacked the spiritualists and the subsequent public meeting held by the Croydon National Spiritualist Church to reply to his criticisms. In the words of the Spiritualist's leader the *Bishop was invited to come along and get some first-hand knowledge of this very important subject and accept the freedom of the platform to state his views.* Unfortunately he did not come. Had he done so it would clearly have been an even more noteworthy occasion than it was.

I reported on the opening of lavish new extensions to Croydon's leading departmental store at which four Rank starlets were present. They were Lana Morris, Jimmy Hanley, Petula Clark and Dirk Bogarde – the latter two destined, of course, to reach the glittering heights of international stardom. Bogarde in particular looked understandably bored with the whole proceedings. He was a short, slight, rather weedy-looking young man wearing shoes with thick crêpe rubber soles. But as I observed him that day I felt there was certainly something about his smouldering dark eyes and disdainful brow which would make him a big romantic star.

I did a good deal of Police Court work and, although being in the newspaper business makes one pretty broad-minded, I must confess that I was somewhat shocked to find that one of the Probation Officers carried a pornographic novelty toy round in his pocket which he sniggeringly brought out to show to reporters on the Press Bench.

During the summer I covered a particularly ambitious fête and carnival with lots of authentic fairground attractions. There was an exotic-looking lady in ocelot fur fabric bra and briefs who performed with a pair of pythons. After her act I was invited to put one of the pythons round my own shoulders. I was not a bit frightened for instead of being cold and clammy to the touch as I had imagined, the python's skin was dry and warm. As long as the creatures are kept well fed and sleepy there is no danger in handling them.

Occasionally assignments took me up to London's West End. At a lavish banquet held by Licensed Victuallers at the Grosvenor House Hotel the cabaret was provided by Anne Ziegler and Webster Booth.

I think the work I enjoyed most of all during my year at Croydon was covering the autumn elections. I saw some of the best-known political names of that period in action . . . Sir Herbert Williams, Reg Prentice, Cyril Osborne and the present Lords Ogmore and Byers. There was one hilarious incident at a meeting for a Labour candidate (a lady solicitor). A titled gentleman came along to speak on her behalf. With him on the platform were several Croydon dignitaries and in the centre was a table hung around with posters saying. *Vote for Miss . . .* He gave the sort of speech one expects on these occasions and ended with . . . *so I wholeheartedly urge you to vote for Miss . . . Miss . . .* – he faltered, having obviously forgotten her name, and had to glance hurriedly at the posters round the table before completing his sentence. The reaction of the audience packed in that large public hall was thunderous.

One of my fellow reporters on the *Advertiser* was Gerry Williams who has since become well known in Fleet Street and on television as a tennis commentator. I went to Wimbledon with him and among the players we saw in action was the glamour girl of that particular season, 'Gorgeous Gussie' Moran.

From time to time the *Advertiser* Editor Bob Taylor was approached by local schools to give talks on *Journalism as a Career* at Parent-Teacher Association meetings. He often asked me to do this in his place and I thoroughly enjoyed it. I remember in the course of my talk at the Lady Edridge School, South Norwood, saying that it was excellent practice for an aspiring journalist to keep a diary. Afterwards a genial, beaming Dad came up to me and said he'd love to see *my* diary!

In actual fact my diary at that time was full of romantic references to one of my fellow reporters on the *Advertiser.* His name was Dennis ('Slog') Wallis and, looking back, *I* suppose he was my first great love. A clever journalist and excellent cricketer, 'Slog' was very left-wing and looked like a sulky Teddy Bear. I watched all the cricket matches he played in and went through agonies when he was hit on the cheekbone by a ball. His nickname for me was 'Maggie Fair Leg'. He took me to the Unity Theatre in London and spooning by the lake at twilight in St. James's Park. We drove down to Brighton together in a vintage car and bounced gleefully around all evening on the 'dodgems' at Penge Fair. But although I was genuinely in love 'Slog' was known as a confirmed bachelor among his mates and before long he left Croydon to become a sub-editor up in Leicester.

Throughout the post-war years I had kept in regular touch with my good friend Jennifer Clark who was now married to Vangeli Couroucli, a prosperous businessman in Athens. While I was at Croydon she came over to England to have her first baby at a nursing home near Watford. To everyone's great grief the child – a son – was stillborn. She accepted her loss with characteristic courage and later had two daughters, the elder of whom is my god-daughter. When I went to see her at her mother's home she suggested that I should visit her in Greece. The invitation came at a time when I was feeling restless and wistful about 'Slog's' departure. I had also long had a passionate desire to travel and the country I most wanted to see was Greece – partly because of its associations with Byron.

The last story I covered at Croydon was a notably human one. In the men's ward of a hospital for incurables lay a 17-year-old lad named Michael. Although severely spastic and bedridden from birth he took a great interest in and was very knowledgeable about cricket which he followed avidly on television and in newspapers and books. The Captain of the England XI at that time heard about Michael and sent him a cricket bat autographed by all the team. Despite his great difficulty in speaking I was able to understand what Michael said and got an extremely interesting story from him.

On the afternoon before publishing day I received a telephone call. The cultured man at the other end of the line said that he was Michael's father and requested me not to publish the interview with his son. 'My wife and I have always told our friends that we have no son' was the reason he gave me. I at once discussed the situation with my Editor, who deplored the father's attitude as much as I did. In the end we printed the story omitting Michael's surname.

I stood my newspaper colleagues the customary round of farewell drinks at a pub near the office and, early in 1951, I set off for Greece. I made this first solo long-distance trip with my parents' full blessing and encouragement – a fact I record with eternal gratitude, for many more stuffy parents of that era might well have tried to dissuade me. I found that I was a born traveller, able to adapt myself easily to new scenes and circumstances and eager to venture into remote parts well off the tourist track.

CHAPTER SIX

GRECIAN JOURNEY

GOOD LUCK HAS ALWAYS played a significant part in my experiences as a globe-trotter. Time and again I have arrived by chance in a certain place when something particularly interesting was happening or met people who have proved valuable contacts.

In February 1951, I crossed the Channel and continued overland down to Genoa to board the Greek steamer bound for the Piraeus. Thus my first taste of traveller's luck occurred, for I arrived in Genoa during the pre-Lent carnival and found the city filled with gaiety and excitement. Students were out in force, their red and green mediaeval huntsman-style hats hung about with glittering medallions and their pockets full of confetti which they showered merrily over passers-by – including me. Trumpets blared and guitars strummed far into the night. Having booked in for one night at the Bristol Palazzo Hotel, I explored the picturesque old quarter of the city after dark and supped at a wine shop in an alleyway closely associated with Christopher Columbus.

Next morning I went on board ship. Eight hours out of Genoa we ran into extremely heavy weather and she was obliged to reduce her speed to only three knots. The pills I had taken as a precautionary measure lived up to their reputation fairly well, but the best cure for nausea on the high seas is undoubtedly a brisk stroll on the top deck, and I never tired of watching the terrifying beauty of a storm at sea.

At meal-times I had my first introduction to Greek food and found all the dishes very much to my taste. There was lamb basted with lemon juice over a charcoal fire, chicken pilaff, macaroni *au gratin,* mincemeat balls and rice wrapped in vine leaves, red mullet, stuffed green peppers, artichokes boiled in oil. Syrupy sweet paklava was a frequent dessert washed down by uniquely flavoured retsina wine, made from pine resin, or potent aniseed-flavoured ouzo – the Greek equivalent of absinthe.

My shipmates included a newspaperman returning on holiday to his native village in Crete, and a professor of archaeology from Oxford. The latter combined erudition with a keen sense of humour. He had fought with Greek guerrillas in the mountains during the war and thus knew the country and people intimately. He spoke of both with the warmest affection, and returned to Greece as often as he could. Now he was on his way to carry out some research on the island of Delos, sacred shrine of Apollo.

Our ship entered the Gulf of Corinth in the misty dawn of the third day. This stretch of water is the dividing line between northern and southern Greece and forms part of the loveliest scenery in the country. Tranquil silver-green waters were flanked on either side by snow-capped mountains round which garlands of cloud hung like smoky festoons. Sunrise beyond the mountain peaks produced the most glorious lighting effects imaginable. On the southern shore close to the water's edge were clusters of square, ochre houses and vivid green patches denoting terraces of cultivated currants for which this region is celebrated. Beyond the currant plantations and orchards of oranges and lemons are the Peloponnese Mountains, early stronghold of freedom in the Greek War of Independence in 1821, and beyond them Olympia, site of the Olympic Games.

In dramatic contrast, that February morning, the mountains on the northern shore of the Gulf – venerable legend-rich Parnassus, Ghiona and Vardousia – had a dark, brooding magic about them. Along this rugged, desolate coastline lie the ruins of Delphi and, in the extreme west, Byron's Missolonghi. Further northwards stretch the awe-inspiring peaks of the Pindus Mountains, bitter battleground in the winter of 1940-41. I became well acquainted with both shores during my stay in Greece.

Jennifer and her husband Vangeli, born in Cephallonia and now a prosperous businessman in Athens, were hosts in a million. They took me to Sunion, Daphni, Marathon and Salamis, for picnics in pinewoods by the sea, to tavernas and night-spots, to the homes of their family and friends. Jennifer's two delightful step-children Maria and Harry taught me a lot of useful Greek phrases which I noted down phonetically for future purposes.

The Courouclis lived in a very pleasant villa in Philothai, a superior suburb with flower-fringed roads and fine panoramic views of mountains, pinewoods and cypress groves. Like its English counterpart Philothai had a broadway of well-stocked shops and a good bus service down into the city. A travelling greengrocer used to call round the district with a donkey bearing bulging panniers, and another itinerant trader was a wizened old man with a large basket of fresh eggs in one hand and a few live fowls in the other. One of the most familiar morning sounds in Philothai was the dustman's bell as he came round to collect garbage before the noonday heat brought out the flies. By March the weather in Greece is as warm as an average June in England.

Athens is an exciting city which never sleeps and everything about it eloquently reflects the national character. The Greeks are an intense, talkative, quick-witted, warm-hearted, impatient, emotional race who set a high value on family loyalties and the rights of the individual.

They love crowds, celebrations, late nights and talking politics. They are also incurable romantics. Byron is still held in highest regard by the Greeks because of his heroic role in the War of Independence. Many little boys are still named after him and a prominent Athenian journalist told me that even during the German occupation when he was starving and selling personal possessions to buy food, he refused to part with his copy of Moore's biography of the Poet. 'Because of Byron an Englishman will always be made especially welcome in Greece', he told me, and I certainly found this to be true.

The twin landmarks of the Acropolis and Lycabettus Hill dominate the city skyline wherever you walk. Over a glass of wine or cup of Turkish coffee you can sit in Constitution Square opposite the Royal Palace, with its dashing Evzone guards, and watch the world go by . . . rich children with their usually English governesses on their daily outing to the lush Zappeion Gardens, many thin, appealing little boys who have to start earning their living as bootblacks at the age of seven, lottery ticket pedlars, flashily dressed spivs, ultra-conservatively attired bankers, leathery-faced old countrymen in town for the day and wearing the pillbox hat, dark blue fustanella, off-white hose and pom-pom toed slippers which are still the daily dress among his generation in remote mountain villages, priests in flowing black vestments with stove-pipe hats and long hair caught up in chignons.

I never tired of exploring the city – particularly the markets and the ancient Turkish quarter at the foot of the Acropolis. By day the cobbled alleyways there are teeming with picturesque characters, and by night the tiny, lantern-lit tavernas are crowded with tourists who sample superb food to the accompaniment of guitars and folk songs. I dined there and also at some of the less quaint but equally popular tavernas along the road to Phaleron where bazooki music rather than a noteworthy cuisine is the main attraction and many virtuoso performers are to be seen.

There is much party-going in Greek high society. In summer as many as 300 guests may be served with cocktails in gardens gay with illuminated trees. At such a gathering at the home of a close friend of Sophocles Venizelos (then Prime Minister and son of the great Eleutherios Venizelos), I was introduced to General Zervas who won undying fame for his exploits as a guerrilla leader in Northern Greece during the war. I felt very proud to shake hands with him.

The families which nowadays constitute high society in Greece are, for the most part, direct descendants of the corsair captains and mountain bandit chieftains who amassed great wealth during the early years of the 19th century and who served with distinction in the War of Independence. Maria Kalurgis, who entertained me at her fortress-like island mansion on Ydra, is a typical example. Her rich corsair ancestor, Georgios Coundouriotis, built the lovely old house where she still goes every spring and summer, and it contains many family heirlooms dating from his time.

My first long excursion out of Athens was made in early March with Jennifer and Vangeli. Our destination was the monastery of Mega Speleion in the heart of the Peloponnese Mountains. A monk there had just inherited some money from a relation in America and Vangeli was to invest it for him. He had arranged to rendezvous with the monk and the monk's solicitor at the monastery to complete the transaction. With the notable exception of Mount Athos, monkish fraternities in Greece do not exclude female visitors from their establishments indeed, several monasteries offer overnight accommodation to travellers of both sexes.

Mega Speleion stands in a sensationally rugged and remote position on the site of many previous monasteries which were pillaged frequently during four centuries of occupation by the Turks and, more recently, by the Germans. The latest building was restored after the war but still lacked its quota of inner doors at the time of our visit so that the mountain gales swept down the passages from end to end without hindrance.

We started off from Athens by train and the first part of our journey lay along the shore of the Gulf of Corinth. The wild splendour of the sun-bathed rocky heights studded here and there with a small whitewashed chapel, provided a dramatic backcloth to the astonishingly brilliant blue sea. At frequent intervals along the side of the road were little stone shrines adorned with wild flowers and with lanterns burning. All over Greece these are a familiar feature of the rural scene. When we reached the foothills of the Peloponnese we changed to an antiquated Alpine railway which puffed laboriously through a series of spectacular mountain passes to the modest hamlet of Zaklerou. After a meal of fried eggs and sweet herb tea we mounted mules for the remainder of our journey which was made in heavy rain along precariously narrow mountain tracks.

We arrived at the monastery at sunset and were welcomed with glasses of cognac. The room which was to be our dormitory contained three trestle beds with blankets and one oil lamp. We accepted an invitation to attend evening vespers in the chapel and later dined with Vangeli's monkish client in his own apartment. He prepared a delicious meal of lamb and macaroni over an open fire with the aid of a very young novice monk and produced several bottles of retsina wine which had been distilled on the premises. For dessert there were dishes of crystallised fruit. Either this or rose-petal jam is given as a token of greeting, by the way, to visitors in homes all over Greece. It was a very cheerful meal and Vangeli translated much of what his client said. It was interesting to learn that he had been 'given' by his parents to the monastery as a novice monk when he was 12. He was now about 30, shy, unworldly, and extremely handsome.

Plumbing at Mega Speleion (as we had already discovered) was pretty well non-existent, but our bed-time ablutions brought further laughs. We were ushered along to a cell-like room with a stone sink beside which stood a novice monk with a large ewer. First we held out our flannels, he poured on a few drops of water and we washed our faces. Then he repeated the procedure with our toothbrushes. Yet immediately outside the monastery a torrent plunged exuberantly down into the valley far below!

I made a point of being in Athens on Independence Day (25th March) which commemorates the Greeks' first uprising against Turkish oppression in 1821. A week previously I had visited the mountain monastery of St. Lavra where this historic event was secretly planned under the leadership of Archbishop Germanos whose vestments and battle banner are still preserved there.

The Greek capital was gay with blue and white decorations and laurel wreaths and after dark the main buildings were floodlit. Pennants flew on the bonnets of all taxis and buses. Street vendors planted little paper favours among their wares and shoeblacks had them stuck in their foot-rests. Shops staged special window displays and the floor of the flag-decked post office was scattered with myrtle sprigs. For the grand street procession I had a splendid vantage point with Jennifer and her family opposite the Palace. We saw King Paul and Queen Frederika driving to the cathedral with their three children. Guns fired a salute on the heights of Lycabettus. The procession included the armed forces, disabled ex-servicemen, the municipal services, diplomats and youth organisations. Patriotic fervour knew no bounds and a special poetry reading was given by Thanos Cotsopoulos, matinee idol of the National Theatre.

Less than a month after Independence Day came the anniversary of Byron's death at Missolonghi on 19th April 1824. As an ardent Byronian I was very eager to be in Missolonghi for the event. I set out from Athens on 17th April and stayed overnight in Patras where a banker friend of Vangeli's had given me an introduction to a leading hotelier. This jovial old fellow had a daughter Lydia, who was a prominent social worker, and a son Theodore who ran a machine importing business. Theodore at once appointed himself my escort. He was a well-upholstered, happy-go-lucky young man with a good profile and an excellent command of English. Inevitably he was also romantic, but only in a gentle, engaging, non-wolfish way and, while we enjoyed each other's company, we did not get seriously involved. His best friend was a policeman whose fiancee Hermione was a student, and the four of us joined a group of her fellow students to go across to Missolonghi on the opposite shore of the Gulf for the celebrations.

The ferryboats from Patras to the desolate northern coastline were crammed with pilgrims in gala mood singing to the accompaniment of guitars and accordions. We disembarked at the tumbledown hamlet of Nafpaktos and drove 20 miles through superbly rugged and completely wild mountain country to our destination. Along most of the route the precipitous road wound immediately above the sea. When dusk fell the only sign of life to be seen was a shepherd boy crouching on a rock or the amber glow of a fire in a hollow where gypsies were camped.

Missolonghi was ablaze with decorations and pulsating with excitement. Despite its singularly remote position it is today a friendly and fair-sized town with a surprisingly elegant Town Hall and strip lighting in the chief tavernas. I was introduced to the Mayor who invited me to take part in the procession being held that night and again the following morning.

The celebrations began at eight o'clock in the evening with a parade to the Garden of Heroes. Here a statue of Byron had pride of place flanked by Greek and British flags. Nearby was a shrine containing the bones of many who died in the battle for independence including Byron's old comrade-in-arms Marcos Botzaris. Soldiers discharged tracer bullets into the night sky and lit fireworks, and bowls of incense were placed at the entrance to the shrine. Then, through an avenue of fixed bayonets, a colourful pageant came into view. Children in national costumes, local dignitaries, war veterans, and last and most impressive of all, the Archbishop of Patras in rich brocade vestments and jewelled mitre. He was attended by priests in cloaks of green and gold who bore under a tasselled canopy a gold-framed picture of the Exodus from Missolonghi – an heroic military campaign of 1825 which is commemorated annually on the same date as Byron's death. The ceremony was followed by revelry in the tavernas and main square.

Next morning a second lavish celebration was held in the Garden of Heroes. Crowds overflowed the pavements and gathered on balconies, walls and rooftops, to watch the procession. To the accompaniment of the town band little girls dressed in the national colours of blue and white scattered rose petals, and leading citizens made speeches on a leaf-shrouded platform. Later, for the Mayor's special guests there was a banquet, and at five in the afternoon a display of national dances in the main square formed the climax to a great day.

Because of mosquitoes one is still advised at hotels in Missolonghi to sleep with the windows shut, but otherwise the town of today is very far removed from the primitive and dreary place Byron knew. A mile out in the lagoon is the islet of Klissova which Kitzo Djavella and 150 men defended so gallantly against powerful Turkish naval squadrons in 1826. A low-lying silhouette on unruffled waters, Klissova is now famous for its fish.

In the old quarter of Missolonghi a walled garden marks the site of the house where Byron lived and died. In it stands a marble column bearing a profile likeness of the Poet. Every April Greek and British flags are flown there and flowers are laid. The bunch I placed at the foot of the column bore the inscription: *'In memory of Byron through whose endeavours "Freedom's fame finds wings on every wind." Placed here by a compatriot of his who also loves Greece'.* My visit to Missolonghi was greatly enhanced by the fact that I already knew so much about Byron and had read George Finlay's book about the War of Independence.

A few days later I took a train southwards from Patras to the ruins of Olympia, scene of the ancient Olympic Games which dated back to 776 B.C. They lie in a secluded grassy hollow encircled by thickly wooded hills and cover a considerable area, for they were not only the site of a stadium and amphitheatre but also a complete township. The Games were held every four years in July or August when the moon was full, and they lasted five days. A victory in the Olympiad was regarded as an honour equivalent to success in battle. Music and poetry figured in the programme as well as athletics and racing. The chief temple was dedicated to Zeus and in it stood the magnificent statue of Hermes by Praxiteles, which is now housed in the nearby museum. It was hidden from the Germans during the war. The museum also contains a remarkably large collection of other statuary which once adorned either the other temples or the gardens of ancient Olympia. Most are of immense proportions and depict gods, goddesses, satyrs, soldiers, and athletes.

I first viewed the ruins with a guide in the afternoon, but later I strolled back alone by the light of a full moon to take a second look at that wonderful place. The River Alpheus, which had reflected so many of the scenes I was trying to recapture in my imagination, rippled softly nearby. Seeing Olympia by moonlight in the middle of a Grecian springtime was undoubtedly one of the highlights of my travels.

In Greece Eastertide falls a few weeks later than in England and is by far the most important religious festival of the year. With Jennifer, Vangeli and the children, I spent it on the island of Ydra – once the domain of corsair leaders – as the guest of Maria Kalurgis, great-great-grand-daughter of one of them.

The first glimpse of Ydra when one comes ashore in the long boat from the steamer is enchanting. Coffee-houses, tavernas, fish stalls, fruit barrows, a modest hotel, a sprinkling of tiny shops and a church comprise the waterfront, and gaily painted fishing schooners rock gently at anchor on a vivid jade and turquoise sea. Beyond the quay terrace upon terrace of quaint old houses (freshly whitewashed for Easter when I was there) stretch far up the steep hillside which is a maze of alleyways composed almost entirely of age-worn steps. Through archways are glimpses of courtyards filled with geraniums and pink stock. Numerous tiny white chapels, ruined windmills and a fort with rusting cannon still fixed on the battlements add further to the highly romantic scene. The site of the ship yard which was a hive of industry during the War of Independence can still be seen. The breathless tranquillity is broken only by birdsong, bells, the braying of donkeys and the occasional throb of an outboard engine.

Maria boiled scores of eggs and dyed them scarlet – the colour symbolising joy. These she gave to everyone who visited her house and, when the fasting period was over, they were also served at meals embedded in spiced bread. Like all my Greek friends I fasted according to custom. Lentil soup, octopus and squid, potatoes, bread, honey and fruit were on the permitted menu.

I had a special interest in the octopus which was served at one meal because I had watched it being caught during a morning sail. It had been harpooned in the centre of its soft, bag-like body and hauled into a fishing boat. Squid tastes so good that one forgets to be 'squeamish' about it. Being somewhat indigestible, however, it is best washed down with wine.

On Good Friday the deep-throated bell of the quayside church tolled all day long. Flags flew at half-mast on all the ships in harbour as well as on buildings. In the evening the church was filled to overflowing for a long service. Everyone present held a lighted two-foot long candle. Focal point of the ceremony was a richly-carved representation of Christ's bier. To the accompaniment of swinging incense-burners, a shower of rose petals was released from the central dome and scattered over the *Holy Body*. At the close of the service the bier was borne out of the church and made a tour of the waterfront.

Another service on a similarly grand scale was held on Saturday night. It ended at midnight with the joyful cry of *Christ is Risen!* and people exchanged embraces and greetings of *Hronia Polla!* (Long Life). This time everyone crossed their home threshold with their candle still alight, for thus, it is believed, good luck is carried into the house.

On Easter morning the delicious aroma of roasting lambs filled the air. Easter lunch is usually a lavish picnic. Never happier than when they are entertaining friends, the Greeks hold many Easter parties. Social gatherings were held at all the splendid old mansions of corsair memory. Cards were played in stone-flagged halls, fireworks let off on flower-filled terraces. The gayest party of all was held on the quay by the island's oldest families. A long table was prepared at the water's edge outside a taverna and we dined to the accompaniment of guitars. Wine flowed freely and jumping crackers were tossed into the harbour. I was invited to 'lead' the dancing and by this time I had a good knowledge of the basic steps of Greece's highly distinctive and exuberant style of 'tracing the light fantastic'. So we sang and danced and made merry under the clear starry sky on that lovely fragrant night until two o'clock in the morning. The date was Ist May, when circlets of flowers are placed above all front doors and at the top of ships' masts.

The majority of my solo excursions were made by country bus, and the most memorable of all was a 13-hour journey from Athens to the fascinating old Turkish town of Joannina up in the north, not far from the Albanian frontier. The route lay through some sensationally beautiful mountain country steeped in legend of the most romantic kind. Eagles wheeled overhead and emerald green lizards darted among the rocks. I saw storks nesting in ruins, shepherd boys like young Pans, donkey-borne old crones spinning wool on primitive spindles as they rode along, gypsies camping under crude blanket bivouacs. Throughout rural Greece women do the bulk of the work. I even saw some repairing roads near Joannina!

Ali Pasha's old capital lies on the shore of a beautiful lake encircled by mountains, and its skyline is dominated by minarets. Echoes of its former Turkish associations abound everywhere-in its architecture, its arts and crafts, and its food. Joannma is specially noted for the exquisite filigree work of local silversmiths and for brass-ware. The inhabitants speak a dialect which is, I gather, difficult for Greeks from further south to understand.

By the lake I watched scores of peasant women doing their laundry in the shallows. They beat gaily-coloured blankets and carpets stretched out on rocks with flat pieces of wood like outsize butter-pats and then hung them up to dry on bushes and trees. Immediately on the lakeside too extensive parts of Ali Pasha's fabulous castle still remain, and there is a museum housing many items of rich furniture which used to grace his court. Ali was a deceptively mild-looking tyrant who entertained Byron in lavish style when he visited Joannina but who, as a ruler, was capable of great cruelties. In the centre of the lake is a tiny green islet where Ali Pasha was eventually trapped and killed by his enemies. I hired a boat and spent half an hour there.

It was in Joannina that I saw my first karakiosi puppet show one evening. This is a very popular form of adult entertainment in the remoter rural districts. The puppets are the simplest kind worked by sticks instead of strings. Tragic as well as comic plays are performed and many plots are drawn from Greek history. But no matter what the story, the puppeteer always introduces comments of a topical nature.

Over coffee in the main square I met a delightful girl named Elli who took me to see a lovely old Turkish-style house where Byron stayed in 1809. The owner welcomed us warmly and gave us some zaccari paklava – very sweet powdery cakes much eaten at that particular season. The upper room where we sat had rose-coloured walls and a large quantity of exceptionally beautiful embroidery. A fine old staircase led down to a cobbled courtyard where a girl was weaving rugs on a hand loom.

Elli strongly recommended me to make the eight-hour bus journey from Joannina to Kalambaka while I was in that part of Greece, and I shall always be very glad that I did. The scenery on the way over the top of the Pindus Mountains had a spellbinding grandeur beyond anything I had ever seen in my life before.

The bus reached the primitive hamlet of Kalambaka at six in the evening. Although it had now grown into a bustling little community again, signs of its brutal devastation by the Germans during the war still remained. But among the fire-blackened ruins simple white-walled one-roomed homesteads with tins of geraniums beside the door stood out bravely. Piglets, lambs and chickens ran in and out at will.

I booked in at the one and only hotel, a very modest but welcoming establishment kept by a hugely fat woman with a marked air of dignity and cordiality about her. After I had had an evening meal at a nearby taverna she invited me to sit on the second floor balcony with other members of her family. As is the case everywhere in Greece at dusk the entire population moved to and fro along the dusty track below us (which served as the main street) engaged in the communal 'evening promenade'. Everyone wore their best clothes, and unless a couple were officially betrothed, the boys walked together in one group and the girls in another.

When it was time to retire the proprietress told me that I was to have her own bed in the living room. At its head hung a religious medallion and above this a tapestry of Evzones making love in a pastoral setting. The chief reason for my visit to Kalambaka was to see the fantastically-situated monasteries of Meteora which tower above the hamlet on rocky pinnacles, and I ordered a mule to be ready for me at dawn next day.

Accompanied by a young muleteer I started off on the ascent to

Meteora early the following morning. Though not the first ride I had made on mule-back it was certainly my most exciting and hazardous one, and altogether a thoroughly exhilarating experience. It was already very hot but the rippling melody of cattle bells was as yet unspoiled by the clamour of other daytime sounds. After an hour's climb we reached a gorge from which Kalambaka looked like a toy village. We were surrounded on all sides by soaring pinnacles of rock nearly every one of which was crowned by an ancient monastery. How they ever came to be built in their remote, precipitous situations seemed to me little short of miraculous. Incidentally the word Meteora means 'cloud-wrapped'.

By further climbing we gained access to the monasteries of St. Stephen and St. Theodor where we were greeted by shabby, lean-looking monks. I noticed one wearing flannel trousers and suede shoes under his threadbare robes. At St. Stephen's we were ushered into an austerely-furnished apartment and offered chocolate creams, while at St. Theodor's we were shown some rare icons and the shed where the skulls and thigh bones of fifty former brethren were set out on shelves. Both monasteries had cobbled courtyards, fine cloisters and their own bakeries and wine distilleries. I imagine that all the less accessible monasteries of Meteora are similar in style. Nowadays only a handful of monks live there, and they are probably completely blasé about their location which I regard as the eighth Wonder of the World.

When I got back to Kalambaka I had a substantial breakfast and waited for the bus to take me once again to Joannina. One of my fellow passengers was a tubby little man with bloodshot eyes and a battered panama hat. He told me that he was formerly an officer in the Greek Army and had been attached to British forces during the war. Remarking that he read many English books, he produced one and asked if I would swop my own reading matter with him during the journey. So I handed over *Dr. Jekyll and Mr. Hyde* and received in return *Selections from the Best English Prose.*

Travelling on the battered-looking but invincible country buses of Greece was always a highly entertaining pursuit. They never seemed to break down despite the punishment they underwent on pot-holed, rock-strewn tracks. The extreme friendliness of the passengers, the singsongs, the goats in the aisle, the incredible miscellany of luggage piled high on the roof, were a constant source of interest to me. Where any form of toilet was entirely non-existent we alighted and disappeared into the bushes for a few moments. And nobody was a bit shy about it.

Sanitation was also decidedly basic at the many humble rural hotels where I stayed. One privy I recall with particular amusement was the dilapidated earth closet in a courtyard at Delphi. It was necessary to push aside a drowsy pig and goat before the door could be opened. Once inside it was advisable not to waste time as the animals were liable to slip back into their customary positions and blockade the exit. But I found it great fun sleeping in a room where a tin canister of water was nailed to the wall above an earthenware basin, and eating at a rough-hewn table set upon a floor of levelled earth.

I also lunched on countless occasions in peasant homes in remote villages. The fare was generous and the hospitality overwhelming; it even included an afternoon siesta between freshly-laundered sheets. I used to join my hosts in the folk songs I had learnt and never tired of listening to family music-making on a guitar, accordion and shepherd's pipes.

Ydra will always remain my top favourite among the islands of Greece, but three others I visited were Rhodes, Crete and Corfu – a celebrated trio, and all surpassingly beautiful in their contrasting ways. Rhodes, which lies within sight of the Turkish coast, was Italian territory before the last war and therefore has the best roads in Greece. It has been developed as an ambitious holiday centre, and to discover any of its original old-world charm one has to go out into the countryside to villages like Lindos which is famed for its extraordinarily pretty pottery. My host in Rhodes was the Mayor, who owned a factory where this pottery was produced for export. The designs and methods of manufacture were faithfully based on centuries-old traditions. He presented me with a superb plate depicting a fanciful peacock traced in jade, cornflower blue and terracotta.

Crete is a place of rugged splendour, fierce vendettas and rich archaeological discoveries. The menfolk are a princely race with markedly Turkish ideas about women. The very distinctive national costume of voluminous pleated trousers, fine leather top boots and turban-like caps, is still widely worn as everyday attire and not merely for festivals as is the general custom in other parts of Greece.

In a lush green, flower-starred, gentler way Corfu also has scenic beauties that make the heart soar with delight, and the headdress worn by the island's womenfolk is the most becoming one in the whole of Greece.

I returned to England laden with souvenirs (of which my home has since become a veritable treasure trove). Even at a distance of twenty years the atmosphere of Greece remains vivid in my memory . . . the sharp clear quality of the light, the spicy fragrance of wild thyme and vassiliko, the haunting music of shepherd boys' flutes, the sweet balm to mind and spirit which I always felt so deeply when I drove through wild mountain country or watched an Aegean sunrise from the deck of an island steamer.

Nowadays, I hear, even Mega Speleion has flush toilets and good roads have replaced the stony tracks I bounced along so happily. I am glad I saw Greece before tourist-minded promoters made these embellishments.

CHAPTER SEVEN

FUN IN THE FENS

WHEN I RETURNED from Greece I joined the staff of the *Wisbech Standard,* a lively, enterprising weekly newspaper in the heart of the Fen Country, and was there from the autumn of 1952 until the summer of 1954. The Managing Editor was Wally Green, a dynamic character of stocky build and pugnaciously attractive appearance. Like many Fenlanders he was a rugged individualist of fiery disposition, and during the war he knocked down a man on the town bridge whom he knew to be living with the wife of a soldier imprisoned in Germany. The Chief Reporter, George Usher, who later moved to the *Eastern Daily News* at Norwich, was likewise a personality to be remembered. Tall and gangling, a typical Fenlander with his dark looks and lantern jaw, he was passionately fond of music and the author of a musical play.

Wisbech is a fascinating town with the River Nene running straight through the centre of it in a singularly picturesque manner. The most enchanting stretch of all is known as the North and South Brinks where roads run directly beside the river, flanked by interestingly varied Georgian and Queen Anne house-fronts of considerable charm and elegance. I was lucky enough to have a front upstairs flat in a Georgian house called Fenland Court, on the South Brink immediately overlooking celebrated Peckover House on the other side of the river. Fenland Court, like a great deal of other property in Wisbech, was owned by a remarkable old lady named Lilian Ream, who had started out as a street photographer and ended up very rich. Not far away is The Crescent, a gracious, quiet thoroughfare full of more choice period architecture.

Every summer, perpetuating the tradition laid down in an ancient Royal Charter, a splendid fair is held in the town, the sideshows being spread out in medieval fashion along the streets instead of being concentrated on one particular site. The old Horse Fair is another historic venue. A short distance down-river the small port bustles with prosperity, and on the outskirts of the town along the West Walton Road tulip fields in springtime rival their counterparts in Holland.

The rich, black earth of the Fen Country yields crops of outstanding quality and many of the local farmers are fabulously wealthy. On market day they drive into town in dazzlingly expensive cars, though some of them are so illiterate they can scarcely write their names. I remember once going to a very modest-looking homestead on a remote dyke-bordered drove to collect details of a wedding. It appeared to be a nondescript singlefronted house, but once inside I found myself standing amid all the elaborate furnishings which spell opulence for folk whose taste in such matters does not match the size of their bank balance . . . charioteer wallpaper, fur rugs, gilt Buddhas, giant candelabra and so forth. Extensions to the house had been made lengthwise on to the back in a somewhat bizarre manner at different levels.

The flat solitude of the Fen Country landscape may not appeal to everybody but I loved it; both gale-swept and snowbound in winter and gay with blossoming orchards and lark-song above the marshland reeds in summer. One feels a wonderful sense of winged freedom cycling or strolling along a Fenland road, and the sky effects at all seasons are marvellous. I was told (though I never had any chance of confirming it) that black magic was still practised in the remotest part of the Fens. Nowadays when that cult is publicised as being widespread in Britain this does not seem remarkable, but back in the early 1950's it was. Certainly the rural Fenlanders are a secretive and taciturn race who often give the impression that they would have been much happier to remain a community apart, cut off from the rest of their countrymen by extensive undrained marshes.

Although Wisbech lies at the end of a branch railway line at a point on the map regarded by many as decidedly off the beaten track, it was during my residence there – and no doubt still is – a very vital and go-ahead town peopled by some talented and interesting personalities.

Prominent among those who lived with considerable zest and style was Ken Elliott, a somewhat eccentric and very likeable Irish doctor with a pretty wife named Betty. He ran up the Irish Republican flag whenever he held social gatherings at his home (he lived first near Ingleborough Mill and later in West Walton). These occasions were frequent as he used the most minor incident as an excuse for an original and highly entertaining get-together, e.g. an unveiling ceremony to mark the introduction of new French windows at his house. His great ally in these lively affairs was Oliver (David) Barr, the Wisbech coroner who, although always very dignified when presiding over inquests, was when off duty bursting with schoolboy high spirits. It was after interviewing Ken Elliott about some mock hunt ball he had been involved in that I was invited to become a member of his 'club of funsters'. I regarded this as a great honour and spent many happy times with them.

Sometimes the functions organised by Ken and David were on a really impressive scale. A typical example was the *'Ingleboro' Lancers Regimental Dinner'* held on 5th December 1953, at the *Rose & Crown*, the town's premier hotel and formerly a lovely old coaching inn. I received an elegant gilt-edged invitation on which I was styled 'Senior

Commander Sherry' (although in fact I had never been more than a sergeant) and, replying in similarly humorous vein, my acceptance read: 'Senior Commander Sherry has been loaned to the Hungarian Hussars for moonlight manoeuvres, but providing she survives her daily lashings of goulash and nightly renderings of the czardas on the General's dinner table, she will be delighted to accept your invitation'.

In the spheres of music and drama Wisbech possessed some of the best amateur performers I have ever encountered. There was Leonard Teed's prize-winning Male Voice Choir for example, and the shows put on by the Operatic Society under the musical direction of Albert Gay had infinitely more sparkle and polish than is usually found in provincial towns. I saw a local drama group stage a remarkably well-acted production of that challenging play *The Heiress.* Sheila Chesters, wife of the Headmaster of Wisbech Grammar School, and much resembling that splendid comedienne Hattie Jacques in face and figure, directed many dramatic and musical entertainments by the youngsters of the town. One costume she devised for the girls was the traditional straw bonnet and gown of the Fenland strawberry-pickers. The young and glamorous County Music Adviser was shapely, Titian-haired Catherine Baxter.

In Ted and Eva Rigg Wisbech had a particularly charming and accomplished Mayor and Mayoress. The manager of a local chemist shop, Ted Rigg was a first-rate impromptu speaker with natural dignity and presence, while his wife combined striking good looks with exceptional musical talents. Indeed Ted Rigg headed a remarkably able team, for the Town Clerk had a great flair for showmanship when it came to staging municipal 'spectaculars' like the Mayor-making and the Christmas revelry at the Town Hall, and the Council included some wealthy and influential business-men who were keen to put and keep Wisbech very much 'on the map'.

The then Curate of Wisbech Parish Church (Rev. Teddy Boston) was already an ardent collector of the railway items which have since brought him national renown. Another cleric with very special railway connections was the Rev. W. V. Awdry, author of those delightful children's books about *Thomas the Red Engine*, etc. I interviewed him at his country vicarage.

Wisbech had visits from several famous people while I was there. When the Duchess of Gloucester came to open the new maternity home I accompanied her on her tour of the wards. I found her immensely friendly and approachable. *Is this your pretty work?* she asked one proud new mother peeping at the baby in the cradle beside the bed. Later she commented on a picture of the Queen on a biscuit tin lid, remarking that it was an excellent likeness of her niece.

During 1953 Julie Andrews, then a pig-tailed teenager, appeared in a Sunday charity concert at the Wisbech *Hippodrome*, and Gilbert Harding opened a fête in aid of the Hospital. The enterprising Wisbech Music Committee organised regular evening concerts and engaged top-flight artistes of the calibre of Nina Milkina.

Dr. (now Lord) Donald Soper came up to address a large Methodist Conference. One of the most witty as well as personable looking preachers of our time, he was not afraid of filling the church with laughter, and his sermon was well laced with bright wisecracks and anecdotes. Afterwards he picked up a small stool in the vestry and told me that he intended to go and deliver another sermon in the market place. I knew that the local Superintendent of the Methodist Circuit was bitterly opposed to this idea because Dr. Soper's strong Left Wing views were well-known and he had recently been stoned by students while speaking in the market place at Cambridge. I accompanied Dr. Soper to a good vantage point where he climbed on the stool and began a brilliant impromptu sermon. It was nine o'clock on a cold, blustery November evening, but in a very short time he was surrounded by a large crowd who did not heckle or throw things but listened with rapt attention. As I recorded his words I thought how close the spirits of John Wesley and other great pioneering outdoor preachers must have been to Donald Soper that night.

Another distinguished visitor was Gladys Aylward, the courageous missionary on whose life the film *The Inn of the Sixth Happiness* was based. She was a small, middle-aged woman of very homely appearance with a tremendous gift for showmanship. In the pulpit she wore Chinese costume and flamboyant oriental earrings. With compelling words she told her wonderful story of faith and adventure. All the time she was speaking she held the Bible she carried with her during her epic trek across mountains in the wildest part of China when, hotly pursued by Japanese troops, she led a large party of children to safety. She was endearingly frank about her love of publicity and posed with aplomb for Press photographers.

Perhaps the most poignant story I ever covered in Wisbech was about a man who laid out a beautiful garden for his invalid wife. A woman of great charm, she was dying of a particularly painful disease. The garden had a pool and fountain in the centre and fairy-lights among the trees. During the night it was floodlit so that she could look out upon it from her bed when she was unable to sleep. This story sold a great many extra copies of our paper the week it appeared.

One of my own top favourite assignments was lunching aboard a Polish cargo ship called the *Dunajec* when she brought timber to the Port of Wisbech. Named after a river in Poland, she was a fine-looking brand new vessel from Gdynia and this was her first trip to England. Proving an excellent ambassador of goodwill, the captain allowed many local children to go aboard, and at night she was floodlit. Altogether great interest was roused by this visitor from behind the Iron Curtain.

I went on board with Mr. F. C. Rawling of Messrs. Garland & Flaxman, shipbrokers. Enough English was spoken by the crew of 16 for me to be able to ask them their impressions of Wisbech, what souvenirs they had bought from local shops, and how they spent their leisure hours ashore. When lunch was served the captain insisted that I should occupy his chair at the head of the table. The meal started with sauerkraut soup, followed by tender braised Wisbech beef, potatoes, and delicious pickled mushrooms which, the chief officer informed me, had come from the forests of Poland. Sweet grapes formed the dessert and were washed down by a generous quantity of vodka as numerous hearty toasts were exchanged.

Despite my intake of the fiery liquor I managed to negotiate the gangplank safely and without assistance when I disembarked. Far from being clouded my mind was ultra sharp and I turned in an inspired story at the office at record speed. That is the marvellous thing about vodka. It heightens the senses and does not give you a hangover! Later, with appropriate acknowledgments, my report also turned up in a periodical called *The New Central European Observer.*

Knowing that I had been to Greece the Wisbech Round Table asked me to give a travel talk at one of their luncheons at the *Rose & Crown*. Later I gave a similar talk to the Lady Methodists' Guild and was also invited to act as adjudicator at a drama festival at Wisbech High School. The girls had a delightful outdoor memorial theatre in the school gardens and I much enjoyed their performances. Yet another stimulating engagement was being the commentator at a fashion show. I was an associate member of the newly-formed Wisbech Yacht Club which had Commander Dagless at the helm. One Sunday I accompanied them on a cruise down the Nene and out into The Wash. On board the cabin cruiser *Perugia* I was allowed to take my turn at the wheel. Off Boston we saw many seals.

Out-of-office-hour activities like these gave me a feeling of being completely integrated into the life of the town. Also my stay in Greece had taught me a great deal about hospitality and I loved entertaining at my flat. There was a wine shop in Norfolk Street that sold ouzo and retsina. Thanks to a useful tip-off from Ken Elliott I contacted a recording company and cut my first disc of some Greek songs.

It was from Wisbech too that I set off on my first holiday in Paris. I stayed in the Rue d'Amsterdam and went to the Comedie Française, the Grand Guignol Theatre and the Cirque d'Hiver. 1 had long been interested in the history of the trapeze, done a great deal of research on the subject, and had an article entitled *Spangled Swallows* published in a London magazine. This feature was about Leotard, inventor of the trapeze, and other famous aerialists since. I made a special point of going to the Cirque d'Hiver because it was there that Leotard gave his first performance in 1859. Later I had the great thrill of meeting and talking to one of my heroines – Antoinette Concello – the only woman aerialist in the world ever to perform the superlatively difficult and dangerous triple somersault.

Then during 1953 my mother and father died within six months of each other. They had been wonderful parents who, from my earliest days, helped and encouraged me in all my interests and aspirations. Although I had lived the greater part of my life away from them since the age of 17, we had always remained in close touch by long weekly letters.

I stayed on at Wisbech for nine months after my father's death, thankful to be fully occupied, for hard work is undoubtedly the best antidote for grief. In due course I learnt that I was quite well off financially and in a position to be independent for a number of years. Journalism had brought me a great deal of happiness and fulfilment but it was a very demanding profession which left little time for other pursuits which were important to me like creative writing, music, travel and welfare work.

After considering the matter deeply I bought a house at Cambridge and moved from Wisbech in July 1954. It was one of the biggest decisions of my life and I never had reason to regret it.

CHAPTER EIGHT

BROADENING HORIZONS

AND SO I SPENT one of the most eventful decades of my life in one of the most exciting towns in England. At my new home in the pretty suburb of Cherryhinton I planned a varied programme of activities.

One of the first things I did was to buy a Spanish guitar and take lessons with a remarkably versatile character named Derek Tozer. Singing to my own accompaniment was to become one of my favourite hobbies for the rest of my life. I also became a member of the Cambridge Public Speaking Circle, a move which later led to many interesting public engagements.

But the most significant event of my first winter in Cambridge was joining the Writer Circle which at that time used to meet at *The Copper Kettle* on King's Parade. Apart from introducing me to an exceptionally talented group of amateur and part-time professional writers and launching me ardently into the concentrated pursuit of creative writing, it also brought me the second great friendship of my life – with Gillian Edwards. Gillian, at the time we first met, had already published one highly-praised novel and was single-mindedly preparing herself for the outstanding success she has achieved since both as a poet and novelist. In terms of literary experience if not in years Gillian was universally regarded as the Circle's 'elder statesman' and chief adviser. Small and dark, with a particular liking for exotic jewellery which she could wear to perfection on account of her striking Romany looks, Gillian was an expert on the Renaissance period in Italy which has formed the background of two of her finest books. With her clever, penetrating eyes and the wry, worldly curve of her lips there was, in fact, a marked resemblance to subjects of 16th century Florentine portraiture in her own appearance. She gave many people the impression of being a formidable bluestocking but actually (unlike a lot of other very clever women) she also had a keen sense of fun and was as much at home in a swingboat at a fair as in a library of medieval Latin manuscripts. In the first instance we were drawn to each other by a mutual interest in the Romantic Poets – Shelley was her special idol – and later I discovered she had a passion for travel akin to my own. Gillian also possessed that most precious quality in friendship – absolute loyalty as a keeper of confidences. She lived at Old Chesterton and the Cam flowed immediately past the bottom of her garden, providing a ringside view for University rowing activities.

I had the good fortune to belong to the Cambridge Writer Circle during what is still generally acknowledged to have been its heyday,

My Great-grandfatther Henry Nunn, aged 85.
Part-owner of Colchester's Theatre Royal 1878–1889.

My maternal Grandfather, a gifted man and a dedicated Town Councillor.

My Mother at "Rosemount" Exeter, shortly before her marriage, 1921.

My father at the age of forty. Very handsome and proud of being a Devonian, 1928.

My maternal Grandmother when she was known as the "Rose of Colchester".

My parents with Grandpa and Grandma Nunn at our hut, "Sea Shanty" in 1933.

On the Beach with my brothers John (left) and Peter in 1933.

Uncle Churchie.
A direct descendant of the artist
Thomas Churchyard, 1950.

Auntie Audrey.
The kind of aunt everyone would
like to have, 1950.

The garden at their home in Surrey.

The old corsair fort Ydra, Greece.
With me are Jennifer, Harry and Maria, 1951.

Dining out in Istanbul with left to right: Yavuz, Tahir, Afife and Osman.
In my hand is a glass of raki, 1957.

Outside Giuliano's Tomb at Montelepre, Sicily, with the famous photograph of the bandit, 1959.

Marian and I at the time of our Engagement, 1963.

Marian and I on our Wedding day, May 9th 1964.

Johnny aged 2.

and I shall always remember with affection the personalities who contributed so much to that golden era. Founder-member Rene Lister was a warm, endearing matriarchal figure with a rich fund of knowledge on an astonishing variety of subjects. Celia Dale, who lived in a period gem of a house at Histon with a priest-hole and a Cavalier ghost, was a woman of unusually fascinating looks; an intriguing blend of Egyptian princess and Siamese cat. Jack Carter, who had a flourishing clothes-hire firm in Portugal Place, wrote in a breezy, virile way and had a splendid rugged Iberian face inherited from his Basque grandmother.

The delicious Rabelaisian humour of Ron Westbrook from Great Shelford produced some inspired comic short stories and one never-to-be-forgotten evening he had us 'rolling in the aisles' when his hero got his flies caught in an umbrella stand! Mildred Dale's lovely farmhouse home at the end of Grange Road was the scene of many happy literary gatherings. In spite of a disabling arthritic hip Mildred was always elegant and gay and possessed a marvellous gift for spinning impromptu verses of sparkling charm for special occasions. Widow of the celebrated magician and circus-owner *The Great Carmo*, and herself once a music hall artiste of repute, Rita Cameron brought an authentic touch to her stories of the heartbreak behind the tinsel of show business. A little secretive about her age, Rita was still a vivacious, pretty, very feminine woman who continued to live life according to the brave philosophy of the veteran trouper.

These were just a few of the grand folk from all walks of life and with an infinite variety of story-telling material and technique who came together in a spirit of happy, stimulating comradeship. At the meetings where work was read out constructive criticism was given and markets for publication discussed. Successes of fellow members were wholeheartedly applauded.

And during those stirring days of the mid-1950's the most eagerly looked forward to event each month was the meeting of the Novel Group at Vera Batt's flat in Maid's Causeway overlooking Midsummer Common. Through a hallway aglow with brightly polished brassware and up an elegant staircase we would go to our own particular wonderland . . . a large room illumined by friendly furnishings and Vera's own special brand of generous hospitality. There, often until well past midnight, we would listen to extracts from each other's novels, intrigued by the variety of mood and scene presented. I remember particularly Cecilia Smith's wonderful family saga set in the Fen Country, Frank Reeves' unusual love story in the Austrian mountains, Celia Dale's crisply sophisticated *Aunt Dido* and Gillian's rich and turbulent Renaissance drama about Leo Della Fontana. My own contribution was a rumbustious Regency adventure-romance called *The Dark Peacock*. The atmosphere of these gatherings was electric and not even the fiercest blizzards of mid-winter could keep people away.

Apart from the Novel Group the meetings were held either at hotels in the city or at members' homes. I had the honour to serve as Circle Chairman from 1956-57 during the period when our general meetings were held in an upper room at 'The Eagle', a singularly quaint old coaching tavern down Bene't Street. These meetings were often addressed by distinguished writers and I particularly recall a visit from the poetess Frances Cornford who recounted some personal reminiscences of Rupert Brooke.

Thus through a combination of circumstances the time, the place and my frame of mind were abundantly right for creative work. With encouraging frequency I began to see myself in print . . . travel articles . . . historical features . . . childhood reminiscences . . . short stories . . . humorous verse. Somewhat surprisingly perhaps, it was the latter that gave me particular satisfaction, and there was clearly a direct kinship between my Orson Welles Eulogy of long ago and the various satirical verses I now got published. My own special favourite was *A Race Horse Reminisces* which ran as follows:

I hail from a stable in Ballykillskoot
And 'Celtic Coquette' is my name.
My Dad was a sprinter of rakish repute,
My Mum a fast filly called 'Flame'.

T'was Dermot O'Harp first applauded my pace
While trying me out on the straight,
And now I'm the winner in every race
And always first out of the gate.

I'm petted and vetted and widely admired
By top-hatted types in tail coats;
The sleekest and fleetest that's ever been sired,
I get champagne mixed with my oats.

Oh yes! I'm a girl for extravagant fare –
Remember my very blue blood;
Descended direct from an Araby mare,
The pride of a rich Pasha's stud.

From her I inherit each elegant curve,
My Levantine, lustrous *élan;*
She also bequeathed me her desert-hot verve
Which made her the talk of Tehran!

And then there's my grandpa (two centuries back)
Now framed on the Jockey Club wall,
Who caused a bar sinister wooing a hack
With no kind of background at all.

And yet I'll say this for the indiscreet clot –
He ran on the first Derby Day
In 1780, and beat the whole lot
While casually chewing some hay.

My Aunt 'Spicy Lass' next defied protocol,
Eloped with a circus ring mount.
Oh yes, he was one of the Troupe Haute Ecole –
But with *us* that just doesn't count.

Even worse was the saga of poor Aunt Rocheen
Who, wandering alone in the dew,
Was seized by a pony of gypsy-like mien
And lured to his bogland H.Q.

Of course *I'm* a horse of superior sense,
Such lapses I cannot condone.
I've borne on my back in the classic events
Some jockeys whose names are well-known.

Praise was poured on
Me and Gordon.
A gold purse, sir,
Gained with Mercer.
Waved a proud flag
With Harry Wragg.
Shared a hug with
Doughty Doug Smith.
Won a tester
With young Lester.
Did splendid work
With Charlie Smirke.
Was the field's star
With Harry Carr.
Romped home eas'ly
Teamed with Breasley.

There's just one small matter that mars my success,
My vanity shrinks at the thought
Of photos in close-up by newsreel and Press
While I am all steaming and taut.

I ask – is it fair to a beautiful girl
To picture her covered in sweat,
With mane all awry and a wild rolling eye,
And maidenly muzzle all wet?

One day I will leave all this glory behind,
Be put out to pasture and ease.
But do not imagine I really will mind –
I've other plans certain to please.

I'll meet a nice stallion,
Indulge in some dallyin',
And start a new line
As famous as mine.

Incidentally I sent a copy of this to the Jockey Club at Newmarket and received a most cordial acknowledgment.

I also wrote my top favourite short story at Cambridge. A ghost story in a Greek setting, it was called *Kitzo's Tune*, and was inspired by the appearance in my front porch one Christmastide of a schoolboy with a recorder.

It was at this period too that I at last had time to assemble the enormous amount of material I had collected over many years and from countless sources and write a full-length book about Byron's childhood and early adult years before fame. This was noticed most kindly by no less a personage than Sir John Murray, eminent descendant of Byron's own publisher, then resident at the family's house in Albemarle Street off Piccadilly. I spent a memorably happy afternoon there in the upper room once frequented by Byron, Scott and Tom Moore.

It has often been observed about Cambridge that the ordinary citizen in general has little contact with the life of the University. Everyone is certainly free to enjoy the pageantry of The Backs in springtime, listen to a recital of madrigals on the river in midsummer, get momentarily involved in the high jinks of Rag Week, attend carols by candlelight in Kings College Chapel. But actually to set foot in the inner sanctum of the University and take wine in the private apartments of a Don is a much rarer privilege and one which I enjoyed on three occasions.

Most intriguing by far was my visit to Dr. 'Freddie' Brittain of *Jesus College*. A man of surpassing charm with the humorous face of a music hall comedian (he was in fact a most versatile entertainer), Dr. Brittain was the friend and biographer of Sir Arthur Quiller-Couch and an authority on troubadour ballads and medieval Latin literature. But my particular reason for visiting him was to write about his remarkable collection of 400 cockerel ornaments. A cockerel has been the emblem of *Jesus College* since 1496 and in more recent times this led to the formation of the College's famous club called 'The Roosters'. Both as student and don 'Freddie' Brittain ardently identified himself with all the activities of The Roosters and there was a roost held in his rooms every Sunday evening during the Michaelmas and Lent terms. Viscount Snowdon was a Rooster while up at Cambridge.

Dr. Brittain's college rooms were filled with cockerel motifs of every imaginable description . . . the brass door knocker, the carpets, firescreen, cushion on his favourite chair and even his tea pot. Most of the ornaments came from students, the girl friends of students and other folk who had enjoyed his lively company. Some were of great value and some cost a few pence. The oldest was a 2,500 year-old clay cock from Cyprus, the smallest a gold bracelet charm. Of more homely origin were a church weathervane, a gingerbread mould and a Spanish olive oil jar, and there were toys of plastics, twigs, straw and wire.

Behind several lay amusing stories. There was, for example, a money box into which a notoriously talkative character in the college was required to drop a penny every time he interrupted a conversation. By the end of the day the box was full. The only snag was that every morning he of the over-active tongue crept into Dr. Brittain's room while the latter was away at breakfast and retrieved all his cash from the box!

After the publication of my article Dr. Brittain elected me an 'Honorary Hen' and sent me an invitation to the Rooster Club's next Sunday luncheon party. I treasure the autographed menu among my souvenirs.

On another occasion I accompanied Mildred Dale through the lantern-lit cloisters of *St. John's* to spend an evening with Professor Hobson. He was an expert on the origin of languages and his great delight was to tune into various foreign radio stations and identify, for instance, an announcer speaking German with a Greek accent. His ear was infallible and he could detect not only a man's nationality but also the actual district of the country from which he came.

The third of the distinguished dons with whom I took wine was Dr. Sidney Smith of *St. Catherine's*. This time my fellow guest was Gillian.

We saw the Doctor's priceless collection of Chinese porcelain and were also treated to some brilliant playing on the harpsichord which shared pride of place in his apartment with a grand piano.

Worthy in his own right to be mentioned alongside these three intellectual giants although he was not at the University is Professor Rheinhold Regensburger, who lived in Coleridge Road, Cambridge. His house was remarkable for having more books than furniture. Practically the entire wall space upstairs and down was given over to books in many languages, beautifully bound and carefully indexed. While I was writing *The Dark Peacock* I visited him on several occasions to do some research on carnival-time in early 19th century Venice and the activities of Barbary Coast pirates. The professor turned up the information I required with no trouble at all, brewed some excellent coffee, and set a box of Continental chocolate creams at my elbow. A frail, bespectacled man with a shock of white hair and exquisite manners, Rheinhold Regensburger was a man of rare courage as well as scholarship. At the time of the Nazi take-over in Germany he was a High Court judge in Berlin. Being a Jew he was on Hitler's black list. One morning as he was about to preside in Court he received warning that Storm Troopers were coming to arrest him. He slipped out of a side door and spent the next twenty-four hours riding round and round on the Berlin Metro. Despite his dangerous situation he passed the time teaching himself Persian grammar. Altogether he could read in fifty different languages. When the hue and cry died down he left Germany and lived for some time in Ireland before going to Cambridge. Miraculously he also managed to smuggle a large number of his most precious books out of Berlin.

For the theatre-goer Cambridge offered some marvellous opportunities. At the Arts Theatre I saw the two outstanding performances of my life: Siobhan McKenna's *St. Joan* and Michael MacLiammoir's towering virtuoso piece on Oscar Wilde. The atmosphere in the crowded auditorium on these occasions was absolutely electric and one felt a thrill at sharing in such great theatrical experiences. In a less profound but equally enjoyable way I had this same feeling when I saw the original *Beyond The Fringe* revue starring Jonathan Miller, Dudley Moore, Peter Cook and Alan Bennett. It was without doubt the funniest show I have ever seen.

Theatre fans in Cambridge had a great friend in F. Cyril Turner who owned a hairdresser's shop in King's Lynn. A diminutive bachelor who wore tinted glasses on account of an eye complaint, his frankly nondescript appearance belied his considerable taste and skill as an artist and, above all, as an organiser of theatre-going excursions to London and Stratford-on-Avon. He arranged these outings with immense efficiency and style for they were a true 'labour of love' in his life. I was one of the party which attended a performance of *Swan Lake* at Covent Garden, and afterwards he took me round to prima ballerina Beryl Grey's dressing room and introduced me to her. He was in fact on friendly terms with a large number of theatre folk, including Vivien Leigh and Sir Laurence Olivier. Later we all had dinner at a top London restaurant and a cake which had been specially designed with a 'Swan Lake' motif was cut.

Not long afterwards Mr. Turner was again my host when I attended the King's Lynn Arts Festival at which Sir Frederick Ashton, Joyce Grenfell (whom I idolise) and John Betjeman were the foremost celebrities. When I had tea at his home in Avenue Road I met his very remarkable mother. An artiste almost as good as her son and clearly once very beautiful, she had a trapeze hanging from the ceiling on the upstairs landing which she regularly exercised upon until she was well into her seventies!

Throughout my years in Cambridge writing dominated my life, but the variety of my other activities was considerable. I used to attend an evening class of some kind every winter. My tutor at the sculpture session had been a pupil of Henry Moore and my photography instructor had originally taught Viscount Snowdon his craft. I lost count of the number of talks I gave on travel and journalism to Townswomen's Guilds, W.I.'s, Rotarians, church fellowships and other miscellaneous societies. I appeared on an *Any Questions* panel and in several public debates and much enjoyed being guest speaker at the Forum Club's annual dinner.

I had long wanted to learn Italian and contacted the Faculty of Modern Languages in search of a likely teacher. And thus it was that the third great friendship of my life was forged when I began to take lessons with Loredana Baccovich at 5/- an hour in the Bohemian atmosphere of the students' 'Soup Kitchen' in Petty Cury.

When I was introduced to Lory (as she was generally known) I immediately realised that I already knew her by sight. The first time I ever saw her was while having tea with a friend under the apple trees at the Orchard Cafe, Grantchester, one Sunday afternoon. Lory was helping to serve and I watched her carrying a tray with the langorous grace that was so characteristic. Her strong featured, arresting face was very like a youthful Anna Magnani, though framed by long blonde hair instead of black. She had a compact, well-endowed figure and a style of dress that was all her own . . . flowing skirt with billowing petticoats, tight sweater and soft leather pumps. Her whole appearance was head-turningly attractive in a decidedly off-beat way. Even in a city noted for colourful characters Lory stood out.

The Faculty told me that she spoke 'beautiful' Italian and when we met I learnt that she was the daughter of a wealthy glass-factory owner who had a palazzo on the Grand Canal in Venice. Her mother was a celebrated society beauty from Milan. Lory was in Cambridge as an *au pair* girl and her fiance Lino, who hailed from Calabria, was a trainee hotel manager in Florence.

Thanks to Lory's admirable tuition I quickly learnt to speak and write Italian fluently. In the process we became firm friends and she invited me to go and stay with her in Venice. And thus I was introduced to the city that has captured my heart more completely than any other in the world.

A true *Veneziana* to her finger tips, Lory knew all the gondoliers by name and showed me all the enchantments of her birthplace with a deep knowledge of its history and customs. We took afternoon tea in grand style at Florian's in St. Mark's Square and also had many meals in tiny, out-of-the-way cafes where I was able to listen to the soft, beguiling Venetian dialect and watch the age-old local game of dice *(dadi)* being played. She knew a little shop in a secluded alleyway that sold exactly the same sort of *polenta* pudding that was much favoured as a delicacy by rich and poor alike during the 18th century. Indeed one traditional song still survives about the Contessa Benzoni, a renowned beauty of that period, who used to glide along in her gondola with polenta pudding hidden in her bodice! I never tired of wandering through the maze of alleys watching craftsmen at work in their dark, cramped shops, nor of standing beside the Grand Canal at sunset marvelling at the famous rose-tinted afterglow which illumined the whole city.

Lory took me to the Venice Opera House, to the island of Chioggia (noted for its amber-sailed *bragozze* and as the birthplace of Carlo Goldoni), to the haunted solitude of the island of Torcello and to the islets of Murano and Burano celebrated respectively for glassware and lace. I went to the Palazzo Mocenigo, where Byron once lived, and to the enchanting little islet of San Lazzaro far out in the lagoon where the Armenian monastery often visited by Byron still stands. It houses the presses on which all the world's Armenian literature is printed.

I also had the rare privilege of seeing a *squero,* one of the small, hard-to-find boatyards hidden well away along the side canals of the city where gondolas are made. Like so many old crafts that of gondola-making has been handed down from generation to generation in the same families. Eight kinds of wood are used in the making of a gondola and if two or three men are working together on one it can be completed in a week. All the construction is still done with hand tools as it has been down the centuries. The *ferro* (swan-like prow ornament) has a special significance. The axe-like top represents the head of the Doge and the arch at its base the Rialto Bridge, while the frets below symbolise the districts into which the city is divided.

I stayed on the Lido at the luxury flat of Lory and her mother in the perpetually gay, lantern-lit Gran Viale. The Lido, which lies on a separate spit of land a few miles beyond the old city of Venice, is one of the glittering playgrounds of the international set and the scene of the Venice Film Festival which was in progress while I was there. With two friends Adriana and Roberto, Lory and I virtually gate-crashed the ultra-exclusive Hotel Excelsior one afternoon and, on the strength of a cup of coffee apiece, had our cigarettes lit by a passing waiter and some request numbers played by the resident orchestra.

But my happiest memory of Venice-in fact one of the happiest memories of my whole life – was when Lory, Roberto, a young English theological student named John and myself went 'out on the town' from nine o'clock in the evening (the fashionable hour for dining in Venice) until five o'clock the next morning.

We started off with a typical Venetian meal served in the vine-canopied courtyard of a small trattoria overlooking a side canal. It was washed down with the deep red local wine called 'ombra' which makes you feel wonderful without making you tight. Then we explored the oldest, quaintest parts of the city by the light of a full moon, slipping into some tiny bar *en route* whenever we felt in need of further refreshment. We took a gondola ride through a liquid wonderland of dancing shadows and reflected lantern light and joined the gondolier in his songs. Later, like an exuberant bunch of kids, we jumped on and off the massed *sandali* (trading barges of the city) which were moored alongside a quay. We ran hand in hand across deserted squares and turned cartwheels in jasmine-scented courtyards, and the laughing spirits of those carnival revellers of long ago seemed to be all round us. It was a unique and joyous experience. At dawn we caught the first water bus of the day back to the Lido.

I just cannot see how anyone can be disappointed with Venice. The moment you walk down the flight of steps out of the railway station you find the splendour of the Grand Canal spread out before you. To my eyes everything about Venice is superlatively artistic right down to such minor details as the design of the lamp standards, the red carnations the gondoliers fix on the prows of their craft and the flower-patterned bags in which purchases are wrapped at patisseries and confectioners' shops.

Lory was always very entertaining and – as with all true friendships – we never ran out of conversation or tired of each other's company. Despite her upper class background her politics were extremely left wing. Versatility was her middle name. She was a talented artist and writer, a champion swimmer, a clever linguist and (a most unusual feminine accomplishment in Italy) a dashing and fearless motor-cyclist.

I visited her in Italy for the second time shortly after her marriage. At that period she and Lino were living in an enchanting, secluded little cottage set amid vineyards and cypresses in the grounds of a famous old villa on the outskirts of Florence. There she kept a powerful motor-cycle and a Lambretta motor-scooter. On the latter I took many rides with her during my stay. Florence is the stateliest of cities, very historical and exceedingly beautiful though with a somewhat austere atmosphere. It is as different from Venice as a dowager contessa from a sprightly courtesan. Nevertheless Lory would drive at a spanking pace through the cobbled streets in the heart of town and when we got out into the ravishing Tuscany countryside she would really open the throttle and keep up a steady seventy, accelerating still more for a playful race with any male motor-cyclists we encountered on the road. I held on for dear life, trusting in Lory's skill but at the same time secretly philosophising that if I had to come to a violent end there was no lovelier place to do it than here!

Near the market place in Florence we dined at Armando's tiny restaurant not far from Annigoni's studio. In his box-like open fronted premises where tables spilt out on to the pavement, this celebrated chef prepared his superb cuisine in full view of his customers with a flair and showmanship that defied description.

One of Tuscany's greatest charms is the abundance of small hilltop towns perfectly preserved in their medieval state. They are encircled by sturdy walls and entered by massive gateways. The narrow cobbled streets echo with the rumbling wheels of primitive looking wagons piled high with grapes and drawn by oxen. I visited two of the most perfect of these ancient little townships – San Gimignano and Assisi. The latter – birthplace of my favourite saint – is especially beautiful with its arches, flowers and clouds of white doves.

In 1958 I was again in Italy, this time with Gillian. Our ultimate destination was Sicily but we stayed in Rome for a few days on the way. Our hotel was a modest *pensione* in the Via Margutta, a narrow side street close to the Spanish Steps, and much frequented by the artists' colony. We saw all the celebrated local sights . . . the Vatican, the Castle of San Angelo, the Appian Way, the Coliseum, Hadrian's Villa and the wonderful gardens and fountains of Tivoli. But two of the places I remember best are less familiar to tourists. One was the Protestant Cemetery where Keats is buried. It would be hard to visualise a more beautiful resting place anywhere. Just outside the cemetery stands a pyramid, one of Rome's most prominent landmarks, and the waste ground surrounding this is inhabited by a group of cats which are fed daily by cat lovers and provided with newspapers on which to lie luxuriously in the sun. They are magnificent creatures in the peak of condition.

While we were in Rome the Circus Togni was pitched close by St. Paul's Gate. Being a great circus enthusiast I attended an evening performance. Gillian did not share my passion for sawdust and spangles so I went alone. I got an excellent ringside seat and during the interval Signor Togni invited me to his caravan for a glass of wine. The highlight of the second half was the most spectacular trapeze act I have ever seen. For the climax of this the arena was plunged into total darkness and the aerialists, wearing phosphorescent costumes, swung to and fro on invisible trapezes like fireflies and made some hair-raising leaps from bar to bar which had all the illusion of flight through space.

Later Gillian and I moved on to Naples where we went to the San Carlo Opera House. Because it was April (a slack time of the season) the management invited us to exchange our modest seats for the grandeur of a box. We drove along the superb Amalfi Coast, explored the ruins of Pompeii and dined at Sorrento. Then we caught a steamer to Sicily, landed at Palermo about eight o'clock next morning and booked into a decidedly seedy but conveniently central hotel.

My intense desire to visit Sicily had been sparked off by Gavin Maxwell's admirable book about the bandit Salvatore Giuliano entitled *God Protect Me From My Friends,* and four hours after setting foot on the island I caught a bus out to Giuliano's native village of Montelepre where Maxwell had lived while writing his book. Gillian preferred making a tour of Palermo's churches so, as should be the case with all good friends who go a-travelling together, we happily went our separate ways that hot April afternoon.

My excursion to Montelepre proved to be one of the most interesting experiences of my life and I cannot do better than quote the travel talk which I gave about it some years later on *Radio Colchester*:–

'Even today banditry is still a widespread occupation in the lovely island of Sicily away from the tourist centres. But, as I can vouch for from personal experience, a foreigner – and an unaccompanied woman at that – can safely venture into the heart of bandit territory and be most hospitably received.

I visited two of the most notorious bandit strongholds in Sicily: *Montelepre* – birthplace and subsequent battle H.Q. of the late celebrated Salvatore Giuliano, whose sensational career as an outlaw was constantly in the world's headlines between 1946 and 1950, and *Favara* – a hamlet tucked away in the hills not far from Agrigento, where surprises lurk round every turn of the dark, twisting alleyways.

The bus from Palermo to Montelepre starts from a square just off the busy thoroughfare where Giuliano used to kidnap wealthy hostages in broad daylight. On the way out of town it passes the plush restaurant where the bandit used to dine openly while police were searching for him in the mountains.

The steep, winding road to Montelepre is lushly green and ruggedly barren by turns. In spring the hour's ride is an especially beautiful one for much of the landscape is aglow with wild flowers. Amber marigolds and an outsize species of petunia-coloured clover predominate. The air is heavy with the fragrance of orange groves.

On this mountain road so ideally suited for ambushes, the full flavour of the Giuliano saga still lingers though it is now 20 years since he met a violent end at the age of 28. Everywhere there are landmarks associated with him. The lonely *carabinieri* barracks he once attacked regularly, the farmhouse where he held secret meetings. A mile or so before reaching Montelepre is the walled cemetery where he is buried. The atmosphere there is one of whispering cypresses, the drowsy hum of bees and the rustle of emerald green lizards among dry twigs.

Montelepre itself lies in a fold in the mountains. Giuliano's mother still lives in his old home. The back door through which the bandit once made so many dramatic exits looks out onto steep cultivated terraces of figs, beans and prickly pears. It was siesta time when I strolled through the village and there were few people about. My camera was in action constantly for Montelepre is picturesque in the characteristic Sicilian manner. Houses cluster along narrow streets of steps. Iron balconies are festooned with washing. Ducks, chickens, dogs and cats wander at will amongst the garbage. By some doorsteps is a hen in a coop or a tethered goat. Pack mules are plentiful.

While I was crouching in the shade of a church porch to reload my camera a podgy but not unpersonable young man came up and offered to be my guide on a tour of the village. I would have been perfectly happy to explore Montelepre on my own but (as is bound to happen in Mediterranean parts) he remained a fixture for the rest of the afternoon and – as things turned out – I did not regret it.

While we were drinking coca-cola 'on the house' in the one bar that was still open during siesta-time, my companion was joined by four of his friends. One was a photographer who worked for a Palermo newspaper but lived in Montelepre and ran a small fancy goods shop there as a sideline. He it was who took the original dashing photograph of the handsome Giuliano which has been reproduced in countless publications all over the world and which is now displayed in the front of his tomb.

I sooned learned that all five men had known Giuliano well and they asked me if I would like to drive out to the cemetery to see his grave. We got into a car, which I very much doubt if any of them could have acquired by honest means, and drove off at breakneck speed. I must confess that I was surprised that all these able-bodied characters in the prime of life should be free to "take the afternoon off" like this but in Sicily – and above all in Montelepre, it is wisest not to inquire how a man makes his living!

Among the humble graves of the peasant-folk who idolised him as a Robin Hood, Giuliano rests in a princely marble sarcophagus inside an impressive shrine. While we were there the photographer insisted that I should pose for a picture outside the shrine holding the bandit's portrait. Quick as a flash he removed the photograph from the niche in front of the tomb, thrust it into my hand and "snapped" me with my own camera. It turned out to be an excellent photograph and remains proof to my friends that I am not telling a tall story about this memorable episode. When I caught the evening bus back to Palermo the whole village turned out to wave me farewell.

Though *Favara* may lack the romantic aura which surrounds Montelepre on account of Giuliano, it is a fascinating place to meet bandits on their home ground. I travelled there by country bus from Agrigento arriving at about one o'clock in the afternoon. Directly I saw the maze of alleyways with cobbled steps and the one-roomed homes with whitewashed tins of geraniums outside, I knew my camera was going to have another field day, but to my dismay I found that I had forgotten to load it with a fresh film before leaving Agrigento. The chances of getting a 620 reel in this very primitive tumbledown village at one o'clock on an extremely hot afternoon seemed very remote indeed, but being a supreme optimist I made my way to what passed for the main square and scanned the buildings for any sign of a chemist shop. I cannot say I was really surprised when I didn't find one. As a last resort I approached an old woman who was sweeping her step and asked if there was anywhere I could obtain a film.

She beckoned over a lad of about eight and gestured me to follow him. For ten minutes, without saying a word, he led me through a network of alleyways and stopped at last at the door of a small, cramped house. In answer to his knocks heavy bolts were drawn aside, the door opened furtively and the boy stated his business. The door was then opened wider and I was beckoned inside while my small guide departed without having exchanged a single word with me.

To my amazement I found myself standing in a room filled with photographic equipment of every imaginable kind – quite obviously stolen property of course! I was handed the film I required and, having paid exactly the same price as I would have done in a more reputable establishment, I departed fascinated by the cloak and dagger quality of the whole transaction.

As I strolled through Favara taking photographs, women called friendly greetings from their windows and ran out to show me their babies or press a flower into my hand. As I was passing one house a woman came out, seized me by the arm and drew me inside. Then she triumphantly bolted her door so that no neighbours should 'share' her guest.

She seated me at a well-worn table, laid a freshly laundered, lace-trimmed serviette at my elbow and poured me a glass of wine. As I sipped my drink I glanced round the typical Sicilian interior. A good deal of space was taken up by an enormous bed. On the wall immediately above it was a picture of the Madonna and a little oil lamp burning. The rest of the furnishings were very sparse and poor except for . . . I could scarcely believe my eyes . . . except for a magnificent new radiogram. And it worked too. For with the ingenuity all Sicilian peasants possess, means had been found to introduce electricity into this humblest of abodes.

My fat, bouncing hostess went over and put on a record. It was 'Granada' which is a fairly loud tune in any case, and she turned it up to full volume which was absolutely deafening. Then she reseated herself beside me, threw an arm about my shoulder and proceeded to shout cordially into my ear. This was a taste of Sicilian hospitality that I would not have missed on any account.

Before I left Favara I photographed a bandit father with his pretty little daughter in his arms, a mother with her bonny baby son perched on the saddle of his father's mule, and a tiny church containing a huge, hauntingly lifelike effigy of the crucified Christ. This church stood at the end of a long, dusty track which appeared to mark the centre of the village. I did not learn the significance of this track until I returned to Agrigento. There I was told that all the folk living on one side of the track had a deadly feud with all those who lived on the opposite side. It was more than a youth's life was worth to fall in love with a girl on the other side of the road.

Yet I had been treated to an equally warm display of friendliness by both factions. For in Sicily – as in other places where violence and vendettas are an accepted part of the everyday scene – there is a strict code of honour which ensures that strangers may travel safely and happily.

In Agrigento and Taormina we stayed at excellent *pensioni* which had been recommended to us by Olive Cook (Mrs. Edwin Smith), the well-known East Anglian writer and artist. Olive had lived and painted in Sicily and adored the island and its people. At a cafe in Taormina Gillian and I had a chance meeting with Daphne Phelps, a remarkable Englishwoman who owns a villa there and is a generous benefactress to the islanders. There was a BBC programme about her in 1965.

Taormina is situated in a sensationally beautiful coastal setting but is much too commercialised for my taste. It is possible to stand on the terrace of a former monastery (now a highly exclusive hotel) at dusk and watch Mount Etna erupting in the distance. A memorable and decidedly awe-inspiring sight.

Although my travels had already taken me to some of the loveliest places on earth there was still one city that drew me like a magnet . . . *Istanbul.* In the spring of 1959 I started making preparations for the most ambitious journey I had yet undertaken. Determined to learn a few hundred words of Turkish in advance I approached the Faculty of Modern Languages for a second time and they proved most helpful. I was given the address of a delightful Turkish girl named Beylan who had rooms over at Newnham in a house quaintly called *The Little Pyghtle*. A doctor of psychology doing a post-graduate course in Cambridge, Beylan was a petite, dainty brunette with ravishing eyes and colouring that suggested she hailed from the Circassian district of Turkey, long famed for its exceptionally beautiful girls.

In a large notebook I wrote down phonetically all the words she taught me, paying the closest possible attention to a really accurate rendering of the pronunciation. Instead of paying Beylan in cash for my lessons I gave her painting materials, for she was an artist of very great merit. Her work was prodigiously bold and colourful and several of her paintings hung in well-known art galleries on the Continent.

During one of my lessons a Turkish student named Yilmaz happened to call, and when Beylan told him that I was shortly going to Istanbul he gave me the address of his family who lived in the suburb of Kadikoy on the Asiatic shore of the Bosphorus, a 20-minute steamer trip from Istanbul proper. This was a tremendous stroke of luck and my contact with Yilmaz's family added vastly to the pleasure of my stay in Turkey.

I set out in late May for Italy and spent a few days with Lory in Venice before continuing by sea to Istanbul from the Zattere aboard an Italian steamer. It was a memorable voyage which lay for part of the route among the little golden islands of the Aegean that I already knew so well. I shall never forget the thrill of my first glimpse of the fairytale skyline of Istanbul – exactly like an illustration from *The Arabian Nights.*

I booked in at the Park Hotel, a quite expensive westernised one in the heart of the city, and within an hour I was out making a tour on foot of the surrounding streets. Although a great deal of modern town planning has taken place in recent years I saw several fine examples of the old-fashioned style of ornately gabled, wooden houses in muddy backstreets. Only five minutes' walk from the hotel I found myself standing on the shore of the Bosphorus confronted by all the mosques, minarets and oriental splendour my heart could desire.

On my first evening Yilmaz's family came to the Park Hotel, and over drinks we got to know each other. The father Osman was a widower and a retired merchant, the eldest son Tahir was a specialist mechanic who spoke excellent English, the third son Yavuz was a teenage student, and there was one daughter Afife aged 14 who already showed signs of growing into a great beauty. She loved drawing and spoke good Italian so it was in this language rather than in Turkish that we usually conversed. They were a charming family and we became immediate friends. With their assistance I moved from the Park Hotel to a much more modest but perfectly adequate one in Kadikoy, close to their own home.

As it was Afife's school holiday she was my companion during daytime excursions, and in the evenings Tahir was my escort to cinemas, theatres and night-spots. On what proved to be one of my happiest evenings of all in Istanbul I accompanied the whole family to an open-air night-spot called *Tepebasi.* This was not a smart westernised rendezvous but one at which the ordinary folk gathered every evening between 8 p.m. and 2 a.m. to eat and be entertained by typical traditional style Turkish music.

Our menu was salami with a salad of tomatoes, carrots, nuts and raisins, served up with a side bowl of *chejik* (garlic-flavoured yoghourt and water with sliced cucumber added). Then came rice wrapped in vine leaves and goat's milk cheese, followed by fruit and sweetmeats. And to wash it down, of course, we had the very potent, aniseed-flavoured national drink *raki.*

While we dined one of Turkey's top 'pop' singers rendered songs in the tremulous, wailing, melancholy style one associates with the East. When she ended there was the tinkling applause of hundreds of forks on dinner plates and cries of *'Tekra'* (encore). Despite the strange discordance of the melodies to Western ears the titles and lyrics of the songs were extraordinarily like those we are familiar with. For example . . . *'I am still in love with you'* . . . *'If you are not really in love you will get tired easily'.* The words 'gul' (meaning rose) and 'bulbul' (nightingale) appear frequently in the lyrics and are common expressions of endearment in the Turkish language.

In all their forms of entertainment the Turks are very emotional. Lurid melodrama is the keynote of all Turkish-made films and a similar mood is reflected in their various fiction magazines. The national sport of wrestling is followed with passionate interest and I was taken to a tournament one afternoon being, as far as I could see, the only woman present in the stadium.

The wrestlers wear leather knee-breeches, fight barefoot and are liberally coated in oil. Before commencing their bout they do a strange ritual dance, bowing in obeisance to an imaginary sultan and making elaborate salutations to each other. Adding a unique touch to the proceedings is a band of musicians who supply a sort of musical commentary on the progress of the fight. As the bout begins the drum beats slowly and the reed instruments blow subdued, steady notes. Then as the combat warms up so the tempo of the music quickens and rises to a frenzied crescendo. The audience refresh themselves from time to time with pickled pancakes and a drink made from yoghourt and water. This sport dates back centuries and was once a regular spectacle at the court of the sultans.

After the tournament we went along to Luna Park, the city's famous pleasure gardens, to have samovar tea on a terrace overlooking the Bosphorus. As dusk fell the illuminations were switched on. The multi-coloured lamps were shaped like tulips, this flower being the emblem of Istanbul.

One Sunday I was taken to Princess Island, a favourite weekend haunt further down the Bosphorus. It was an idyllic spot with pinewoods and holiday villas and – apart from donkeys – the only other form of transport was provided by brightly-painted open carriages with fringed canopies and cascading geraniums for decoration. Another weekend we went to Sile, a small coastal resort on the Black Sea. The antiquated bus which took us there did not have a hooter. Instead the driver operated a siren with a piece of string.

But my greatest delight was exploring the old quarter of Istanbul with Afife or Tahir. I was awakened every morning by the rumble of the water carrier's dray beneath my hotel window. The water carrier has been a familiar figure for centuries. At dawn he goes up to the ancient fountain of pure water on Camlica Hill, fills a large number of glass flasks and places them in files on his long, moss lined cart. Then he descends into the town and delivers the water from door to door. After breakfasting on yoghourt, fruit, bread, butter and rose-petal jam with a tall glass of very sweet but milkless tea, I would go and meet my friends and we would take the ferry steamer across to the city, disembarking at the Galata Bridge which spans the commercial waterway of Istanbul, the romantically-named Golden Horn. On the further side of the bridge lies the old quarter; teeming, dusty, rather smelly here and there, and incomparably picturesque.

Along one tree-shaded pavement men sat at typewriters. They

were the modern equivalent of the public scribes of long ago and wrote letters for anyone at a very small cost. Then there were the *humuls* (porters) who carried fantastically heavy loads on leather saddles strapped to their backs. Fortune-tellers stood in the gutter with a pet rabbit or bird which picked your *'kismet'* from a box filled with slips of paper.

One of the most colourful figures I saw was the lemonade or sherbet-seller. On his back he carried a container like an outsize brass coffee pot, the lid of which was adorned with ribbons and coins. Round his waist was strapped a tray of tumblers. When one ordered a drink he merely tipped the spout of the great container under one armpit and poured out. He also sold bread rings which he displayed on his arms like massive bracelets.

I never ceased to be fascinated by the sight of countrywomen in town for the day. They wore baggy floral-patterned trousers and carpet slippers. Their head and shoulders were completely covered save for brow and eyes – by a vast black hood-cum-cloak called *a bashlik*. If she was young and pretty the effect could be ravishing, but if she was old and withered it was terrifying! The *bashlik* was outlawed by Kemal Ataturk when he came to power, but in recent years the custom has crept back among countrywomen. If the women carried babies these were wrapped in swaddling clothes. In complete contrast the Turkish city-girl was very stylish and fashion-conscious.

All the buses and lorries had prayers painted on the front of the drivers' cabins. 'Go on your way happily' and 'May Allah give you good eyes' were typical ones. Taxis often had miniature copies of the Koran fixed to their windscreens, and were distinguished by a black and white chequered band round their coach-work. When hired for a wedding a taxi had its bonnet decorated with red and white flowers and a white silk handkerchief was flown from a little mast on the nearside mudguard.

The gorgeous Topkapi Palace was the home of the sultans for four centuries. A large portion of it consists of a series of splendid, ornate pavilions set in lush green tree-shaded gardens. Inside are rich carpets, couches with jewel-studded draperies, magnificent tilework and coffee tables made of ivory, ebony and mother-of-pearl mosaic.

The relics of luxurious living which are housed in the Palace Treasury make Aladdin's cave pale by comparison. There are articles once used by the women of the harem: ivory mirrors, jade toilet bowls, pearl-studded velvet purses, diamond-encrusted combs, richly-worked girdles and fans, and necklaces of crystal, coral, amethyst and amber.

Also on display are the turbans and scarlet and gold fur-lined robes of the sultans, together with their superb turban ornaments of rubies, emeralds and diamonds. There are solid gold thrones studded with rubies and diamonds, and golden chests brimming over with emeralds the size of pigeons' eggs. Solid gold swords with prayers from the Koran embossed on the hilts. Richly-worked saddles of the finest leather. Jewelled daggers. Five-foot-long smoking pipes of amber and ebony banded with pearls and turquoises.

Istanbul has more than 500 mosques and one of the most memorable moments for any visitor from the West is seeing and hearing for the first time the *muezzin* calling the faithful to prayer from the balcony of a minaret. He still uses the age-old cry: 'Allah is great! There is no God but Allah!'

Inside a mosque there is wonderful colour at all levels. The floor is covered with brilliantly-hued mats. The high circular windows are sapphire, rose, amethyst and amber. But the greatest beauty of all lies in the tile-work adorning the walls. The incredibly lovely colour combination of the tiles is lilac, turquoise and jade and the motifs are usually roses, tulips, carnations and flowing foliage. The effect produced is like that of a particularly rich peacock's tail. Outside the courtyard is dominated by an ornamental fountain where the devout wash themselves with ritual significance before going in to pray. There are clouds of pigeons which are regarded as holy birds and pedlars squat on the cobbles selling prayer caps, copies of the Koran and phials of perfume. On the domes of many mosques are great, untidy storks' nests – one of the most picturesque sights of all. The birds are never disturbed for they are considered to be symbols of good fortune.

One day Tahir and Afife took me on a steamer trip up the Golden Horn to the ancient tumbledown district of Eyup where the holiest of all the city's mosques is situated. Adjoining it is an equally old cemetery. The tombstones have much artistic distinction. They are tall and slender and those of the men are surmounted by carved turbans the patterns of which indicate the trade or profession of the deceased. We walked through the steep hillside burial ground, where sheep now graze, up to an old gabled coffee house known as Pierre Lotti's. Lotti was a 19th century French writer who fell in love with Istanbul and decided to make his home there.

Another place of enduring fascination is the enormous covered bazaar, centuries-old commercial meeting place of East and West and once the destination of rich camel caravans from all over Asia. Merchandise of every description is on sale there. Carpets, ceramics, gold and silver work, jewellery, armour, weapons, furniture, textiles and perfumes. Many stories are recounted of the bargains bought there. One tells how a Frenchman bought a cameo brooch for a song and later discovered it had once belonged to Catherine the Great. Another how an Englishman bought a painting for only three guineas and later found it to be a masterpiece by Bellini.

While in Istanbul I spent one afternoon at the home of Beylan's mother, a distinguished-looking woman who had once known and greatly admired Kemal Ataturk. She told me that as a child she had often seen camel caravans resting outside the walls of St. Sophia which is situated close to the Covered Market.

I made one solo excursion out of Istanbul to the former ancient capital of Bursa which lies some distance inland beyond the shores of Anatolia. Like all Turkish men Tahir was askance at the idea of my making the journey unaccompanied, though I assured him that in England girls travelled round quite freely on their own. He contacted a friend of his in advance (a likeable and enterprising young man named Mehmet who ran a travel bureau in Bursa), asking him to book me a hotel room and meet me off the bus.

After a three-hour steamer trip eastwards through the Bosphorus I went ashore at a primitive hamlet called Yalova and continued to my destination by country bus. On my arrival Mehmet escorted me to Bursa's Park Hotel ('Park' seems as common a name for hotels in Turkey as 'Red Lion' is in England). This proved to be a remarkably westernised hotel for such an ancient and remote town. Here Mehmet treated me to an evening meal which included an over-generous helping of runner beans cooked in oil. This was clearly one of his favourite eatables and to be polite I consumed it with as much simulated relish as I could muster – though I was to suffer agonies during the night as a consequence!

Later we strolled through the town in the dusk and Mehmet indicated various notable landmarks for Bursa is a place steeped in history. As tactfully as I could I thanked him for booking me into the Park Hotel but pointed out that I would much rather stay at an authentic 100 per cent. *Turkish* type hotel. He was very much against the idea and listed all the disadvantages. However, I gently but firmly insisted and, making it clear that it was very much against his better judgment, he took me to exactly the sort of hotel I was looking for. The sleeping accommodation was immediately above a restaurant impregnated with exotic cooking aromas and the window of my room overlooked a very picturesque bazaar. Ablutions consisted of a line of antiquated sinks. Lone female tourists were not catered for in any way at all, so I used to arrange to go for a wash when none of the male guests was about and ensured a degree of privacy by putting one of the heavy fire precaution tins of sand against the door.

When I retired to bed on the first night I had a pretty uncomfortable time of it. My digestion rebelled violently against all those oily beans; it was an airless, sweltering night, and I got bitten by bugs. But I never for a moment regretted exchanging the civilised amenities of the Park Hotel for two nights of discomfort in truly native surroundings.

I bought a pair of sandals in the nearby bazaar and took photographs of scenes I am only likely to see once in a lifetime. On market day in Bursa farmers came into town with their sheep travelling from the country in covered wagon-type carts. They appeared completely unconcerned as I 'snapped' them, but the women of Bursa fled round the first available corner directly they saw me merely holding a camera, and if they had babies in their arms they covered the mites' faces with their cloaks. Belief in the power of the evil eye is still widespread and children are protected by blue-beaded talismans pinned to their underclothing. The month I spent in Turkey was certainly one of the most fascinating of my life.

CHAPTER NINE

IN VALIANT COMPANY

MY YEARS IN CAMBRIDGE proved an important period of self discovery on many levels and the voluntary welfare work I did had a profound influence on me. Through my experiences as a nursing auxiliary at a hospital for chronic sick and as a general helper and escort with the local St. Raphael Club for severely crippled folk, I found that I was not repelled by the sight of disease, deformity and mutilation, and that I could strike up warm, easy, unembarrassed friendships with handicapped people. The dignity, courage and, above all, the humour with which they faced life made me feel very humble in their presence. Anyone who has been involved in this kind of work will know exactly what I mean.

I think it was the work with St. Raphael's that appealed to me most, though I also thoroughly enjoyed entertaining the St. Andrew's Club for the Blind and the Trumpington Darby & Joan Club with my guitar or with travel talks. The former was run by Mrs. Irene Law, an incredibly energetic octogenarian who had clearly been a great aristocratic beauty in her day. She had close connections with the family who owned the famous Hope Diamond and on the days I gave recitals to her Club I used to dine at her treasure-filled house in Newton Road. The Trumpington Darby & Joan Club was run by two charming, lively women named Joy Slater and Margaret Scott who had made it one of the cheeriest rendezvous in the district. In addition I read once a week at an old people's home and periodically visited two housebound invalids. These were no mere 'do-gooding' chores for I felt genuinely drawn to this sort of work and found it tremendously worthwhile.

Towards the close of 1961 the death of a man who was very dear to me made my world stand still. Marriage had been the shining beacon on my road ahead and now it was extinguished. For seven years my life in Cambridge had had a halcyon quality about it. I had found fulfilment in creative work and had never worried much about tomorrow. Now, at the age of 39, my future was to be entirely reshaped by a major decision. The social welfare work I had been so happily engaged in at Cambridge proved to be my signpost. I wrote to Sue Ryder offering my services to her Foundation in whatever capacity she considered most suitable, and she asked me to go and see her at her home in Cavendish.

My first meeting with Sue Ryder, O.B.E., the wife of Group Captain Leonard Cheshire, V.C., took place one afternoon in April just before Easter, 1962, in the *'Red Room'* at The Sue Ryder Home, Cavendish. Besides being the family home of these two remarkable people, this gracious 16th century house close to the village green is the permanent haven of a group of gravely disabled concentration camp survivors and patients of all age groups.

All visitors to The Sue Ryder Home were received in the *'Red Room',* a small, homely apartment with a brick fireplace and cream paintwork. Dark oak furniture was set against a red carpet and matching curtains. Figurines in Polish national costume danced on the window sill. On the walls hung a flower study, a ballet scene, a magnificent piece of framed embroidery worked on black linen and a painting of a troika being driven through deep snow.

Prior to our meeting, I had no idea what Sue Ryder was like in appearance. I knew of course about her service with Special Operations Executives and also her idea formed during the war of founding a Living Memorial to relieve suffering in Europe and elsewhere, of her relief work and also her countless marathon solo drives to different places in Europe where she had provided desperately needed Homes for the disabled, including many sick children. Somehow I had pictured her as tall, strongly built, perhaps a trifle formidable in looks and manner. Nothing could have been further from the truth.

I found myself being held in the frank, steady gaze of a pair of very expressive and very blue eyes. They completely dominated the delicately-boned face that was wan and tired from 18 years unceasing work for the relief of suffering. The nose was sharp, the lips full and compassionate. The fine gold hair was worn in a softly curled style which gave her a remarkably girlish appearance. This impression was heightened by her slight physique and slender, pretty legs. She had a delightful way of raising her eyebrows quizzically when in animated conversation. Her voice was low-pitched, her manner of speaking decisive and to the point; she never hesitated or fumbled for words. One sensed that she had no time for 'flannel' or small talk. 'Deeds not words' had always been her maxim. On this particular day when we first met she was wearing a voluminous fur coat and I had no idea that she was within a few days of the birth of her second child. In fact nobody outside her immediate circle knew and her pregnancy had not been allowed to interfere with her usual long-distance drives on the Continent. I was aware of an immediate rapport between Sue Ryder and myself.

'This is quite extraordinary', she said. 'As you probably know our work is based very much on faith. We have been praying that someone like yourself would come along to do public relations work for us.'

She explained that an hour-long film about her work was just nearing completion and that by the end of the summer it would be ready for showing all over the country. It was called *These Are They* (a quotation from Revelation). Some of it had been made by her husband (I knew the Group Captain was an expert photographer) and the editing was being done by a professional film maker named Wyn Cooper. There was a commentary spoken by Sue Ryder herself. Would I be willing to accompany the film round the country and answer questions from audiences after its screening? She also needed someone to speak about her work at functions which, for one reason or another, she was unable to attend herself.

I replied that this sort of assignment was just up my street and thus in the most informal way imaginable, I became that afternoon Honourary Public Relations Officer to the *Forgotten Allies Trust*, as it was then called.

After the interview I was shown round the house and gardens and met many of the patients and survivors who would have had no future at all in the post-war world if Sue Ryder had not brought them over to be cared for in England for the rest of their lives. The single patients had their own bed-sitting rooms, while married couples lived in bungalows specially built in the grounds. All the accommodation was gay and attractive with colour schemes and soft furnishings personally chosen by Sue Ryder herself. The majority of the patients at Cavendish were Polish, though Sue Ryder's work as a whole embraced many nationalities.

I spoke to two patients with particularly sad background stories. Stefania lost both arms when she was thrown out of a train window by Nazi guards. Holding a needle between her teeth she was able to do exquisite embroidery. Mr. Bor was in the Ministry of Finance in Poland before the war, and during the occupation of his country he was a leader in the underground resistance until he was captured. The only survivor of a large family, his constitution had been shattered by typhus and T.B. At Cavendish he belonged to a new family circle. A gentle, distinguished man with a white goatee beard, he worked happily in the garden and kept poultry.

In the blue and gold Chapel of St. Christopher adjoining the house I saw a memorial tablet dedicated to the 20,000,000 men, women and children who perished in concentration camps. Much of the chapel's beautiful interior was made by patients. Like her husband, Sue Ryder was a Catholic convert.

When my tour was over she invited me to stay for supper, but a glance at my watch told me that the last train back to Cambridge was due at Cavendish in little more than five minutes' time. The Group Captain, who had now joined us, drove me to the station. Tall, dark and very slender, he was informally dressed in windcheater and light trousers and had a singularly attractive speaking voice. I remember looking at his hands on the steering wheel and thinking, 'Those are the hands that guided a 'plane on so many skilful and gallant missions during the war.'

An exciting year lay ahead of me during which I made a journey into Poland, knew the friendship of some of the bravest men and women in Central Europe, acted as Sue Ryder's emissary all over England, and met the man who was to become my husband.

To enable me to learn more about her work I spent a few days in early May at *Hickleton Hall* in Yorkshire, another Home which Sue Ryder had established in England for survivors and other disabled patients. Once the house for a short while of the Halifax family, the Hall fell into disrepair when they moved to their other estate at Garrowby. To save the once-lovely mansion from demolition, Lord Halifax sold the property to Sue Ryder for a nominal sum in 1961. During the spring of that year a legion of Yorkshire volunteers helped to make it habitable and beautiful again to receive 50 particularly tragic cases Sue Ryder planned to bring over from the Continent, and others admitted from British hospitals. They were able to move in during the summer.

Hickleton lies six miles out of Doncaster along the main road to Barnsley. It is a pretty hamlet, green, well-wooded and completely unspoilt thanks to the harmonious grey stone of which all the houses are built. On the left as one enters the village are the castle-like walls bordering the grounds of the Hall. Within glades and broad lawns lead to the house. Behind the old mansion stone steps descend into terraced rose gardens adorned with mossy statuary. Beyond lies a disused pond and more woods. It is an idyllically beautiful spot. One finds it hard to realise that it stands in the heart of a flourishing mining area where shaft wheels and slag heaps scar the landscape just over the horizon. Arriving there for the first time in early May I saw Hickleton at its loveliest.

Before travelling up from Cambridge I arranged a meeting with my good friend local bookseller Teodor Szotek and asked him to teach me a few Polish words. After an evening of instruction over drinks in Miller's Wine Parlour on King's Parade I was able to journey north with ten useful phrases learnt by heart.

At Hickleton meals were served in the magnificently-restored Wedgwood dining room, and at supper on my first evening I had an opportunity of meeting the staff. The housekeeper was Grace Devine, a good-looking, auburn-haired Yorkshire woman. Married and with two grown-up sons, Grace had been one of the first helpers when the Hall was being renovated. For weeks she camped out in the vast empty house tackling jobs that would have daunted most people, and when the patients came her warm, loving way did a great deal to make them feel at home immediately.

After supper I went to help Grace wash up in the kitchen and there she introduced me to a sad-eyed, broodingly-handsome man with a limp. Thanks to Teodor's tuition I was able to wish him *'Good evening'* in his own language. His name was Marian Podgorski and he was the chef. As I was to learn later, to see him cook was to watch an artist at work – and he had a temperament to match! He ruled the kitchen with a princely arrogance and thought nothing of tossing forty pancakes an hour. His goulash was superb, his schnitzels a dream.

Before the war he had owned a flourishing restaurant in Southeast Poland. When this was confiscated by the invading Germans he became a fighter in the underground resistance. (Incidentally Poland had the largest and best-organised underground army in the whole of Europe). Bearing the code-name 'Fox' Marian had been engaged in many guerrilla exploits that make James Bond's adventures pale by comparison. Then in 1944 during a skirmish in woods near his hometown, he had been severely wounded in the leg, captured and taken to Germany where he spent a year in hospital. After the war he passed many hard and sad years in Germany as a displaced person until Sue Ryder helped him to come and settle in England.

Little did I realise as we exchanged formal greetings that evening that before the year was out Marian and I would be deeply in love and engaged to be married.

While at Hickleton I was given access to the medical and personal histories of the folk being cared for there. They made extremely poignant reading with their details of beatings, tortures and bestial medical experiments.

I also had a chance to meet quite a number of the patients themselves when I swept and dusted their cosily-furnished individual apartments. Vladek was an ex-colonel aged 82, a very jovial old soul with an outsize sweater stretched over his enormous tummy. He was a 'do it yourself' enthusiast par excellence which made any attempt on my part to set his room in order decidedly difficult!

He washed his own socks, made his own clothes, cooked his own meals and dried his own tobacco leaves, and evidence of all these activities was manifest in his room. His cooking methods involved various Heath Robinson-like contraptions which I had not the heart to disturb. But when I had sampled some of Vladek's beetroot soup and pirogis (Slav version of Cornish pasties) I came to regard his outlandish equipment with much more respect. Vladek often used to go and have tea and play chess with the squire of the next village.

There was a frail, wizened old man with fierce eyes who had made a most beautiful model of a Polish church from the simplest of materials, and a marvellous wood carver who was hunchbacked as the result of spinal injuries caused by beatings. Telefors was an ex-major mentally-deranged by head wounds received in the Warsaw Uprising, Irena had seen her family shot before her eyes, Jozef had lost both legs, and Michal in addition to extensive physical scars, still had nightmares about the week he had spent travelling in a crowded cattle truck without food or water to a concentration camp.

Later whenever my public relations work took me north, Hickleton was my base and I regarded it as a second home.

Between May and September Sue Ryder arranged for parties of sick and disabled men and women with gallant war records to come over from Poland for three weeks' holiday in England. They travelled from Warsaw via Ostend to Dover. From there they were driven up to Suffolk where they found extremely attractive accommodation awaiting them in the south wing of Long Melford Hall, a splendid Tudor mansion three miles from Cavendish. Rent was paid to the National Trust for the use of part of this house as a Holiday Home for the Sue Ryder Foundation Holiday Scheme. The Foundation feels that providing a holiday or convalescence for these survivors is a small token of recognition and gratitude for all they have endured. Knowing the pitifully drab conditions in which so many of her guests lived in the ordinary way, Sue Ryder spared no effort to make their holiday surroundings as beautiful and comfortable as possible. I was one of the team who helped to prepare for and entertain the first holiday group to arrive.

One morning at the end of May I was sent down to Dover to meet a group off the boat. My transport was *'Boadicea',* a secondhand single-decker bus which had been doing sterling service on this run for several years but was now frankly ready to be 'put out to pasture'. During the winter months she was parked out in the open on a piece of waste ground near Cavendish railway station. When May came round she would be swept out and sent along to the local garage for tuning up.

As the usual driver (Mrs. Jill Buxton) was no longer available, Sue Ryder had advertised widely for someone to take her place but with no luck. At the eleventh hour a local farmer, Jeremy Dylan-Robinson, offered to drive *'Boadicea'* down to Dover. He was an ex-Naval officer, the husband of one of the Friends of Sue Ryder Circle which was made up of supporters in that part of East Anglia. When he went to the garage to collect the old bus the mechanic said that he should drive her slowly as in his opinion she could not do much more mileage and he would never get her to Dover let alone cover the return journey as well. A Viking in spirit as well as appearance Jeremy had the glint of challenge in his eyes when he told me the garage man's verdict.

We set out from Cavendish at about noon; the ship we were meeting was due to dock at Dover at half-past six that evening. It was a pretty agonising journey. The gear changes were excruciating but Jeremy tussled with them grimly in the hot driver's cabin. His hand was cut and bleeding and perspiration was pouring down his face. Many were the hills that *'Boadicea'* shuddered and stalled on, many the times when her engine spluttered and coughed and seemed on the point of giving out. I sat willing her with all my might to keep on the move.

Miraculously the miles passed by and our spirits rose as we began to cruise quite smoothly through the Hop Country of Kent. Frantically nursed and coaxed all the way by Jeremy, *'Boadicea'* reached Dover on time. We were parked on the quayside facing in the direction of our homeward trip when the group from Poland disembarked. There were 25 in the group and their ages ranged from 38 to 75. I was moved and amazed to notice that despite all they had been through and their terrible experiences they still took a real pride in their appearance. No doubt this could be attributed to their personal endeavour to rise up from the degradation which they had been forced to suffer. I was touched to see one woman wearing a necklace of milk bottle tops. Despite their long journey they were in high spirits and intensely interested in everything.

At that time my knowledge of Polish was still extremely sketchy, but several folk in the group spoke English and one in particular – Hanka Mierzejewska – spoke it very fluently as she had studied at Oxford many years previously. Through her I was able to chat with everyone during the drive up to Suffolk.

We made one brief stop on the road for cups of tea. On the whole *'Boadicea'* was behaving quite well although she stalled and cut out several times on hills. When we had left Braintree behind us we were on the home stretch – only about 15 more miles to go. I had been instructed to telephone through to Cavendish to let them know when we were nearing our destination so that supper could be prepared and driven over to Melford to be ready when we arrived. Jeremy stopped at the next phone box and while I was making the call he made the only mistake in all his long day's masterly busmanship – he switched off the engine. When he tried to restart *'Boadicea'* there was not a murmur from her. He tried using the starting handle. No luck.

The men in the party alighted and tried pushing her first from the back and then from the front but all to no avail. In that dark Essex lane *'Boadicea'* finally expired. I rang Cavendish again and they said they would muster up all the transport they could to come and collect us. When the relief cars arrived and *'Boadicea'* had been unloaded, she was pushed into the yard of a nearby pub for the rest of the night. I wonder what the landlord thought when he looked out of his window next day! If he had known the full story I think he would have felt honoured to give haven to such a gallant old lady. And what Jeremy had accomplished was a remarkable feat by any standards.

In specially-chartered coaches we made daily excursions with our guests to places of interest . . . Hatfield House, Clacton, Walton, Frinton, Colchester, Ipswich, Thaxted, Bury St. Edmunds, Norwich and, of course, London. In Ipswich we went to the County Show and at Thaxted we joined the Whit-Monday street dancing by Morris Men. Some of the outings were arranged and financed by Rotary or Inner Wheel Clubs and similar organisations.

Shopping expeditions were also great occasions. The survivors themselves only had a small amount of money to spend, but they never coveted anything and showed no jealousy of people who had material goods; they regarded Woolworths and Marks & Spencers as delightful places. Shirts, woollies, blouses, lingerie, nylons, cosmetics, knitting wool and Nescafe topped the list of items that appealed most.

In Cambridge they were shown round the Colleges by Teodor Szotek and had tea at my house. On our second trip to London we were entertained with great hospitality and kindness at the Polish Embassy.

Apart from the daily outings there were gay impromptu parties most nights in the spacious entrance hall-cum-lounge of the south wing at Melford. The furniture would be cleared from the centre of the floor, some bottles of vodka opened and poppyseed cake produced. One-legged Jan Sikorski would be lured to the piano to play an apparently endless repertoire of waltzes and tangoes interspersed with Polish dances. Many folk from The Sue Ryder Home came over to join us at these merry gatherings. Sometimes Sue Ryder and her mother came. Mrs. Ryder was a grand old lady who, despite her advanced years, took a very lively interest in her daughter's work and was revered by everyone. Sue Ryder was the youngest of her five children and when her work was becoming internationally recognised and she was searching for an H.Q. in England, Mrs. Ryder took the immensely generous step of moving out of what was her own house at the time to let her daughter use this accommodation for a Sue Ryder Home and Headquarters in the U.K.

Both the Cheshires had a great sense of humour excelling particularly at the deadpan variety. Sue Ryder's talent for fun came into play at one of the parties at Long Melford when she arrived in heavy disguise and was introduced to everyone as a late guest from Poland. Her hair was screwed up under a beret, she wore heavy horn-rimmed glasses and a set of protruding teeth which had clearly been acquired at a trick shop.

The immense gaiety of these simple get-togethers at Melford still remains vividly in my memory. Poles thoroughly enjoy a musical evening and it was often difficult to remember that our guests had all suffered horribly in concentration camps and witnessed innumerable acts of sadism. The one poignant reminder always present was the 'Auschwitz' number branded permanently on their left forearms.

One old lady in the party had spent six months in solitary confinement in pitch darkness as a punishment for allowing underground fighters to meet at her home. But the Nazis had been unable to break her spirit.

The quietest member of the whole group was a small, insignificant-looking woman with a sphinx-like quality about her flat peasant face and a very withdrawn air. A woman who had once been in a concentration camp with her told me: 'She is the bravest person I have ever met.' She had undertaken the extremely risky job of passing messages round the camp and had lived for many months under the shadow of a death sentence.

The men's stories were similarly dramatic ones. Tadek, who had been a teenage underground fighter, had been regularly strung up by his wrists with his toes just touching the ground for many hours at a time. Romek, a merry-eyed balding little man barely five feet tall, was a master printer. During his years in the underground resistance he had travelled about Poland on a bicycle smuggling equipment for producing clandestine newspapers from one town to another.

The Poles, like the Welsh, are natural-born songsters and it was magnificent to hear them singing as if they had rehearsed together many times. On coach trips and in the evenings there were many singsongs.

On the last night of their holiday the group was invited to coffee in the main part of Melford Hall by the owner, Danish-born Lady Hyde Parker. She took them on a conducted tour and showed them the family portraits and heirlooms.

During the period between the departure of the first holiday group and the arrival of the second I stayed at 'Headquarters' and saw at first-hand the pattern of Sue Ryder's life when she was at home. Although she seldom stopped working she arranged things so that she could enjoy the company of her children to the full. Their nursery adjoined her office and she dictated letters while nursing baby Elizabeth on her lap. The amount of work she got through in one day was quite phenomenal by ordinary standards. She slept little and ate even less.

Her feats as a regular long-distance driver were fantastic. Forty-eight hours was her record time for the 1200 miles from Cavendish to

Warsaw with her celebrated van *'Elijah'* packed tight inside and out with medicines, comforts and gifts. Bad weather never interfered with her missions. During the exceptionally severe winters she travelled alone through snowbound mountain passes in Jugoslavia, digging herself a route through with a spade when the snow rose higher than her headlamps.

In her upstairs office adjoining the bedroom occupied by herself and her family, she had a cabinet filled with pathetic mementoes of concentration camp life. Perhaps the most poignant of all were the humble examples of creative feeling like the pattern traced on a broken eggshell and the crucifix painstakingly marked out on a fragment of wall. The office was a charming room and her desk was set before a huge lead-paned bay window overlooking a tree fringed lake with a thatched boathouse.

When the next holiday group arrived from Poland they stayed overnight at Melford Hall and then travelled north to spend a memorable fortnight in Gateshead, County Durham, as the guests of Rotary Clubs in the Newcastle area. Danuta, a Polish-born worker for Sue Ryder, and I accompanied them. *En route* our coach stopped at Hickleton Hall for lunch and Marian excelled himself with the menu he produced. We reached Gateshead at eight o'clock in the evening and were accommodated very pleasantly indeed at St. Cuthbert's, Chowdene, a large retreat house run by Anglican Sisters of the Company of St. Francis. We each had a small individual bedroom. Meals were simple but well-varied and appetising.

The head of the house was Sister Ursula, a fine woman in her seventies much resembling Eleanor Roosevelt in her looks and particularly in her smile. She came from Suffolk where she had formerly been a prominent figure in County society and mistress of a large estate. Late in life after she was widowed and her children had grown up, she had forsaken wealth and social position to don the simple brown habit of St. Francis and dedicate herself to all-the-year-round Christian hospitality at St. Cuthbert's and also a considerable amount of active evangelism in the surrounding district. Her resident staff were two accomplished girls in their twenties. Sister Teresa was a versatile artist with a bubbling sense of humour, and Sister Berenice practical and quick-witted in all domestic matters. The three of them invested the old house with an atmosphere of great warmth and happiness.

Among the Polish survivors was a distinguished-looking man with a thick mane of white hair and a terrible scar across his throat. His name was Pawel (Paul) and his Name Day fell shortly after our arrival at Gateshead. In Poland Name Days are regarded as more important than birthdays. On the evening before Pawel's was due several members of the group asked me if I could possibly get a bunch of pansies for them to present to him at breakfast at the same time as they handed him his gift. I mentioned the request to several Rotarians and within a short time a very generous number of pansies had been gathered from Rotarian gardens. Ribbon in the Polish national colours was produced to tie the bouquet.

After the presentation ceremony next morning Pawel explained why he had such a special affection for pansies. While in Majdanek Extermination Camp he had managed to get hold of a few pansy seeds and the cultivation of them in a tiny plot had helped to keep him sane in the midst of all his sufferings.

Then he sprang a surprise on Sister Ursula and those of us who had not shared in the secret preparations. Early that morning, we learnt, the women in the group had gone out to local shops to buy bread, salami, cheese, lettuce, radishes and so forth which they had made into delicious savoury snacks. Poppyseed cake, which had come over with them from Poland, completed the spread which had been set out most attractively with all manner of improvised materials in one of the upper corridors. So we all went to Pawel's Name Day party.

Every day we made excursions to different places of interest . . . to Hexham Abbey, Hadrian's Wall, the spectacular waterfall at High Force, the rhododendrons and woodlands of Craigside, the beautiful Wear Valley, the solitary splendour of Holy Island, the stretch of coast associated with Grace Darling, the old home of George Washington's family. At Saltburn we visited a famous smuggler's cavern bar where a ghost was purported to drink a tankard of ale specially left out for him by the management every night.

The Polish communities in the surrounding district also rose to the occasion magnificently. One Saturday night was spent in the elegant ballroom of the Newcastle Polish Club, while the following weekend another grand social was organised by the Poles at Morpeth.

Thanks to Janina, a plump, jolly housewife from Kosalin, I greatly enriched my Polish vocabulary during this period, and I shall always remember Antonin (who wore his medals every day) asking me with astonishment as we walked down a street: 'Does one family really have a whole house to itself?'

I was to see four members of the party again when I visited Poland two months later: Stefan Teper, keen photographer and fluent linguist; Jozef Bielewicz, an excellent ballroom dancer despite losing a leg in the Warsaw Uprising when he distinguished himself as a gallant teenage fighter; Lucjan, a devoted wartime comrade of Jozef's; Stefan Lapinski, a journalist with smiling eyes.

On the final night of our stay at St. Cuthbert's Sister Ursula organised a farewell party in the dining hall. Rotarians came along with their wives and children to join in the fun.

I shall never forget Sister Ursula. Although I knew her for such a brief time she made a profound impression on me. If I should find myself in circumstances similar to her own during the winter of my days I should like more than anything else to follow her way of life in the name of St. Francis. I was baptised into the Church of England and I suppose my religious faith would be regarded by learned theologians as simple, child-like and unquestioning. But it has always quietly coloured and warmed the background of my life and I believe implicitly in the power of prayer.

CHAPTER TEN

POLISH PILGRIMAGE

BY NOW I HAD an extensive knowledge of Sue Ryder's work, but I felt very deeply that, in order to complete my qualifications as her P.R.O., I should actually go to Poland at my own expense, make a personal pilgrimage to Auschwitz Concentration Camp, and visit one of the Homes which Sue Ryder had set up in that country. She gave me a letter of introduction to the Minister of Health in Warsaw. I took a steamer from Harwich to the Hook of Holland and thence went direct by train to the Polish capital, a journey altogether of about 32 hours.

It was dusk when the train drew into Warsaw on Sunday evening. The station entrance hall was very similar to a large English one with its newspaper stall, cigarette booth and so on. I made a bee-line for the refreshment counter which opened straight out on to the hall and had no seating accommodation. In my now quite adequate Polish I ordered a tall glass of lemon tea, a plate of anchovies with Russian salad, and a slice of delicious crusty bread.

Afterwards I went out into the station forecourt to look for a taxi to take me to the Grand Hotel where I had reserved a room in advance through a Polish travel agency in London. It did not take me long to realise that the Polish method of getting a taxi differed considerably from the English one. From what I could see one left one's luggage on the kerb and leapt onto the running board of a taxi as it swung into the station entrance yard. Queueing up and awaiting one's turn did not appear to be the form at all. I inquired about buses and, having obtained the necessary information, made for a tree-shaded square nearby and joined the crowds already waiting there.

Striking up a conversation with the woman immediately in front of me, I remarked how difficult it was to get a taxi in Warsaw on a Sunday night. She explained to me that the taxi drivers were very independent and often sped by even when they were hailed. This casual snatch of conversation led to my first unforgettable glimpse of the kindness of the people of the Polish capital. Before I realised what was happening half a dozen folk left the queue to station themselves at various points round the square and energetically hail on my behalf every passing taxi. After many fruitless attempts they were at last successful. The lady to whom I had first spoken shared the taxi with me. She was not going along my entire route but when she alighted she pressed my hand warmly and told the driver not to overcharge me.

The Grand Hotel in Warsaw is considered, I am told, one of the finest hotels in Central Europe. Few people outside Poland seem to realise that 90 per cent. of Warsaw was totally destroyed, and it has been reconstructed entirely without financial assistance or help from other countries. The hotel is situated in the heart of the new city which has risen on a completely devastated site and is certainly impressive. I walked up the broad entrance steps into the spacious, ultra-modern foyer. At the reception desk was an austere, mannish-looking woman in a high-necked, navy serge outfit, and this, I would say, was the first sight in Warsaw that reminded me I was in Communist territory. She, like other members of the reception staff, spoke fluent English. The first thing required of me was to hand over my passport which, I was told, would be returned to me on the day I left the hotel.

Then I went up by lift to my bedroom which was furnished in a bright, elegant, contemporary style with streamlined, light wood furniture and soft furnishings of excellent quality. There was an adjoining private bathroom. The price per day for bed and breakfast compared very favourably with that of a similar grade hotel in the West. I have been told since that all the rooms in the Grand Hotel were *'wired for sound'*, but nothing in my pleasant apartment led me to suspect the presence of a hidden microphone. The dining room was enormous; modern and tasteful in decor and tableware. There was apparently a serious shortage of pepper for very modest quantities of it were carefully measured out in little dishes on each table.

I have always believed that the best way to get to know a city is to walk through it rather than take a bus or tram, and I decided the next morning to make my way on foot to the office of the Minister of Health in Miodowa Street, aided by a map. It was the height of the Polish summer and the weather was very hot. My walk led through some of the busiest city thoroughfares and I watched the passing scene with great interest – especially the people.

I noticed the very inferior quality of the clothes being worn. Materials were shoddy and the women's dresses lacked variety, while the men's suits looked as if they would crumple disastrously when caught in a shower. Shop window displays (with the exception of one or two exclusive art shops and souvenir marts) were extremely drab and limited by English standards. As in so many other Continental cities the magazine and cigarette kiosks situated at regular intervals along the pavement added vivid splashes of colour to the scene with their advertisements, postcards, cheap jewellery, plastic toys and dolls in national costume. I came to a broad boulevard with beautifully laid-out gardens and very green grass. Away to my left the skyline was dominated by the towering silhouette of the Palace of Culture – said by some to be the most hated symbol of Communist power in Warsaw.

As I walked through the elegant city on that bright morning I found it very hard to realise that it was only 18 years old. Every building, every street, every green and blossoming garden had been created anew on a site of absolute devastation where Nazi flame-throwers and demolition squads had methodically completed the work of merciless bombardment from the air.

I remembered the way in which the people of Warsaw, when they were at last able to return to their stricken capital, had immediately set to work in a great united effort to restore the city. Everyone contributed to the reconstruction – even little children carrying one brick at a time. Warsaw meant so much to her people that they felt Poland's heart would only start beating again when the capital had been rebuilt. My thoughts also went to the network of sewers beneath the pavements where I was walking. The widely acclaimed Polish film *Kanal* gave a terrifyingly vivid picture of the desperate days when the sewers were the last stronghold of resistance fighters in the city.

In back-streets near the River Vistula I saw the shells of shrapnel-scarred houses, but repair work was in progress. It was noticeable everywhere that while public transport was as plentiful as in any city, there was a conspicuous lack of private cars.

And so I came at last to the Ministry of Health in Miodowa Street and was ushered into the Minister's presence. After reading Sue Ryder's letter of introduction he called in his aide who was to escort me at a later date to the Home for children with rheumatic diseases at Konstancin.

Scion of a distinguished old Polish family, my escort was tall, dark and very handsome. Although he had never been to England his admiration for everything English was boundless. He spoke the language fluently and smoked a pipe with exactly the air of an Englishman. He struck me as being an extremely sad man and later I learned that he now held a good position despite the fact that it was said an uncle of his, a prominent man, had greatly offended the Communists during the war while living outside Poland. Even after all these years poignant memories are bound to remain.

When I left the Ministry I continued further down Miodowa Street on more informal business – to call at the office address of Lucjan, one of the holiday makers I had helped to entertain in England earlier that summer. I gave my name to the janitor at the gate and a prompt telephone call brought Lucjan down to the courtyard where I was waiting. Somehow or other he managed to get the rest of the day off. He took me briefly up to his office to introduce me to some of his colleagues and to ring his great friend Jozef whom I had also met in England. Then we went off on an intensely interesting sightseeing tour.

For me the highlight was the Old Market Place. This architectural gem of Warsaw was totally destroyed during the war, but with the aid of historic prints and plans it has been faithfully restored in every detail exactly as it used to be. Everything about it looks genuinely medieval . . . the cobblestones, the lanterns, the wrought-iron grills, the roof tiling, the stonework. Even the colours of the paintings adorning the outer walls of the houses have a muted, mellow, centuries-old look.

We met Jozef at a little wine shop and then caught a bus out to the suburb where Lucjan lived with his wife and three children. Despite the short notice of my visit Lucjan's wife provided an excellent lunch of cold chicken and salad, cakes and apricot liqueur. Lucjan's fiat was not bad compared with other accommodation in Warsaw. It was similar to a London County Council flat in layout and there was a television set in the living room. The furniture was old-fashioned but adequate and there were the usual homely items everywhere . . . family photos, religious and patriotic emblems, a vase of dry, decorative grasses, toys belonging to the children.

At dusk I drove with Lucjan and Jozef to the latter's fiat. Jozef was a skilled technician who had lost a leg in the Warsaw Uprising and I should have thought this might have entitled him to an above-average standard of accommodation. But such was not the case. Apart from a small entrance hall, a toilet and cramped kitchen, Jozef, his wife and small daughter lived, ate and slept in one room. However, that one room was spotlessly neat and when supper-time came I was much moved by the generous fare which must have made a large hole in the domestic budget. I had brought presents from England for both families.

The following day I caught an evening train from Warsaw to Cracow. Through the travel bureau at the Grand Hotel I had booked a room in advance at the Francuski Hotel in Cracow. Jozef and Lucjan went to the station with me, found me a seat on the train and bought me cigarettes and orangeade. I told them the time at which I would be returning to Warsaw a few days later.

It is a four-hour journey from Warsaw to Cracow but the time passed quickly and pleasantly thanks to a fellow passenger. She was a student on her way down to the magnificent mountain country of Zakopanie for a camping holiday. With the aid of my Anglo-Polish phrase book for words strange to me, and our mutual knowledge of French we conversed on all manner of topics and she shared her picnic supper with me.

The train drew into Cracow about one in the morning and this time I found it easy enough to get a taxi. Soon I was at the reception desk of the Francuski Hotel which had a Victorian decor and heavily-shaded lights. When I told the receptionist that the Grand Hotel had reserved a room on my behalf he replied that every room in the hotel was occupied on account of some conference which was being held in the town. Even at that time of the night I was not particularly worried by this news. I asked to be directed to another hotel but was told that every hotel was full. The clerk took a list off a hook on the wall and ran his finger down it, then scribbled an address on a piece of paper and handed it to me. I was told that the price I would pay there would be the same as if I were staying at the Francuski. I asked him to ring for a taxi, and when it came I handed the scribbled address to the driver. As we set off I lay back in my seat perfectly relaxed and ready for anything. It was very dark for the street lighting was poor by English standards, but I assumed we were driving to a residential suburb, which was in fact the case. The taximan stopped at a house and carried my luggage inside up to my room. Although I had been told it was not the custom to tip Polish taxi drivers I did so on this occasion because I was so relieved to have found somewhere to rest my head. Besides the man was very shabbily dressed and wore rough straw sandals. But it was not an unduly big tip and I certainly did not expect him to sink to his knees and kiss my hand as he did with an eloquent display of gratitude.

My landlady was a dark, handsome woman of very respectable appearance. Indeed I sensed that she came from a superior background and was only forced by reduced circumstances to let rooms in her house now. My bedroom was a spacious high-ceilinged apartment furnished in an over-elaborate, old-fashioned style. Just across the corridor was a bathroom for my private use.

No breakfast was provided at the house so, having washed and dressed, I hurried eagerly out determined not to waste a single minute in exploring one of the most historic and beautiful cities in Europe. Ten minutes' walk from my lodgings I found the tram terminus and rode down into the city centre, alighting where the fancy took me.

My first stop was for breakfast at a modest cafe adjoining a bus station. I was amused to notice that some public toilets did not bear the Polish equivalents of 'Ladies' and 'Gentlemen' but instead had symbols painted outside: a circle for the women's convenience and a triangle for the men's. This, of course, was a reminder of the illiteracy which years ago existed among large sections of the older age groups in the poorer classes.

Unlike Warsaw, Cracow was undamaged during the war because the German Commander made it his headquarters. There is a fairy-tale quality about the old part of the town which is extremely quaint and colourful. Most famous landmark of all is Wawel Castle set in a romantic position on top of a hill. This was once the home of the kings of

Poland who were, incidentally, elected to the throne and did not succeed by right of heredity. The Castle's magnificent rooms are full of art treasures, antique furniture and royal bygones. I went through the splendid gilded apartments on a conducted tour. The atmosphere and character of Wawel Castle can best be described as a blend of Windsor Castle and Hampton Court Palace.

I lunched at a cheap working folks' cafeteria where I had some excellent beetroot soup followed by meat and two vegetables, caramel blancmange and lemon tea. The Cracowiaks were as friendly as Warsaw folk.

The other highlight of a day's sightseeing was my afternoon stroll through the Old Quarter past the round, sturdy tower of the Barbican and through an ancient arched gateway into a vast, beautiful square filled with flower stalls and pigeons. On the left side of the square stands St. Mary's Church, its green spire encircled by a golden crown, and to the right are the stone arcades of the medieval covered market.

I bought a picture postcard and sent it jointly to Grace and Marian at Hickleton.

But my main reason for being in Cracow was to make a pilgrimage to Auschwitz Concentration Camp which is situated in the close vicinity, and the next morning I breakfasted in the restaurant at Cracow railway station before setting out on my journey. It was very stodgy and Victorian in style, but the cuisine was excellent.

All the seats in the train were wooden ones and when I alighted at Oswiencim (Polish version of Auschwitz) I climbed straight down onto the track. A long goods train had halted alongside completely barring the way to the exit platform. All my fellow passengers started climbing over the couplings of the goods train wagons so I did likewise.

Even without its now eternally tragic associations Oswiencim would be a singularly unattractive provincial town. A bus from outside the station set me down at the concentration camp gates. Auschwitz was the largest of the 3000 camps run by the Nazis all over Europe and it is estimated that 4,000,000 men, women and children perished there. Now it is a permanent museum and memorial of man's inhumanity to man. People come from all over the world to see the heart-searing relics preserved in the colony of sombre brick buildings.

Behind huge plate-glass partitions are displayed enormous mounds of shoes, suitcases, toys, spectacles, false teeth, artificial limbs and other personal possessions which once belonged to people of many different nationalities who were done to death there. Widely assorted implements of torture are exhibited, prisoners' uniforms, battered mugs and dishes, details of the near starvation diet on which men and women were expected to do heavy manual labour. In one glass case are items showing the many ingenious ways in which secret messages were smuggled round the camp by prisoners. The very air of Auschwitz is still haunted by the terrible cruelties perpetrated there. The original gallows still stand by a grassy track.

More horrifying to me than the Death Block, gas chambers or even the crematorium furnaces, were the double brick-walled stand-up cells in which four prisoners used to be wedged together at one time. To enter these narrow oven-like structures the prisoner had to go down on his knees and crawl through a low, kennel-like entrance which was then slammed to and bolted from the outside. It was rare for a prisoner to survive a night passed in these conditions as it was tantamount to being walled up alive. Another sight which specially moved me was an enormous mound of human hair which had been set aside to make cloth for the Third Reich.

Before I left England Sue Ryder had told me: 'When you go to Auschwitz do try and see Birkenau (Brzinka) Camp as well.' This I now proceeded to do. Whereas Auschwitz Camp is situated beside a main road only a short distance from town and is visited by crowds of sightseers, Birkenau lies at an isolated spot two or three miles further out and is seldom visited by anyone. Rusting barbed wire fences and rotting watch towers stretch as far as the eye can see. I did not meet a soul.

Making my way through what had once been the main gate, I walked to the lines of primitive wooden barrack huts which used to house at least 1000 human beings each. Most of them were locked, but finding one door ajar I went in and passed slowly down the whole length of the hut, pausing now and again by the numbered tiers of flimsy wooden bunks which were once filled to overflowing with human beings in the last stages of degradation.

Out-of-doors the ground underfoot felt strangely light and spongy and my shoes got covered with white powder. I realised that this was because the rough grass covered many layers of human ashes. Jews and gypsies were the chief inmates at Birkenau.

Although Auschwitz is the official show place of sadism I personally was even more profoundly moved by Birkenau. As I stood there alone in the summer sunshine amid the utter silence and desolation, I felt closer to the true meaning of Sue Ryder's work than ever before.

So the time came to return to Warsaw, and once again a fellow passenger made the miles pass swiftly. She was an elderly lady professor and, although she constantly read books in English, this was her first opportunity to converse in the language for many years. Among other subjects we compared the merits of Cracow and Warsaw, and she warmly declared that while Cracow was certainly a city to *visit,* Warsaw was unquestionably the only city to *live* in.

A wonderful surprise awaited me at Warsaw station; I was met not only by Lucjan and Jozef but also by Stefan Teper and Stefan Lapinski whom I had met earlier in the year at Melford. A bunch of red roses was placed in my arms and after I had washed and freshened up, my friends bore me off to a very good party.

On my last day in Poland the Minister's aide drove me out to the village of Konstancin to see Sue Ryder's Home for girls with rheumatic diseases. This Home is typical of all those she has provided. The buildings are prefabricated at a factory in England and then shipped out to a prepared site. It is a combined operation between the Polish Authorities and the Foundation. The furniture, linen etc., are provided by the Sue Ryder Foundation and some of the equipment given by the Institute of Rheumatic Diseases in Warsaw.

The Home at Konstancin is set among pinewoods and the ages of the girls range from five to seventeen. Before they came there many of them were so severely affected by their painful and disfiguring disease that they could not walk and had never been to school. Thus side by side with expert medical treatment the children also receive regular lessons for the first time. In many cases wonderful improvements in health have been achieved, while the children who are incurable are assured of devoted care all their lives. There is plenty of laughter and a real family atmosphere. I gave them a Beefeater doll and in return they presented me with a set of embroidered mats and a bookmark with delicate paper mosaic motifs.

My stay in Poland was nearly over. My escort took me out to lunch and then drove me straight to Warsaw Station. My homeward bound train was already at the platform, and waiting there to bid me farewell were Lucjan, Jozef and Stefan Lapinski. Lucjan gave me a mermaid brooch (the emblem of Warsaw) and carnations, Jozef's gift was a record of my favourite Polish songs, and Stefan filled my arms with marguerites.

When the train moved off I waved my scarf from the window until Warsaw Station disappeared from view. I now felt truly qualified to become Sue Ryder's Public Relations Officer.

CHAPTER ELEVEN

EMISSARY ON THE MOVE

THE TIME I SPENT as Sue Ryder's travelling representative proved to be an extremely happy period in my life. In addition to showing the film (which was of a remarkably high quality both technically and artistically), I addressed clubs and organisations of every conceivable type – schools, public luncheons, fetes and bazaars and, on one occasion, a fashion show held specially to raise money for the Sue Ryder Foundation. My work also entailed making new contacts, canvassing for new support groups, organising sales of work and preparing the way for personal appearances by Sue Ryder. She gave me a completely free hand in the way I tackled my various tasks and in the composition of my speeches, and my journalistic training stood me in very good stead.

I was constantly on the move . . . from Torquay to Durham to Liverpool taking in the Isle of Wight, Richmond, Harlow, London, Harwich and Huddersfield on my way, for example. I usually took pot luck in my eating and sleeping arrangements and never allowed bad weather to hinder my activities. It was a pretty hectic sort of existence but it was thoroughly congenial to my temperament, and I loved every minute.

Quite often I enjoyed overnight hospitality with friends of Sue Ryder and stayed at beautiful and interesting houses in various parts of the country. At Sidmouth in Devon my hostess was a remarkable old lady of 85. She was still full of vitality and had a wonderful memory. When dinner was over we lingered a long time at the table together over our wine, and I listened to some of her fascinating reminiscences. In her youth she had often stayed with a girl friend in Germany. She had shared a box at the theatre with Bernard Shaw, seen Ellen Terry and Sir Henry Irving perform. At Bayreuth she had met Siegfried Wagner, son of the great composer and his beloved Cosima. Although the offspring of such notable parents he himself, she told me, was a very unexciting personality and no great shakes as a conductor either. The same applied to the son of Robert Browning and Elizabeth Barrett, whom she met in Florence. He was a very indifferent artist who was accepted in Florentine society because of his celebrated parentage. My hostess had lived in Ireland too and was a personal friend of Lady Gregory.

I do not think any assignment gave me greater pleasure than the preparation for our Christmas Fair at Chelmsford in November 1962. It was Sue Ryder's custom to hold such a Fair in a different East Anglian town every year. This time the setting was Chelmsford Corn Exchange, and the opener Anna Neagle. My stay in the Essex county town during the greater part of October was destined to be one of concentrated activity because we had few if any existing contacts there. I had to find at least 12 local organisations that were willing to run stalls and sideshows for us. At the same time I had to contrive to get a banner made free of charge to drape across the Corn Exchange balcony, mount a window display somewhere, distribute posters, feed advance news items to the local Press, and canvass as many shops as possible asking for free gifts for our stalls.

Someone who claimed to know the place well warned me grimly that Chelmsford was a 'stony-hearted town' – but I found precisely the opposite to be the case and Chelmsford will always have a warm corner in my memory. At every turn I found the people exceptionally kind and helpful. Local organisations turned up trumps and provided splendid stalls and sideshows. The Principal of the Art College solved my banner problem. The Editor of one of the town's newspapers allowed me to mount a publicity display in a well-appointed window on his premises. Pubs, fish and chip shops, hotel foyers and cafes as well as shops displayed our posters.

The pseudo-Venetian palazzo style Corn Exchange had decidedly primitive kitchen and washing amenities which presented some catering problems, but to counterbalance these disadvantages the caretaker proved extremely co-operative. Nearly 70 shops both large and small donated gifts for our stalls. In several instances these were very generous indeed, being items priced at five guineas. Wholesale fruit and vegetable merchants gave some really luscious looking decorated baskets of fruit. Luxury crackers, exquisite baby clothes, toys, cakes, groceries, cosmetics, stationery, nylons, jewellery, household equipment, flowers, confectionery, ceramics . . . the variety and attractiveness of the gifts from local firms was boundless.

The problem of collecting and storing all these items was solved for me by Mrs. Howe of New Street. She loaned me one of her husband's hire cars for an afternoon, and then let me store all the goods at her home.

Soon all sections of the community in Chelmsford seemed to be involved in some way or other in helping our Fair . . . churches, Scouts and Guides, Toc H, St. John Ambulance Brigade, a Parent-Teacher Association – and even the Police. Word got round fast in town who I was and folk used to stop me in the street to ask how things were progressing. Even the little woman who worked in the ladies' toilet near the bus station used to inquire every day how I was getting on.

My accommodation while at Chelmsford must be the smallest hotel room in Britain. The proprietor dubbed it *'Uncle Tom's Cabin'*. It contained a bed, a small table, a wall radio – and that was all. To get in I had to put my luggage on the bed, and to bend down I had to open the door first! But I heartily relished the novelty.

A week before the day of the Fair our huge scarlet-lettered banner, which had been sewn by many willing hands, went up over the façade of the Corn Exchange. The night before the event all our helpers rallied round magnificently and converged on the Corn Exchange with their stocks and equipment. At eight o'clock next morning there was already intense activity within the walls of the pseudo-Venetian palazzo. Stalls being erected and decorated, goods being artistically set out, side-shows assembled. Before long Sue Ryder herself arrived from Cavendish in *'Elijah'* which was packed with goods made by the patients. By the entrance she set up a stand of brochures, pamphlets and Christmas cards. At one end of this was laid a faded concentration camp uniform scattered with fresh freesia blooms.

Despite rain large crowds gathered to watch the arrival of Anna Neagle and her husband film director Herbert Wilcox, shortly before 10.30 a.m. Miss Neagle, looking far younger than her years and with the slender figure of a girl, wore a red velvet suit with fur at the neck and a large-brimmed off-the-face hat in matching velvet. She performed the opening ceremony with considerable charm and zest, and afterwards sold her autograph to many admirers in aid of our funds. Then trade began in earnest. It remained flourishing all day, and when the Fair closed at half-past five well over £600 had been raised.

Looking back now I realise I must have been pretty busy at Chelmsford. It was a real high-voltage campaign but I did not feel at all tired after my exertions. If I worked like a being inspired I knew the reason why – I was in love.

It was in the early autumn of 1962 that I really first became aware of Marian in the romantic sense. I noticed that his face always lit up when I appeared on the scene, and when I returned to Hickleton from assignments in that locality his welcomes became increasingly warmer. At mealtimes he treated me with marked deference, hovering attentively round my table, seeing that everything was laid just so, that my plate was well filled, that my chair was a comfortable one.

Grace Devine told me how Marian always spruced himself up when he knew I was due to arrive at Hickleton, and someone else commented, 'You have certainly melted Marian' (for he had the reputation of being rather temperamental and aloof). There was now something electric between us whenever we encountered each other about the house. Long years of hardship and suffering had left their mark on his face, but I could still see that he must have been dashingly handsome in his youth. His hair was thick and dark, his brow high and open. He had a stubborn mouth and a firm, cleft chin. It was a strong, manly face; a face one would notice in a room full of people.

Immediately after the Christmas Fair at Chelmsford I had canvassing assignments in Stafford, Manchester and Liverpool. Everywhere I travelled my thoughts were full of Marian, and I regularly sent him gay picture postcards with messages written in a mixture of English and Polish. I told him what I was doing and what I thought of the town where I happened to be staying. Good-humouredly I grumbled about the coldness of the weather, saying I would like nothing better than to have a mug of his choicest beetroot soup in my hands.

Liverpool has a very large Catholic population which could be expected to give strong support to Sue Ryder's film, and my first call there was at the Arch-Diocesan Offices on Brownlow Hill. On the doorstep I met Cardinal Heenan who is a close personal friend of Sue Ryder. He had no idea who I was but gave me a merry greeting. I got to like Liverpool very much. Its lively, cosmopolitan atmosphere greatly appealed to me. By the time I had completed my mission there Christmas was close at hand and I spent my last day buying presents for Marian and for several other patients at Hickleton. As a gift for the home at Hickleton I bought a statue of the Madonna with a halo of stars about her head. I chose her because she had the most beautiful face of all the Madonnas in the shop.

When I got back to the Hall I found Grace hard at work assembling and inscribing the parcels which were to be distributed to the patients, their personal tastes being carefully borne in mind. How she used to love this job! Local Borstal boys had built a Holy Stable in the pillared entrance hall and the life-size figures in the Nativity tableau had been most skilfully made by Grace's husband. There were several tall, illuminated trees about the house and the long corridors were decked with streamers and evergreens.

I gave the Madonna statue to the House Mother, Molly Trim, who decided that it should be displayed on the fine marble mantelpiece in the Wedgwood dining room where the greatest number of people could see it. Word soon reached Marian that I was back. He hurried to meet me and kissed my hand in the Polish style of greeting. Then he accompanied me as I went round the house to deliver the gifts I had brought from Liverpool. I had already planned to ask three of the folk at Hickleton to be guests at my home in Cambridge over New Year, and when I gave them presents I also issued this invitation. One was to be Irena Kunc, because she had a friend living at Fulbourn only a few miles from my home. The second was to be Stanislaw Geniusz, a former dental surgeon now in his seventies, because he had a doctor friend who lived only ten minutes' walk from my house. The third, of course, was to be Marian because I decided that the time had come to indicate that I was as interested in him as he obviously was in me.

Marian knew that I was leaving after breakfast the following day to go down to Cambridge for Christmas, and he asked me to meet him in a place where we could say 'Goodbye' in privacy. I went to him at the appointed rendezvous and for the first time he took me in his arms and kissed me.

My brother Peter, a schoolmaster at Ipswich, came to join me for Christmas, but for the first time in several years we did not invite any friends round over the holiday. Instead I worked hard getting everything ready for the arrival of my three guests on 28th December. I wanted the house to look its cosiest and prettiest. On the appointed date I met them at the station and bore them home by taxi to a good tea beside a blazing fire. It was bitterly cold and snow was beginning to fall heavily. That evening Teodor Szotek, my bookseller friend, came round as he had promised with Polish magazines and books for my guests. A bottle of vodka was uncorked, toasts exchanged, memories of pre-war Poland recalled. And I rejoiced that the man I loved would be sleeping under my own roof for the first time that night.

Next morning Irena came down wearing her best dress in readiness for her visit to her friend at Fulbourn. When Stanislaw went to call on his friend Dr. Schiller, a few streets from my home, the medical man was delighted to see how well the old fellow looked. When he had first arrived in England two years previously he was still in pretty bad shape as a result of concentration camp life.

Stanislaw was the easiest of guests. As long as he had an unlimited supply of cigarettes and plenty to read he was content. He also had a passion for drinking tea and was always asking for a cup at the most unexpected times. We promptly complied with all his requests. And I gave Marian the free run of the kitchen.

On the 29th I had to make a flying trip to the Foundation H.Q. to discuss New Year assignments, but I was able to go knowing that all my guests were happily occupied. When I returned in the evening Peter entertained Irena and Stanislaw while Marian and I went into the adjoining room to play darts and cards.

My aims at the dart board were not very accurate, I remember, and I found it equally hard to concentrate on our card game. I do not know whose decision it was eventually to throw the cards aside. For a little while we sat there side by side in the firelight not saying very much. Then quite suddenly, in one of those rare moments of time that have the touch of eternity, we spoke our declarations of love to each other and tension gave way to joy. I took a foil-covered chocolate heart from the Christmas tree and gave it to him. He has lovingly preserved it to this day.

Next morning being Sunday, we all went by taxi to church. Snow was now lying very deep. After a roast chicken lunch we gathered round the fire to plan the New Year's Eve party we were going to have on the morrow . . . Sylvester as the Poles call it. Marian was eager to make the traditional dish called *Bigos* and together we drew up a list of the ingredients we must buy at the Continental shop in town.

We telephoned to Cavendish to invite Jan Wawryn to come and join us. He was a great friend of Marian's as they hailed from the same district in Poland. Jan had an incurable disease which caused him to tremble and walk unsteadily. Although he was getting progressively worse he gallantly continued to look after himself. His bed-sitter at The Sue Ryder Home was always neat and his clothes well-pressed.

Marian spent much of the afternoon with Jan listening to Polish records and talking over old times. Then he busied himself with preparing the *Bigos*. The longer one cooks it the better its flavour. While it is actually cooking the smell is far from appetising, but its taste when served up is really delicious.

Early in the evening more guests arrived: Maria Kastrowicka, a Polish agriculturist working in Cambridge, and her young niece Marisa; my good friend Gillian Edwards; my cousins Bernard Nunn, a lively up-and-coming young businessman from Monks Eleigh, and Gerrit Sheppard, an enterprising young Colcestrian who was at that time an Engineer Officer in the Merchant Navy. Altogether 11 of us sampled the *Bigos*, which was washed down with choice Starka vodka, and later we all enjoyed ourselves vastly in a hotly contested darts tournament.

When my guests had departed and Irena and Stanislaw had retired to bed, Bernard and Gerrit invited Marian and myself to drive down to a pub in town with them to see in the New Year. We went to the *'Eagle'* in Bene't Street – a good choice with its cobbled courtyard, old timbered gallery and coloured lights. The bar was crowded with students, and when midnight struck the boys and girls started to *'Twist'* madly. Marian and I held hands and felt very, very happy.

On New Year's Day my three visitors returned to Yorkshire. When we parted Marian and I considered ourselves officially betrothed.

I was held in the South for another week by several public relations engagements, but when I eventually went up to Hickleton I found Molly Trim and Grace Devine excited and delighted by Marian's and my news. Sue Ryder also knew all about it, of course, and wished us every happiness. She had always referred to him as 'dear Marian' and he was clearly one of her favourites among the many survivors she had helped. As we went into the dining room for supper Marian called my attention to the candles he had set on either side of the Madonna statue I had brought from Liverpool and he proceeded to light them with great ceremony before we sat down to our meal. Indeed it became his regular practice to kindle the candles beside the Madonna every supper-time.

I will always remember with intense pleasure those winter days of our courtship at Hickleton Hall. The old house and surrounding glades presented a lovely sight under deep snow-particularly by the light of a full moon. My assignments, by a happy coincidence, were all in the north of England during the next eight weeks. Whenever I rose early to set off on a trip Marian cooked me a substantial breakfast, packed sandwiches, carried my luggage to the bus stop immediately outside the grounds of the Hall and kissed me 'Goodbye'. This always got me off to a wonderful start and although my excursions at this time were undertaken in some of the worst weather of a phenomenally severe winter, I went cheerfully about my work in howling blizzards and never caught a cold. When I addressed a Rotary Club luncheon at Selby the Speaker's Host assigned to me was Ken Johnson, close friend and flying comrade of Douglas Bader.

Whenever I was actually in residence at Hickleton there was much correspondence to keep me busy and, of course, Marian was also fully occupied all day. But we spent all our evenings together, and how glad I was that I now had a good working knowledge of Polish, for Marian's English was rather sketchy. He told me about his childhood and youth. He spoke knowledgeably about the nature lore of the Polish countryside, about birdsongs and wild life, the pleasures of hunting, his passion for dogs and horses, his service in the Polish Cavalry. Sometimes he told me of his adventures as an underground resistance fighter and of the many terrible atrocities he had seen committed by the Nazis. I learnt that I was not to be the first 'Margaret Podgorska' in the family. He had a great-grandmother of that name (the Polish version of Margaret is *Maogorzata*) who had lived to be 105. Sometimes he sang me Polish love songs and I discovered that he loved all music, not only that of his own country. Marian displayed a quick, practical mind, a good head for figures, considerable shrewdness and a remarkable memory which helped to make him a crack card player. I loved his simplicity, sincerity and great sense of fun.

We went to several Polish parties in the neighbourhood of Hickleton. These were always wonderfully gay affairs. Poems were recited, speeches delivered and songs sung with patriotic fervour. The food provided by the womenfolk was always superb, vodka flowed freely and there was music and dancing far into the night. Yorkshire, like many other parts of the North, has a large Polish population.

Marian enjoyed himself vastly on these occasions, and although his lame leg prevented him from dancing he was always most insistent that *I* should do so.

As Spring approached I set out southwards again for assignments in Devonshire, the Isle of Wight, Worcester and various parts of East Anglia. Calling in at Cavendish *en route,* I found a new face at The Headquarters. His name was Eugen and he had performed some incredibly brave deeds during the war. He had been in the Warsaw Uprising and had fought in the maze of sewers beneath the city. Outstripping all his other adventures, however, was his six-month long impersonation of a German Air Force Officer who was still alive at the time though fighting on another front. Eugen bore a strong physical resemblance to him and spoke perfect German. So he was assigned to masquerade as this man on a German air base, and while doing so he regularly sent valuable information to the Allies.

In between jobs I managed to find a sunny house in a pleasant part of Doncaster close to the Race Course, and I moved from Cambridge in June. At that season my new garden was full of stock, peonies, tiger lilies and fine roses. After I moved in Marian came over from Hickleton on his days off and loved to potter about the garden and in the old disused greenhouse. I had not seen much sign of life in there but he discovered a very withered geranium in a chipped flower pot. It looked dead to me, or at least past saving. But Marian nurtured it lovingly and the plant flourished. In the kitchen he cooked delicious meals and gave me many useful culinary tips.

In July I held a small party to mark Marian's birthday. Grace Devine and her husband were among the guests and afterwards she wrote to me: 'I wanted to tell you how happy we felt walking home on Sunday evening after seeing Marian so happy and "belonging" at last and you glowing in every sense of the word. Bless you both and speed the great day. One glimpse of your faces then and I am sure there will truly be rejoicing in Heaven.'

Marian and I were married on 9th May 1964. It was a true love match and has remained so ever since. My last public relations engagement five days previously was at Lincoln, home-town of Rose McIntosh, a charming, accomplished musician and traveller who had for some time been rendering devoted service at Hickleton. We had tea with a friend of hers at a delightful flat in the Cathedral Close, and later I showed Sue Ryder's film to a large audience at St. Andrew's Church. This was followed by an informal supper party at 'Miss Mac's' lovely Georgian home in a secluded court near the Cathedral.

The 40 guests at our wedding included several patients, survivors, and members of the Hickleton staff. I wore a white lace day length dress and coat, and a net hat decorated with white silk roses. My bouquet was red roses and white freesias – the Polish national colours.

Sue Ryder's present was a set of engraved wine goblets. She also gave me a charmingly inscribed book called *One, of Great Price,* by Sergei Hackel, and a wonderfully-worded letter of thanks for my work which I now have framed on my study wall.

In her closing paragraph Sue Ryder wrote: 'Needless to say I shall miss you a great deal and only wish you could stay on and enlarge the scope of the work which you have carried out so well under great difficulties and appalling weather conditions. I have often admired you for the way in which you unhesitatingly set forth undaunted by cold, rain and high wind. I hope that from time to time you will not mind my asking for your help'.

From a gallant woman who had many times cleared radiator-high snow from the road ahead by the light of headlamps during solo marathon mercy drives on the Continent, these words meant a great deal. After my marriage I continued to give talks on her behalf from time to time at fund-raising events.

CHAPTER TWELVE

THE CONTENTED HEART

AFTER WE RETURNED from our honeymoon in East Anglia another dream came true for Marian; he opened his own business. As a D.P. in Germany he had attended an American-sponsored rehabilitation centre to learn a new trade and had gained a first class diploma as a master shoemaker. When he came over to England in 1961 he brought the tools of his trade with him. At Hickleton he had managed to obtain a second-hand finishing machine and in his spare time did shoe repairs for a faithful following of customers in the immediate neighbourhood.

Now, thanks to permission from the Doncaster Town Planning Committee, we had been allowed to build a handsome, fully equipped workshop in the rear garden of our home. We bought all the extra up-to-date apparatus necessary to make it a thoroughly competitive concern. I devised a trade motto *'Our skill is at your feet'* as our personal advertisement, and this was no idle boast. News of Marian's splendid craftsmanship did not take long to circulate and soon he was firmly established.

Unlike so many northern towns Doncaster is not a drab, soot caked place overshadowed by forests of factory chimneys. The residential quarters are airy and attractive, and up around the race course there is some charming Regency architecture and a picturesque old tavern. The famous St. Leger is run at Doncaster in early September and then it is a town *en fête* with celebrity banquets, hotels filled to overflowing, crowds of gypsies, horse boxes under heavy police guard, and a mammoth fair on the fringe of the course. I quickly made many new friends and, I hope and believe, helped to dispel the chilly image Northerners have of Southerners. Like all Doncaster housewives one of my favourite haunts was the vast covered market that sells everything under the sun at cut prices. My customary 'elevenses' at one of the tiny cafes sandwiched between the stalls was that traditional Yorkshire snack bread cake with pork dripping and a cup of tea (total cost 10d).

Doncaster (or *'Donnie'* as it is known to the locals) is, of course, in the heart of Northern Clubland now famed nationally for its rumbustious uninhibited pleasure palaces. These clubs are notable for their flashy finery, deafening electric organ music, gargantuan beer consumption, one-armed bandits and extremely near-the knuckle cabaret turns. An evening spent at one is an education in itself!

But in direct contrast to this there are many scenic splendours too. I loved going up to the Brontë Country near Keighley. In the bleak hilltop village of Haworth the Old Parsonage where the famous family lived and wrote still stands on the very edge of the moors. It houses their furniture, personal possessions and manuscripts. Nearby is the Black Bull Inn, the interior of which remains very much as it looked when Bramwell Brontë went there to drown his frustrated ambitions in drink, and was warned by Emily tapping on the window when his formidable old father was approaching down the cobbled alley in search of him. And strolling across the moors today one encounters the windswept ruins of old grey stone houses such as Emily clearly had in mind when she wrote *Wuthering Heights.*

Nottingham too is relatively close to Doncaster. I re-visited Newstead Abbey many times and also forged a warm friendship with Dolly Sewell, a sparkling and dynamic Nottingham writer, tutor and business woman who was later to be my son's godmother.

After our marriage Marian and I kept in close touch with the Sue Ryder Home at Hickleton Hall. We attended garden fetes and Christmas parties there and kept 'open house' at our own place for many of the patients. And I 'came out of retirement' on three occasions to speak about the Foundation – at a County Guide Rally, a garden fete, and a Christmas Fair. I also found time to resume my literary activities. I made the small bedroom above our hallway into my study and den . . . little realising that it would soon be assuming the even more important role of a nursery.

Early in 1965 I found that I was going to have a baby and I regarded being a mother for the first time in my forty-third year as a bonus blessing beyond all price. At the ante-natal clinic and relaxation classes I felt a bit of an ancient monument among the many very young mothers-to-be, but I had a trouble-free pregnancy with no trace of morning sickness, swollen ankles or varicose veins. Just before lunch on Friday 19th November, 1965, our son John Richard David was born at the Western Hospital Maternity Unit in Doncaster. He weighed 7lb. 15oz. Marian came up almost immediately to see us and gave me a bouquet of red carnations. Flowers and messages poured in from many well wishers. To me – as to any woman – having a son was the greatest happiness of my life.

Because Marian is a Roman Catholic and I am Church of England our marriage had taken place at Doncaster Register Office but this civil ceremony had been followed by a Service of Blessing at St. George's Anglican Church. With Marian's complete agreement, John was christened on Mothering Sunday in 1966 at St. George's.

I bought the christening gown but made the accompanying bonnet and christening pillow myself. John's little white slippers were a gift from his great-great aunt Daisy Nunn. Now they are all carefully packed away for John's children.

After the ceremony a party was held at our home and a blue and white cake was cut. Many beautiful gifts were received, including baby clothes from Sue Ryder's mother Mrs. Mabel Ryder.

When Johnny was six months old he visited East Anglia for the first time. Savouring every new scene and experience with obvious pleasure he proved an excellent traveller.

We realised very early on that he was a bright little boy. At two-and-a-half he began to take a passionate interest in books and showed an excellent ear for music. He learnt his numbers by studying the figures on garden gates as we strolled along the street. At three he could work a radiogram on his own including the various speed changes, and loved playing records, with classical music high among his favourites; he called this 'grand' music.

By his fourth birthday he could write his name very well, and the full extent of his interest in the written word became apparent four months later when, entirely on his own initiative, he began to write words he saw on television or copied from newspapers and household items. When we were out he continually asked me what various street signs, advertisement hoardings and shop fronts said. To this period also belongs the memorable bath-time when he spelt out correctly from memory TAXI, ZOO, EGG, APPLE, CAKE, FIRE, GOLD, HOUSE and EMBASSY.

A parent's life is constantly illumined with wonderful 'first times'. The packaging of the bolster on that first Christmas Eve, the first birthday preparations, the first decorated harvest festival basket, the first pantomime, the first sight-seeing trip to London, the first school play, the first star for good work, the first handmade greetings card with its crayonned picture and lovingly scrawled message . . .

Here are my favourite anecdotes about Johnny as a four-year-old. One day in pouring rain he walked along with face raised skywards and mouth wide open explaining that he was a gargoyle. On being told that Cavendish railway station had been closed down because it was very old he asked if it had been built by the Romans. While listening to one of his favourite records he remarked that it couldn't be much fun being a ghost because ghosts had no ears and couldn't hear music. After watching a stag beetle on a very hot summer's day when he himself was wearing next to nothing, he inquired if insects had birthday suits.

Marian and I spent the first four years of our married life in Yorkshire and they were by no means unhappy years. But in 1968 the lure of living once again in East Anglia became too strong to resist any longer. Severe northern winters proved tiresome to Marian's old war wound.

In June of that year I spent a week in Colchester, viewed seven houses and made my choice. Two months later, with the temperature in the upper eighties and Marian plying the removal men with frequent beers which they fully earned, we moved into our charming little period cottage in the heart of Colchester's West End, close to many of the best-loved haunts of my childhood. I have always particularly liked the West End of town.

There is a rich abundance of Georgian and Regency domestic architecture. The municipal hill-top church of St. Peter's has a joyous peal of bells. Behind quiet little backstreets a rustic path leads to the gorse-clad uplands and panoramic views of archaeologically-rich Sheepen Meadows. Further westwards are the aristocratic Victorian facades and fine old trees of Lexden Road.

Sadly missing nowadays are the sort of 'characters' who added so much to the local scene during the '30's, but at least there are two worth mentioning. Donato is a diminutive dark-suited figure of typical Neapolitan aspect whose only concession to wintry days is a muffler. His chief occupation (in the words of the song) seems to be 'standing on the corner watching all the girls go by', and his cheery greetings of *'Buon giorno!'* do not go unacknowledged. Then there is the elderly gentleman who goes shopping in an old army greatcoat elaborately embroidered in wools of many colours. On his half-belt and back are worked religious texts.

We bought our house from an old merchant seaman who had modernised it in a style very much to my taste. There is a good deal of cyclamen pink paintwork inside – a shade usually associated with Hollywood boudoirs and chi-chi hotel powder rooms. But as used in our house it gives a warm rosy glow of singularly pleasing effect. The small, snug black and pink bathroom, which the old seadog converted most efficiently from a wash-house, is in scale and layout very like quarters aboard ship. On the upper floor is a splendidly proportioned 17 ft. long drawing room which is regularly the scene of happy social gatherings. Both Marian and I love company.

Nor did the Town Planning Committee disappoint us. They gave Marian permission to build a workshop in the back garden on the site of an old conservatory, and it did not take Colcestrians long to recognise his exceptional skill. A pretty little old-world garden remains with roses, honeysuckle and giant dahlias. Beyond is a pleasant airy vista of poplars and elms on rising ground.

One of my great delights is visiting antique shops in various Essex and Suffolk villages to buy old china, pewter and country craft items which look so well in a house like ours. Among my favourite purchases is a model of a gypsy caravan made by an aged craftsman at Long Melford.

Also – though only in a very modest way at present – I have started to collect work by local artists. There is a fine bronze bust of our little son – a really stunning likeness – by my good friend Betty Curtis, who has a studio down in the Dutch Quarter in partnership with two equally gifted friends Isabel Gregory and Neil Syer. Betty excels in many media but admits that sculpture is her favourite.

I am also delighted with a water-colour I commissioned recently from a young Lexden artist named Gerald Walden. The subject I chose was that beguiling portion of Balkerne Lane incorporating Parker's Dickensian general stores and the unique little bow windowed cottage (demolished, alas, on 26th March, 1971) with St. Mary's Steps and a glimpse of the church tower above. Gerald, aged 24, is self-taught and particularly skilful at painting water reflections and brick textures. His handling of the Roman wall in my water-colour is masterly.

At regular intervals Marian and I join in the revelry at parties held by Colchester's Polish community. The lively music is provided by a group of scarlet-coated Poles from Witham. Dishes of piping-hot *Bigos* and sugar-frosted doughnuts are served halfway through the evening and vodka flows freely. We also retain close links with Sue Ryder's home at Cavendish and go over there several times a year.

When the time came for Johnny to start school my natural choice was the New Church School where I had been a pupil from 1927 to 1930. Today Muriel Gill has a worthy successor in Hilda Waters, a wise, vibrant and open-hearted woman with exceptional teaching ability. The present pastor and headmaster is the Rev. Bjorn Boyesen, a distinguished preacher and an engaging personality.

Early in his first term Johnny made his mark by reciting the First Psalm word-perfectly from memory (no mean feat for a child still under five at the time). He loves to recite poems and stories aloud with a wealth of expression (as befits the great-great-grandson of an actor-manager).

Not long ago my very dear friend Jennifer Couroucli said to me: 'Mags, you are one of those people who know how to handle happiness when they have got it.' I am certainly aware of a deep inner contentment as I gaze out across a hay-scented, lark-haunted East Anglian landscape to bright new horizons.

THE END OF BOOK ONE
(1922 – 1970)

The Way of My World

Book Two

1971 – 1995

Courtworth Publications
Colchester

To the Dear Memory of My Husband
who was
The Cornerstone of My Happiness
for
Thirty Years

CHAPTER ONE

IN THE LITERARY ARENA

MY RETURN TO COLCHESTER after so many years of travel and adventure awakened nostalgia of the pleasantest kind, and it was after contributing a number of reminiscent articles to the local newspaper that I decided in 1970 to write my first volume of autobiography. I worked on it in the evenings after I had read Johnny a story and tucked him up in bed. As the book progressed I was astonished to find how much I had to tell.

Early the following year I submitted it to a publishing company called Precision Press which was then located at High Wycombe. It was quite by chance that I chose this particular publisher. Watching television one evening I learnt that an autobiography called *The Mayor & the Matron* had just been brought out by Stanley Wilson, an extremely well-known figure in Saffron Walden.* I made a note of the publisher's name and address and sent off my own typescript without delay.

To my delight Precision accepted it and soon I was in regular touch with George Loman, J.P., head of the firm. He was a scholarly-looking middle-aged man who wore a black astrakhan hat on chilly days. I followed the various stages of production with intense interest and was invited down to High Wycombe to watch the books being bound.

By late Autumn *The Way of My World* was ready for the bookshops. George Loman thought that Colchester Town Hall would be an ideal setting for the launching party and he approached the Mayor, Alderman Nancy Smith, to seek permission. A petite, vivacious and elegant Welshwoman, she not only allowed us to hold our party in the splendid surroundings of the Mayor's Parlour and adjoining Grand Jury Room, but also consented to be our guest of honour with her genial husband. The catering was done by Last's who at that time had a business in High Street close to the Town Hall.

Friday, 17th December, 1971, was the great night and the whole event was very well stage-managed by the Precision Press team. Around 100 guests attended mainly comprising my family and friends, although a number of representatives from the bookselling trade were also present.

Chandeliers in the beautiful civic apartments shone down on a lively scene. Camera bulbs flashed, toasts were drunk, speeches made and the books on show perused. Johnny presented the Mayor with a bouquet and she in turn gave him a copy of my book which Precision Press had bound specially for him in green and gold.

* Later I met Stanley and his equally remarkable wife Kitty at their home.

Although I had seen myself in print so many times before in newspapers and magazines, this was my first book . . . a dream come true. I still vividly remember how, towards the end of the evening, I moved across to the window that opened out on to the balcony where election results were traditionally announced. My thoughts turned to my grandfather and the night he had come top of the poll nearly forty years before. Now here I was feeling a similar sense of elation only a few feet away from the spot where he had once stood so joyfully. It was a heady start to the 1970's which were to prove a full and exciting decade for me.

Reviews of *The Way of My World* in various newspapers and magazines were all favourable and in some instances much more than that. I have never had an inflated idea of my own importance, but I must confess that it gladdened my heart when Edmund Orwell of the *East Anglian Daily Times* wrote: 'Many well-known people have come within the scope of her quick gaze and eager mind. Her enthusiasm for life and her determination to see the best in people are qualities constantly demonstrated. One feels that meeting her would be a stimulating experience'.

I also much appreciated the comment by Frank Tonkinson of the *Evening Star* that 'This book is an admirable piece of lively, uninhibited journalism'.

From her home near London's Regents Park, Doris Langley Moore, the distinguished writer and Byron scholar, sent me a letter saying: 'It is indeed a very happy book full of natural ebullience. I found your descriptions of places most evocative. It is a really good read'.

Later I had the great pleasure of meeting her. The date was 19th April, 1974, when I went up to London on the 150th anniversary of Byron's death. This was marked by a moving service of commemoration at Westminter Abbey which was attended by some of the Poet's descendants, members of the long-established Byron Society, and Sir Robert Boothby who was M.P. for Aberdeen where Byron spent his early years. I felt very privileged to be there.

Afterwards Mrs. Langley Moore invited me to dine with her at *Ye Olde Cheshire Cheese* in Fleet Street. This surpassingly picturesque and historic landmark is my favourite London eating house.

As famous for her wonderful Costume Museum at Bath as for her authorship, Mrs. Langley Moore was one of the most fascinating personalities I have ever met. Although certainly not conventionally beautiful, she had an unusually striking and attractive face even in old age and dressed with considerable dash and originality. On the night we dined together she was wearing yellow and gold and her hat was inspired by one of the most becoming regional headdresses in Greece.

At the time of our meeting she was working on her biography of Byron's daughter, Ada, who died of cancer at the age of 36, and we discussed the book at some length over our meal, She told me that she had discovered evidence beyond doubt that Ada's mother Lady Annabella Byron had a sadistic streak. She was certainly described by people who knew her as 'cold and calculating' but there was a far darker side to her nature than this.

Ada was only a few weeks old when her mother left the Poet after one year of stormy marriage and she never saw her father again. Yet it was her dying wish to be buried beside him in the family vault. This Lady Byron found totally unforgivable and, during Ada's last agonising days, her mother denied her painkilling medication. It is good to know that Ada's husband Lord Lovelace refused to let his mother-in-law override his wife's last request. Lady Byron did not attend the funeral. Byron students owe a great debt to Doris Langley Moore on many counts.

Sales of *The Way of My World* were brisk and I received many appreciative letters. They included one from Muriel Brittain, widow of that most lovable Cambridge Don Dr. 'Freddie' Brittain who had made me an *'Honorary Hen'* of the Roosters Club at Jesus College while I was living in that city during the 1950's. I accepted her invitation to lunch at the College where she was still very actively engaged in University life and the Roosters Club in particular.

We dined in Dr. Brittain's old rooms where his gown still hung in its accustomed place and his genial presence could be felt everywhere. My fellow guests were Alan Percival and his wife Moira, both leading members of The Roosters, whom I had previously met some 15 years before at one of the Club's unforgettable Sunday luncheons.

During the meal Alan told me one of the most remarkable coincidences I have ever encountered. He referred to the chapter in *The Way of My World* in which I described my interview in 1951 with Michael, a cricket-loving teenage spastic who at that date was a patient in the men's geriatric ward at the Mayday Hospital, Croydon. Alan said that from the circumstances I had recounted the Michael in question was almost certainly the same young man who regularly attended a summer holiday camp he ran for the disabled at Woodlarks, Farnham, Surrey.

It was altogether a most enjoyable reunion and before we parted Muriel autographed my copy of her husband's autobiography *It's a Don's Life* – a rare treat to grace any bookshelf.

Through my friend Grace Baalam news of *The Way of My World* reached Dame Anna Neagle who was naturally interested to hear that there was more than a passing reference to her in one of my chapters about Sue Ryder. After playing the harrowing rôle of French wartime resistance heroine Odette (Hallowes) in the powerful film of that name

Dame Anna became closely associated with Sue Ryder and her work.

Writing from the Adelphi Theatre the great actress asked if she could obtain a copy of my book. By that time all copies had been sold except for a few in my own possession, so I gladly sent her one of these on open-ended loan.

I received a number of further charming letters from her bearing either the address of the Adelphi or of her home in Hamilton Terrace, St. John's Wood. Most were written in her own hand – a very firm and distinctive hand that was full of character. I very much enjoyed all the films she made about famous women and I would love to have met her again, but sadly this was not to be. She died in 1986 only a short time after her last stage appearance in pantomime.

Later when I called at her home to collect my book Joyce, her devoted friend of many years, invited me in. There was a beautiful bust of Dame Anna in the hallway and the gracious drawing room was filled with momentoes of her husband Herbert Wilcox and herself. International trophies, awarded for films they had made in such happy partnership, were displayed in a large glass cabinet and there were countless nostalgic photographs of memorable moments both on and off stage. Having read her autobiography *There's Always Tomorrow* I knew Dame Anna was a great cat lover and this was abundantly reflected in the pictures and other accessories with cat motifs.

Spin offs from the appearance of my book were varied and interesting. There were radio interviews, *Any Questions* panels and similar events. It was great fun taking part in a Colchester version of *Going For a Song* (inspired by the very popular TV programme of that period). My fellow panellists were antiques specialist Derek Lamberth, jeweller Garth Cooper and Barbara Jones, wife of the then Garrison Commandant.

I was asked to give talks about my adventurous travels or my work for Sue Ryder and venues ranged from church halls and art galleries to schools and social clubs.

One of my favourite places was a charming house at Weeley set amongst the strawberry fields of Ken Muir, a prize-winning grower of international repute. My hostess invited me to speak at the height of the strawberry season and after the meeting I came away with a gift punnet of luscious freshly-picked fruit and a carton of cream.

May, 1974, marked another literary event which gave me great pleasure. After attending the Chelsea Flower Show (an occasion on no account to be missed), I decided to call on the publishers to whom I had submitted a short romantic novel. It was called *The Golden Garland* and was set in my beloved Venice. To complete what had seemed a charmed day they told me that my story was to be published in November.

This acceptance meant a great deal to me because *The Golden Garland* was my favourite among all the fiction I had written up to that date. The characters I had created were intensely real to me and I had painted in the Venetian background with all the loving detail of personal acquaintance. Even today, so many years later, I still retain a special affection for this story.

CHAPTER TWO

SUNFLOWERS AND BLACK CHERRIES

IN THE SUMMER of 1976 Marian, Johnny and I spent two months holiday in Poland travelling all over the country and staying at the homes of different relations. It was a very special journey for several reasons. To begin with it was the first time Marian had returned to his native land for more than 30 years and was, therefore, marked by emotional reunions and poignant memories. I had been to Poland before as Sue Ryder's emissary, but now I came as the wife of a Polish exile to meet Marian's many relations.

It was a memorable occasion for Johnny, aged 10, to meet his half-brother Zygfryd and his half-sister Izabela and get closely acquainted with his Polish roots. Among fields of sunflowers and black cherry orchards, surrounded by his own people, Marian and I were to enjoy a second honeymoon.

Our first hosts in Poland were Marian's cousin Kazik and his wife Teresa who lived in Slonsk (Silesia) near the German border. When our train reached Opole they were there to greet us and we drove to their home in the nearby village of Trawniki. Teresa was the principal of the school and their home adjoined the schoolhouse. Although it was smartly furnished they had no indoor plumbing. Water was supplied by a traditional hand pump in the garden, while the toilet was an earth closet on the farther side of an orchard populated with chickens and geese.

Kazik was a skilled mechanic who worked at a garage in the neighbouring town of Kozle. Teresa was dark eyed, vivacious and attractive. They had three daughters Malgosia (Margaret), Lilla and Ewa aged 16, 12 and nine respectively. Ewa was extremely keen on card games in which we often joined her. The family pet was a dog of indeterminate breed called Misha. As there was a spare bicycle Johnny was able to go out on rides with the girls or on his own and he soon made friends among the village children.

Trawniki was a pleasant, well-maintained village with a handsome church and a recently-built community centre that actually had a flush toilet. Among old one-storey cottages were quite a lot of modern houses with intricate stone wall patterns and colourful gardens. A good bus service to other towns and villages ran along the main tarmac road through the centre of Trawniki.

In the older part of the village each cottage had an adjacent smallholding and some a stable or cowshed. This was also the location of a large general store with bare wooden floor boards, antique scales and plentiful sacks of miscellaneous provisions. Wide ranging merchandise included some singularly tasty bread rolls and – somewhat surprisingly – delicious chocolate creams which were dispensed to customers in sturdy cone-shaped brown paper bags.

What intrigued me most in Trawniki was the mouldering beauty and shuttered silence of an impressive mansion on the outskirts of the village. Before the war it had belonged to a wealthy landowner. In a cobbled farmyard nearby some folk still lived in the humblest of dwellings. Johnny and I were invited into one of them by an old lady named Alexandra.

She had just baked an extremely good chocolate cake in her primitive oven and, while we sat down to enjoy generous slices of this, she carried on with her ironing. We were much amused by the basic but undeniably effective method she employed to moisten the items on her ironing board. She simply sipped a mouthful of water and then sprayed it over the garment in question.

Facing the old mansion was an extensive wood and we discovered that in the heart of this secluded sylvan retreat the menfolk of Trawniki had their own comfortably appointed club where they played cards and drank liberal quantities of vodka.

Food was plentiful and wholesome in Trawniki in high summer. Like her fellow villagers Teresa cashed in on her own resources. She gathered honey from her own hives, brewed drinks from the fruit in her orchard, made her own yoghurt and collected eggs from her free-ranging poultry. The roast served for Sunday lunch meant one less among our feathered friends in the grassy paddock. Milk and vegetables came from her brother-in-law's smallholding.

One of the most striking characters in the village was a rosy-cheeked farmer's widow named Stanislawa whose primitive wagon, piled high with hay and clover, was drawn by two dairy cows. We always returned her cheery greeting.

Mail was delivered daily by a grey-uniformed postman on a motor cycle. Since he lingered at most of the homes he went to for a chat and some vodka, his progress astride his machine became increasingly erratic.

While we were based at Trawniki I took Johnny on a three-day visit to Crakow which was relatively close and readily accessible by train from Kozle. I was keen to show him the extremely beautiful medieval city that had won my heart, even on brief acquaintance, back in 1962.

We stayed at the pricey, centrally-situated Hotel Europelski which had elegant en suite bedrooms but did not serve breakfast. To off-set accommodation costs we had most meals at the very inexpensive Bar Tempo nearby or, alternatively, bought bread, cheese and fruit for picnic snacks. Mid-morning we drank coffee at an ornate marble-topped table in the grand surroundings of what had originally been the Clothiers' Guild Hall. This ancient architectural gem stood on one side of the vast market square which was bright with flower stalls.

On either side of the square an exhibition of paintings by art students was displayed on railings. Fields of sunflowers and forests of silver birches were popular themes and the work was excellent. We purchased dumplings wrapped in serviettes from a street vendor. They were shaped like pineapples and had a saffron glaze. Later we took a ride on a horse-drawn bus along narrow cobbled streets.

Dominating Crakow is Wawel Castle, majestic hilltop citadel which was once the home of Polish kings. Having donned obligatory felt footwear to protect the marble floors, we toured the sumptuously furnished rooms. One of the features that charmed us most was a magnificent clock on which angels with trumpets ushered in every hour with a fanfare.

In complete contrast we then took a tram to the poorest quarter of the city in search of a certain 'Podgorska Street' which had caught our eye when we scanned a map of Crakow. Friendly fellow passengers made sure we alighted at the correct stop. The unpretentious little street that bore my name immediately overlooked the River Vistula and was bordered by ochre-walled cottages with geraniums in window boxes.

Our curiosity having been satisfied, we took a walk beside the river which was of majestic proportions at this point and had steps leading down to the water. What fascinated us most of all, however, was the number of men playing cards and chess on makeshift table tops in thick bushes.

Crakow is noted for its talented street musicians and we encountered a group performing in an underpass in the heart of the city one rainy morning. I could not resist asking them to play a universally popular romantic ballad which I knew well called *Malienki Znak* (Little Rendezvous). As they gave a melodious rendering of the catchy tune passersby stopped to sing the words with me. It was a joyous experience and I paid the music-makers generously.

Johnny and I returned to Trawniki with plenty of anecdotes to recount about our stay in the lovely old city where Pope John Paul was Cardinal before being chosen for the holiest appointment of all . . . a source of immense pride to all his countrymen.

A few days later the three of us said farewell to the good folk of Trawniki after strolling for the last time through cherry orchards and sunflower fields. We caught an overnight train to Marian's home town of Zamość close to the Russian border. At sunrise I watched the passing scenery. Cornfields were interspersed by woods where silver birches predominated. I noticed that the haycocks were a different shape from those round Trawniki and had fetching top-knots. On the distant skyline were mountains.

Zamość was a picturesque, historic town. In a pleasant leafy suburb we stayed at the flat of Marian's favourite cousin Bogousha and her husband Vassek. She was tiny, bright-eyed and highly strung with bossy ways that were good-naturedly tolerated by Vassek and their two buxom, pretty daughters Elsbiéta and Grazynka.

Because of many ordeals they had faced together during the war Marian shared a particularly close bond with Bogousha and their reunion was very touching. She also gave me a warm welcome and we got along very well together. Vassek who, as Johnny observed, bore a strong resemblance to the actor Sid James, was equally hospitable and soon we were clinking glasses of vodka with him. Then I met Bogousha's mother Stefania who had been Marian's affectionate substitute mother after he was orphaned as a small boy. I knew how much he loved her and I held her in my arms for a long time.

Marian's son Zygfryd, whom he had last seen as a boy of ten, lived nearby with his wife Helena and two children and the next day we went to have lunch with them. As gifts we took a bottle of fiery Spiritus, a packet of Carmen cigarettes (far superior to those usually smoked) and a box of chocolate stars. Zygfryd had last seen Marian before he had become an underground fighter and received his permanently disabling injury. I was moved to tears as father and son embraced and caressed each other's faces. What had originally been planned as a lunchtime visit continued until well after midnight. There was so much to talk about.

I had of course seen several photographs of Zygfryd which he had sent to Marian at various times, but he was even more handsome in the flesh and had a grave dignity that charmed me. He was a driving instructor at a heavy lorry training centre but music was the great delight of his leisure hours. He sang to his own accordion accompaniment and also played the organ at his local church. It was an exciting experience for Johnny to meet his half-brother for the first time and their facial resemblance was striking.

We met a large number of Marian's relations during our stay in Zamość. On one occasion there were so many members of the family gathered in the same room that I asked teenager Anna to draw a genealogical tree for me which she proceeded to do with skill and clarity.

I particularly recall Albina an elderly somewhat eccentric lady who loved gardening and also kept pigs at the rear of her carved wooden Russian-style home on the outskirts of the town. One day, in pouring rain, she took Johnny and myself through a maze of back streets (absent-mindedly losing the way en route) to a restaurant where one of her daughters worked. This was called the *Restaracja Centralna* and before the war it had been a famous eating-house among the rich. It was fascinating to have a meal there in surroundings of faded grandeur.

After dining on roast duck, we were joined by Albina's son-in-law Kazik (a very common boy's name in Poland), her second daughter Marisia and four-year-old grandchild Beata. Kazik, a civil servant, was born in Zamość and was very proud of his town. He took all of us to a delightful kawarnia (coffee-house) that occupied the ground floor of the Town Hall. Besides drinks we had kremas, a delectable cross between a blancmange and an ice cream, which Johnny and I were to sample frequently not only in Zamość but in other towns we went to later.

The Town Hall was the most imposing landmark in a large square which had been designed by the same architect who had created much of Padua.This explained why the lantern-lit arcades with vaulted ceilings at once struck me as being so Italianate.

Beneath the arches were romantic-looking little shops while living accommodation above was decorated with rich pargetting and geranium-filled window boxes. At the time we were in Zamość there was an air of dilapidated elegance about many of the buildings but admirable restoration work was in progress.

The Town Hall itself was beautifully maintained. Majestic flights of steps leading up to the main entrance were often used by choirs for outdoor concerts, and the tall graceful central clock tower dominated the town's skyline. The fine interior had marble floors, antique furniture and brass filigree chandeliers.

There was a special staircase giving access to the clock tower and one morning Johnny and I made the steep climb. En route we saw the workings of the time-piece enclosed in a large protective glass case. Standing on the tower's circular balcony we obtained a panoramic view far beyond the rooftops to the surrounding countryside.

A museum was also situated in the Square. Once it had been the home of the noble family who gave the town its name and the atmosphere was similar to that of a wealthy medieval merchant's house in England. There were ancient mural paintings, family portraits, manuscripts, weapons and suits of armour. Glass goblets and decanters were elaborately embellished with gold scrolls and coats-of-arms.

But what appealed to me most was a display of *Korowaj* which are important traditional symbols at country weddings in Poland. They are tree-like structures with boughs made entirely from dough and garlanded with numerous beads moulded from the same material. To this basic framework are added paper ribbons and flowers. A *Korowaj* is fashioned in a wide variety of designs with the emphasis always on exuberant colour schemes.

There were numerous other examples of craft work created with dough, straw, paper and dried flowers. In peasant homes these would be hung from the ceiling or used as a table centre. One outstanding piece was more sophisticated than its companions and clearly made for some patriotic event. Similar to corn-dolly work in England, it was taller than a man and consisted of intricately plaited cornstalks arranged in a series of circles and tied with red, white, green and blue ribbons. The final grand touch was a plaque of Poland's national eagle symbol fashioned entirely in cornstalks of contrasting lustre.

Exploring the town on foot was always intriguing. Outside the old barracks Johnny and I encountered a market. Some of the stalls were presided over by men with flowing moustaches, Tartar-style caps and quilted gaiters. Onions, a form of nettle, snowberries, black currants and parsley filled our nostrils with the subtle aromas of countryside cooking ingredients. Abundant sunflower seeds were on sale. Apart from providing oil they are regarded as a valuable source of vitamins. I noted, too, that sunflower motifs figured prominently among curtain and dress materials.

Other stalls sold miscellaneous household goods, brooms, rush mats, basic clothes, cheap toys and baubles. I purchased what I thought was a small tablecloth with an elaborate pattern of roses and forget-me-nots on a scarlet background. Later I was told it was a peasant headscarf, but down the years I have always used it as a table covering and it still launders beautifully.

On this particular outing we also found to our great delight a whole group of old Russian-style houses very tumbledown but still lived in. Bark slates, moss-covered porches and carved shutters gave them an extremely picturesque appearance. Their small gardens were full of hollyhocks, marigolds, roses, antirrhinums, yellow chrysanthemums, lupins, geraniums and carnations.

Throughout our travels we were never in direct contact with the Police though there were uniformed patrols at all railway stations and police cars roamed the streets. In tourist centres like Warsaw and Crakow a visitor could easily forget that he was in a country under Communist rule, but in a provincial town like Zamość hoardings with political slogans were prominently displayed.

Housewives shopping in Zamość often had a frustrating time. Queues for bread started forming very early in the morning, meatless days were frequent, sugar was scarce and fruit on sale was very poor quality by English standards. Prices were high and the fact that shops opened at irregular hours was another problem.

When we were in Poland in 1976 Russia still regarded her as a 'colony' and everyone worked very long hours for low pay. The cream of all profits went to Russia which, Marian told me, had even taken huge trainloads of Polish soil away.

One place where the people of Zamość could find a welcome escape from their worries was a park which we went to frequently. Being high summer it was full of leafy avenues, lawns and secluded arbours. Beside a large lake a broad flight of steps led up to a glass pavilion serving refreshments.

Close by was a zoo where the animals included llamas, camels, monkeys, armadillos, lions, bears, a yak, a puma, deer, mountain goats and a wild horse without a tail. The bird enclosures contained peacocks, pelicans, storks, vultures, a falcon, parrots, canaries and budgerigars.

There was now great excitement at Bogousha's flat because the wedding of her elder daughter Elsbiéta was imminent. She was marrying an engineering student named Edward who lived in a pretty country town called Namyslow where the ceremony was to take place. Marian, Johnny and myself were invited and we accompanied Bogousha and the rest of the family on the long journey which took fourteen hours. After changing trains at Lublin we fortunately got a carriage to ourselves.For supper Bogousha unpacked cutlets with bread and tomatoes, poppyseed cake and lemon tea.

We reached Namyslow at five o'clock in the morning when a brilliant sunrise enhanced its many charms. Although much smaller than Zamość it too had a Town Hall with a kawarnia at street level. We all stayed at the home of the bridegroom's parents which was a spacious chalet-style bungalow with a garage built underneath.

After a hearty breakfast and a few hours' sleep I went out with Johnny to buy him a new jacket for the wedding. I was amused by the informality of the service in the shops. While attending to customers the assistants would pause from time to time to eat strawberries, munch a bread roll or draw on a cigarette. The counters were mounted on casters and sometimes the pressure of people caused them to shift disconcertingly.

Before returning to the bungalow we strolled beside a river with a weir. The water meadows were full of little green frogs that hopped merrily round our feet. At a café called the *Widawianka* we saw a wedding party in progress and later we learned that the orchestra playing there would be providing the music at our own family celebration.

While Poland was under Communist rule a civil wedding ceremony was obligatory. If, like Elsbiéta and Edward, a young couple were devout Roman Catholics then a church celebration would follow.

Elsbiéta arrived for her civil wedding at the Town Hall wearing an emerald green dress and flower-trimmed straw picture hat, while Edward looked very smart in the grey suit, waistcoat and large bow tie which he would also wear at the church the following day. In his buttonhole was a white carnation.

As we were all ushered into the wedding chamber the familiar strains of Mendelssohn's *Wedding March* burst forth from a concealed tape recorder and this melody, diminished in volume, was played throughout the ceremony. It was an impressive apartment lit by wrought iron chandeliers with clusters of lanterns. The vaulted ceiling was painted terracotta and gracefully draped gold brocade curtains framed Gothic-shaped windows. There were no religious symbols. In the centre was a very large highly polished desk and the taped music was issuing from an open drawer.

Guests sat along opposite walls while the bride and groom had two ornate high-backed chairs facing the desk. A chic, dark-haired woman in a long orange gown officiated and she proffered rings to the couple on a silver tray. At the end of the ceremony the tape recorder played the *Bridal March from Lohengrin* and glasses of champagne were served. Then everyone returned home knowing that they would be attending a far more meaningful celebration in church the following day, and during the evening Edward, Elsbiéta and their student friends held an informal party.

Meanwhile in the garage at the bridegroom's home older male members of the family prepared and assembled all the food and drink that was to be carried out on a tractor-drawn trailer to the country location where the wedding feast was to be held on the morrow. Ducks were beheaded and plucked. Flour, eggs, fruit, vegetables and numerous ingredients for both savoury and dessert dishes were methodically checked and stacked on board in company with a generous consignment of festive drinks. Johnny was invited along for the ride.

When she married Edward in the cathedral-like setting of Namyslow Church the next day Elsbiéta wore a traditional white bridal gown. In accordance with Polish custom the car in which she arrived had fixed to its bonnet a doll wearing a miniature replica of her dress. This is always taken to the newlyweds' home afterwards as a lucky talisman.

At the close of the service a long cavalcade of beribboned cars headed for the green, sunlit countryside. The wedding feast was held in a beautifully restored barn with a well-appointed kitchen where female friends had been preparing a large selection of delicious recipes since dawn.

Outside a portable dance floor had been laid in a cobbled farmyard that was decorated with paper garlands and coloured lights, and alongside was a gaily-painted wagon in which the musicians sat to perform after they had finished playing among the tables at the indoor feast. In a nearby garden tents had been set up so that guests could snatch a few hours sleep if they wished, for the revelry was to last all through the night.

I lost count of the number of courses served but the menu was worthy of a royal banquet. Toasts were proposed and emotional speeches delivered with a theatrical panache so dear to Polish hearts. To give digestions a chance to settle down there was some hearty singing before we rose from the table to dance the night away. I knew some of the songs and joined in enthusiastically. Marian put his arm round me and told me how proud he was because I had integrated so completely into the life of his family.

Not many of the guests took advantage of the sleeping facilities preferring to dance the night away under the stars. Waltzes, foxtrots and tangos were interspersed with obereks and other lively Polish folk dances. Because of his lame leg Marian could not join in but I scarcely missed a dance and he watched laughing and applauding with Bogousha and other relations. Meanwhile Johnny had plenty of fun with fellow junior guests.

Sheer exhilaration kept most of us wide awake all night long and, plied with refreshment at regular intervals, the musicians perched high in the colourful hay wagon played with enormous zest.

At dawn we all returned to the barn where breakfast was served. When our particular party drove back to Namyslow shortly before lunch we left behind celebrations that were still far from over, and we carried away with us recollections of some of the pleasantest hours of our lives.

A few days later Marian, Johnny and I left Namyslow by car for the long drive to Warsaw to stay with Izabela and her husband Romek. Cousin Kazik from Trawniki was at the wheel. En route we stopped at Czestachowa one of the most famous Catholic shrines in the world. Depicting Mary and the Christ Child in crowns studded with diamonds and superbly mounted in the magnificent church there was the icon known as the *Black Madonna.*

It bears this name because the passing centuries have darkened the wood and given her lovely face a dusky hue. She is especially sacred to the Polish people because of a miracle long ago when marauding Cossacks slashed her cheek and real blood flowed from the wound.

All reproductions of this precious icon show sabre scars on her right cheek. We brought home a gilt-framed replica of the *Black Madonna* which was embellished with silver dust to simulate the glitter of diamonds, and it has hung above our bed ever since.

Izabela, her husband and baby son lived in a flat in a Warsaw suburb. In 1968 we had sent her money for her bridal gown and in the wedding photographs she later sent us she looked very beautiful. In real life she was not only just as pretty but also dainty and sweet-natured. Elderly relations had already told me that she closely resembled Marian's mother of whom no photographs have survived.

Because the weather was so hot Romek wore nothing in the flat except bathing trunks and Johnny dubbed him *Tarzan*. Unlike Izabela he was less attractive than in the wedding photographs, for which he had worn a toupé, and sadly he was already proving a neglectful, unfaithful husband.

Before her marriage she had been closely involved in the music and theatre world and her many admirers had included one of Poland's leading actors. Apparently her domineering mother had influenced her decision to marry Romek and Marian was very unhappy about it.

The furnishings in the flat bore eloquent testimony to Izabela's artistic tastes and, as her book-case confirmed, she read Russian fluently. At the time we visited her she was a nursing sister at a children's clinic.

Here – as everywhere else – Johnny and I were made to feel very welcome but, realising that Marian would like to spend as much time as possible alone with his daughter, we regularly took a tram into the city for sight-seeing excursions.

The first place I introduced to Johnny was the surpassingly picturesque *Old Quarter* which I already knew and loved. As we walked by the Vistula I told him the legend about the beautiful mermaid who lived in the river and always came ashore with a sword in her hand when the city was in danger. Symbols of her could be seen all over Warsaw and lapel brooches bearing her likeness were popular souvenirs.

We strolled happily through a maze of narrow cobbled streets and alleyways of steep steps, and had ice creams and lemonade under a parasol in the Market Square. We also went to Wazienka Park, once the holiday retreat of the Polish Royal family. Their exquisite miniature palace in classical style overlooks a swan-filled lake.

On the day before we left Poland we took a 30-mile bus trip to Chopin's birthplace which is now a shrine and museum visited by music lovers from all over the world. Foremost among the many bygones of the composer in the unpretentious house is his own piano on which accomplished musicians regularly perform his works. This music is relayed into the beautiful gardens through loudspeakers concealed among the trees. Incidentally the first few bars of Chopin's best known Polonaise formed the radio signal of the last surviving partisans in the Warsaw Uprising during their final desperate hours.

This long and eventful holiday *en famille* has remained one of the most cherished experiences of my life. It forged even closer bonds of love between Marian and myself and gave Johnny a pride in his Polish heritage which will remain with him always.

CHAPTER THREE

A ROVING NOTEBOOK AGAIN

WHEN JOHNNY WAS happily settled in full-time education I was keen to return to journalism. I wanted a job that was varied and challenging yet did not encroach too much on my domestic responsibilities.

I found exactly the right opening quite by chance while casually scanning the job advertisements in the *Essex County Standard* late one night in the winter of 1972. *'The Standard'* was one of a flourishing group owned by Essex County Newspapers Ltd. and the vacancy was for an advertising feature writer prepared to travel all over the company's territory. I got the job and embarked on some of the happiest years I ever spent on the newspaper scene.

Assignments took me on roving commissions all over Essex and into south Suffolk. It was good to be back with the old familiar tools of my trade.

My feature writing fell into several different categories: To provide a fanfare for the launching of an entirely new enterprise, to be a showcase for an established company that was expanding or celebrating a notable milestone, to give a powerful boost to a flagging business, or to introduce some glamorous new line of merchandise or hi-tech product.

It also covered the refurbishment of town and country pubs, restaurants, hotels and clubs. Sometimes a double spread was devoted to a collection of mini-portraits of personalities trading in one particular street, or to a description of one specific town or village in terms of atmosphere, historic interest and shopping facilities. Easter was the time for lavish bridal features, summer was marked by agricultural show supplements and Christmas themes started in early November.

I usually had a preliminary chat with the advertising sales executive who had obtained the order for a feature in the first place, and my final briefing came from the advertising feature manager who told me the number of words required.

Otherwise the way I tackled the assignment was left very much to my own creative instincts and I soon learnt to sense within a few minutes of interviewing any client exactly the angle and style of writing that would appeal to them most. The essence of the whole job was to be able to write about any subject under the sun in a way that would capture the public's fancy. In the process my own general knowledge widened constantly.

I did the family shopping in whatever location a job took me. Although I occasionally wrote up features at the office by far the greater part of my work was written at home. It was an ideal arrangement for someone with domestic commitments as well and I never found it difficult to produce a feature 'off the top of my head'.

The early 1970's were the period when fitted kitchens, glamorous bathrooms, ornate conservatories and domestic central heating became really big business. Industrial estates were springing up everywhere on the outskirts of key towns. I saw computers develop from huge unwieldly units to compact desktop accessories.

This was a particularly tough decade for motor dealers, yet I always found them extremely cordial. I quickly picked up a vast amount of technical jargon about cars of every make, nationality and life style. Under the pseudonym of *'Roadster'* I wrote a series of garage profiles.

The adjective 'debonair' might have been specially coined for Ronald Lancaster whose motoring empire began in the early 1970's in a stark, hangar-like industrial unit near East Gates, Colchester. I wrote about his initial launching and was to trace his progress on many subsequent occasions when miscellaneous dealership banners flew triumphantly over his ever-expanding territory. His private life style was that of a country squire and he was a distinguished figure on the Hunting scene.

Equally memorable in his way was Roy Tolley a gruff, blunt character whose exuberant French promotions did marvels for the image of the Citröen at a time when, despite being sturdy and reliable, it was very much the 'Plain Jane' among cars.

It was around this period that the Tartan House Night Club at Frating first opened presided over by an unforgettable Glaswegian couple named Colin and Marie. Down the years it was to change its management and identity several times, but nothing could compare with the interior originally created by the Scottish pair. Part Highland Laird's baronial hall, part Hollywood fantasy, it was an astonishing hotch-potch of styles merged head on in a vast building with a single floor level. I have seldom enjoyed writing a story more and predictably crowds flocked there.

In August, 1976, the London family achieved the singularly daunting task of transforming a huge empty shell of a building on the outskirts of Colchester into a handsome upmarket furniture store of great warmth and distinction called Hatfields.

Little more than seven months previously I had walked with Tony London through what had been a bleak girder-ceilinged warehouse covering 50,000 sq.ft. and he had confessed to me that the enterprise was a 'calculated risk'.

On the fashion scene denim was beginning to make a great impact when David Blackwell opened his shop in Eld Lane. He called it *'Denim*

City' and its robust prairie-flavoured image did not only attract male customers, because the merchandise sold looked stunningly flattering on curvaceous lasses as well. 'David's showmanship would have done credit to Buffalo Bill himself', I wrote, 'Colchester is no one-horse town and Denim City is no homespun trading post'.

Roger Carter's T-shirt transfer business at Braintree enjoyed a worldwide distribution. 'They flamboyantly adorn extrovert chests and seductive bosoms as far afield as Australia and South America' I wrote.

Elsewhere in Braintree and also at Halstead, urbane, silver-tongued Norman Holmes specialised in boosting the morale of mature ladies with the stylish and flattering clothes on his rails. Purchases were happily carried away in bags sporting a design worthy of London's Bond Street.

At first glance a fruit and vegetable warehouse might seem a singularly mundane subject for a feature. In my opening paragraph I said: 'There is a juicy fragrance about the place that is synonymous with produce at the peak of its excellence' and further inspiration followed.

While many of the businesses I wrote about became permanent success stories, others were short-lived but great fun while they lasted. My favourite among the latter was Stanley Bacon's *'Tipplers'* in Colchester's Head Street. Described as a 'drinks appreciation venue', it had grape-purple carpeting and craggy white walls that suggested a vineyard château cellar. *Tipplers* did not stock any wines or spirits but concentrated on accessories like tankards, goblets, decanters, flagons, stein mugs, home brew kits, punch bowls and novelty ice buckets.

Amusing incidental anecdotes often came to light while I was gathering material for a feature. A former landlord at *The Castle* in Ramsey was such a tidy-minded man that he constructed a very realistic mock grandfather clock in his public bar to conceal a dart board when it was not in play. *The Fleece* at Coggeshall had a resident dog who loved to sit and watch people playing cards. At *The White Hart,* Nayland, Thomas Gainsborough's ne'er-do-well brother painted two pictures direct on to the walls of an upper room in lieu of paying for board and lodging. The inn sign outside a fun pub featured a portrait of the owner's small son.

On entering a 'Party Shop' at Walton one was greeted by floating life-size character balloons. Miscellaneous novelty attractions for fairgrounds all over Europe were created in a rambling riverside warehouse. Devising an unusual theme for a hairdressing salon an interior decorator created a desert sheikh's tent a la Valentino. An ambitious teenage businesswoman called her trendy shop after her champion bulldog.

Annual previews of the Tendring Show could have been routine and repetitive. To avoid this I would select a few different subjects from the programme each year to make into stories of universal interest. Side by side with reporting on the pigeon classes, for example, I wrote about the history of these brave and beautiful birds.

In 766 B.C. pigeons carried news of Olympic Games victories to Athens. The Duke of Wellington sent a message by carrier pigeon in 1845 from a ship on which he was cruising off the West African coast. The bird covered 5,400 miles in 55 days. On a flight to Ireland in 1914 a cock bird reached a maximum speed of 93 m.p.h. and averaged 40 m.p.h.

Before visiting a town to write a word portrait about it I always did some research in the library which often yielded unexpected points of interest. In the small town of Southminster in the Dengie Hundred (a largely remote and sparsely-populated area which I especially like), I discovered that the wedding register in the parish church was signed on the map table from *H.M.S. Victory*. Dr. Alexander Scott, a nineteenth century vicar there, was Nelson's chaplain at the *Battle of Trafalgar*.

Not far from Southminster I met a fascinating character named Val Chesson-Bagge. This vivacious blonde London hotelier had just become the owner of the Burnham Country Club and she had invested the handsome mid-1930's house with a romantic and stylish new lease of life.

When I met Val she was wearing scarlet satin pantaloons and smoking a cigar. On her lap was a jet black cat named *'Snowy'*. The room had black walls covered with period prints including one of Queen Victoria whose birth sign Val shared and whom she greatly admired.

In fact the glamorous and dynamic Eastender was an enthusiastic collector of Victoriana of all descriptions. Her other treasured show-piece was a perfect small scale replica model of her former palatial home in Southgate to which her hobby was adding exquisite little accessories she had made herself.

When the James Bond film *Moonraker* was released I wrote a suitably light-hearted promotional supplement of which this extract is typical: . . . . 'the film is, as one would expect, well sprinkled with gorgeous girls in ultra sexy gear that would understandably make the most dedicated of astronauts get his controls jammed! But not our cool, intrepid Bond, of course. He dallies with them as if they were so much moonshine'. The film-makers themselves wrote to say how much they liked this supplement.

Incidentally Bond's creator, Ian Fleming, was once seen eating scrambled egg in a well-known Colchester hostelry. A homely glimpse of a man who inspired some of filmdom's most spectacular escapism.

While the very nature of my work was predominantly up-beat a number of poignant behind-the-scenes stories come to mind as I recall all the people I met.

The broken-hearted young wife of a French chef-restaurateur in an estuary village had a miscarriage when a second Gallic eating-house of similar quality and style opened just down the road. Her husband had worked so hard to get successfully established.

On the surface the bubbly, supremely elegant boutique owner seemed to be in sparkling form when I interviewed her, but the following day she took her own life because of her broken marriage.

Throughout my years as an advertising feature writer I regarded every client as a V.I.P. I often received appreciative letters and sometimes gifts. The latter included an *haute couture* hat from a boutique, an orchid from a garden centre, perfume from a chemist, goodies for my two cats from a pet food manufacturer, a pink boudoir lampshade from a lighting shop, a crystal fan trimmed with pink silk roses from a fancy goods shop, and a family-size serving of fish and chips from a plant hire proprietor who ran a seafood shop as a sideline. Sampling free meals was a frequent pleasure – especially when the setting was an unusual one like a converted sail loft or a hunting lodge beside a lake.

Periodically Essex County Newspapers brought out a Leisure Magazine in which I wrote about various pastimes. Without any doubt my own favourite contribution was about greyhound racing. I was sent along one evening to a stadium with a few pounds for betting purposes, had beginner's luck as a punter and soaked up the atmosphere with relish.

I wrote the piece in light-hearted vein: 'Before laying a bet for the first race I went to the paddock to look over the field. One dog dominated the scene. A splendid jet black animal named *My David.* I fancied the look of his owner too. He was tall, dark and handsome and obviously had a very close rapport with his dog. I've always liked dark, dramatic-looking males and here was a pair of the best. So I bet on *My David* for a win or place and he romped home triumphantly well ahead of the rest of the field.

When the next race was due I again went to the paddock to take my pick. It was the name more than anything that influenced me this time . . . *Only You* which happened to be the title of one of my favourite romantic ballads. He was a fine looking white-and-fawn dog with a bright roving eye and lots of sex appeal. I backed him for a win or a place. *Only You* proved an ace. His blue jacket streaked past the winning post at the head of the pack.'

I have always had a soft spot for greyhounds and, having a two-page spread, I was able to add an historical note too. Greyhounds are one of the most ancient and pure of canine breeds. Their origins can be traced back over 7,000 years and they were a familiar sight at the court of the Pharaohs.

By a remarkable coincidence the last advertising feature I wrote before retiring was about the opening of an opulent black-and-silver night club at Clacton in the old Rosemary Road theatre where I had carried out my very first assignment as a cub reporter in 1939.

To mark my retirement a lunch was held at a cosy old world pub which was aglow with festive decorations at the time. The occasion was masterminded by Sandie Lawrence, Barbara Butler and Stewart McDermid – three great personalities with whom I had forged warm friendships during my time as a feature writer.

After a generous presentation and the customary photographs, I sat down to a merry meal surrounded by colleagues with whom I had enjoyed such a happy working relationship.

CHAPTER FOUR

REVELRY IN THE PIAZZA

BEING IN VENICE at carnival time is a magical experience and in February, 1986, I had the good fortune to be at the heart of the pre-Lenten revelry which has been an important part of Venetian life since Medieval days.

This trip was made possible through my close friendship with Loredana (Lory) Baccovich Giordano who had given me Italian lessons in Cambridge during the 1950's. Down the years we had kept up a lively correspondence and in 1974 Lory and her husband Lino came to stay with us in Colchester. East Anglia delighted them as much as Venice had already delighted me. As Marian knew and liked my hosts-to-be he was perfectly agreeable that I should go, and John was at College.

It would be unthinkable to go to Venice at carnival time *without* a fancy costume, so during the weeks before my departure I made a Regency period gown, brocade turban, velvet draw-string reticule and spangled mask on a stick. As a final finishing touch I bought a pretty lace-edged fan when I arrived there. It bore an enchanting scene of eighteenth century Venice.

I am well acquainted with Venice at all seasons, but I think I love her best in mid-winter when a beguiling pearly grey light gives her a strangely dreamlike quality. Lory met me off the train and we immediately took a waterbus down the Grand Canal to the luxurious *Hotel Europa & Regina* where Lino was general manager. It directly overlooks Santa Maria Della Salute Church across the water.

Passing the hotel's main entrance, which is for private waterborne transport only, Lory and I disembarked at the adjoining San Marco vaporetto stop and walked round to the side entrance. Our route lay across a bridge in the shadow of which gondolas were gathered, then down a narrow alleyway and finally across a courtyard with an ancient well in the centre.

The hotel's palatial foyer with marble floors, rich carpets and glittering chandeliers was decorated with red-and-black tricorn hats and traditional white Venetian masks. Lino came out of his office to welcome me and the three of us went through to the Barozzi Bar for drinks.

At my special request the native wine of Venice deep red *Ombra* was served. After this we relaxed over coffee in sumptuously-furnished peach and cream surroundings where each table stood on an individual oriental rug. At a grand piano Tarquinio, the handsome young resident pianist, played and sang golden oldies by Gershwin and Cole Porter.

A very gracious lifestyle went with Lino's post of general manager as I discovered when a lift took us up to the elegant apartment on the fourth floor where he and Lory lived. Chatting over a delicious meal, which was brought up to us on a trolley, I learned that they also had a spectacular flat like a Hollywood film set over on the Lido (the sophisticated island development only a short vaporetto trip from the Old City). This 'perk' went with Lino's job. In summer they commuted daily between the Lido and the hotel by private launch, but during the winter they stayed at the hotel except at weekends.

I shared the best of both their worlds. They gave me the key to the Lido flat where I slept and breakfasted and every morning at about ten o'clock I joined them over at the hotel to spend the whole day in Lory's company. We would go sight-seeing together, lunch in the Tiepolo Restaurant at the hotel and have an evening meal when Lino joined us up in their apartment. After that I would take a late-night water bus back to the Lido. The spacious, opulent flat had every mod con imaginable and I was not nervous about sleeping there overnight on my own. Lory made sure the fridge and larder were generously stocked.

My bedroom window, which had electrically-operated blinds, overlooked a garden running down to a narrow waterway where Lino's launch would be berthed during the summer months. This quiet stretch of water also gave access to the rear entrance of the *Excelsior,* one of Europe's most glamorous hotels. It had figured in my story *The Golden Garland* under the name of *Hotel Glorioso* and I recalled with a smile how, on my first visit to Venice many years previously Lory, myself and other friends had explored its magnificent interior after buying a cup of coffee apiece.

During the days leading up to the official start of the carnival the weather was bitterly cold and snow flurries were frequent. Most serious of all were the worst floods Venice had experienced for many years. Flood alarm sirens sounded as unusually high tides, whipped up by strong winds, trespassed not only across the flagstones of St. Mark's Square but also into the ground floors of palazzos, hotels and shops.

At the *Europa & Regina* water lapped round the legs of Tarquinio's grand piano in the Barozzi Bar and Lino joined his staff to carry out large scale mopping up operations. The Venetians are always well prepared for such an emergency and the speed with which carpeting is restored and parquet floor blocks replaced is miraculous.

On the Lido the powerful waves of the *Adriatic* had demolished a wall of the *Excelsior Hotel*, smashed furniture, torn up floors and destroyed a richly decorated ceiling. Lory and I went to see the débris piled up in the hotel grounds.

Yet when carnival-time was imminent even the elements showed an uncanny sense of stage management. The snow melted away and the floods subsided as dramatically as they had come. When Lory and I strolled round the city on the eve of carnival the starlit night seemed vibrant with happy anticipation.

Every year Venetian shopkeepers enter fully into the carnival spirit and mount colourful window displays. Even staid businesses like chemists and opticians put tricorn hats, masks and streamers amongst their merchandise.

Shops that lend themselves to artistic displays anyway, like fashion boutiques, fan shops, lace shops, jewellers, toy shops, mask-makers and antique dealers create inspired window arrangements so stunning that they are photographed constantly by passersby. Glass-making is an ancient Venetian craft and at carnival-time the spotlight turns on fanciful items like angels turning somersaults, prancing unicorns and exquisitely-wrought miniature orchestras in eighteenth century costume.

There is a fairytale flavour at the confectioners who sell chocolate every colour of the rainbow and hedgehogs moulded from almond paste. Bakers have loaves shaped like angels' heads and lovebirds on boughs and also sell two traditional carnival goodies . . . *fritelle* which are small doughnuts, and *galani* which are curly-edged wafer thin biscuits sprinkled with icing sugar.

Venice is famous for its seafood and elaborately embellished fish dishes are on show splendid enough to grace the grandest of banquets. Butchers display richly garnished boars' heads. In pizza restaurants humorous animal masks are fashioned from dough, trimmed with silver paper and hung round the walls.

A generous quota of shops hire or sell magnificent costumes. As the carnival's heyday was during the eighteenth century the accent is very much on Georgian styles, powdered wigs and fur-trimmed cloaks. Tricorn hats are numerous, embellished with gold or silver lace or white swansdown. Clothes of the Napoleonic period and rich oriental attire are much in evidence (the latter recalling the old Venetian merchant princes' trade with the East). In more restrained mood are black dominoes. In England this term denotes a small mask, but in Venice it applies to a ground length cloak with a hood. Combined with a tricorn hat and plain white traditional mask this particular garb is a familiar sight in many old Venetian prints. It guaranteed – and still does – total anonymity and therefore remains the perfect disguise for illicit amours.

But what intrigued me most of all were the mask-makers' shops where one could stand on the threshold and watch them at work on various highly imaginative creations. While the stark white *'bautta'* is the true traditional mask of Venice to purists, the mask-makers nowadays make many exuberantly colourful and decorative pieces for sale as collectors' items. These are gilded, spangled with sequins or studded with pearls and framed by peacock plumes or brilliantly-dyed cockerel feathers. The sun, moon, golden lions, Apollos and butterflies are other popular themes in fact the variety is endless. Seductive black lace trims are popular on female masks.

The climax of our eve-of-carnival stroll was naturally St. Mark's Square where we saw finishing touches being made to preparations for the revelry to come. Napoleon once aptly described the *Piazza* as 'the most beautiful drawing room in Europe where it is only fitting that the heavens should serve as the ceiling'.

At one end is the glittering splendour of *St. Mark's Basilica* with its oriental domes and, scarcely less magnificent immediately alongside it, is the palace where the *'Doges'* 'once all-powerful rulers of the Republic lived. At the other end is an impressive medieval clock above an archway leading to the irresistibly inviting Frezzeria. Flanking the Square on either side are very fine colonnades in the shadow of which are luxurious shops and cafés including *Florians* one of the most celebrated coffee-houses in the world.

We watched an elaborate stage being set up where various entertainers would perform and saw extensive garlands of gondola-style lanterns being installed. Immediately outside *Florians* a gilded pavilion had been erected. From its roof flew seven banners of *St. Mark* depicting a gold winged lion on a scarlet background. Then we actually went into this legendary café and, after cups of coffee, walked through the rooms which radiate from the dome-ceilinged and mosaic-floored entrance hall.

Florians, which is *the* place to see and be seen, especially at carnival time, was opened in 1720. Down the years it has been a favourite rendezvous for writers, artists, musicians and actors and the atmosphere is both Bohemian and glamorous. The interior décor remains much the same as when if first opened . . . chandeliers, gilt-framed mirrors, ornate plaster ceilings, panelling painted with flowers, marble-topped tables and opulent red velvet seating. We knew that twenty four hours from now it would be filled with Europe's high society wearing the most gorgeous carnival costumes money could buy.

As we returned to the hotel I paused to admire the artistic merit of wall posters advertising carnival events. There was nothing garish or crude about them as is usually the case with mass-produced street bills intended only for a brief life span. My favourite one, announcing the traditional opening of the opera season on the first day of carnival (in 1986 it was *Otello*) depicted the extremely beautiful interior of the Fenice Theatre.

Later that same evening I was introduced to Maurizio Scaparro, a celebrated man of the theatre in Italy, who played a major rôle in restoring the Venetian carnival to its rightful, glittering place on the winter calendar. After Napoleon conquered the Republic in 1797 and even more during the later occupation of the hated Austrians, the carnival became a pale shadow of its former self. When Mussolini came to power he banned it completely. Now, thanks to Signor Scaparro and other dedicated men like him, the carnival has been revived with all its traditional gaiety and spectacle.

Next morning was crisp and bright and Lory and I set out early for St. Mark's Square which was less than five minutes' walk from the hotel. Already many people of all ages were parading in their carnival costumes among numerous photographers and pigeons on the wing. Commanding universal attention was a young man I dubbed the *'Sun King'*. He was attired in eighteenth century costume with everything flamboyantly overstated in a colour scheme of blue and gold. Cascading blue and white plumes on his outsize gold tricorn hat, ermine-trimmed blue velvet cloak, blue and gold shoes with huge bows, a gem-encrusted cane and a gold lion mask on a stick.

There was a group of people cleverly disguised as chess pieces and an oriental maiden with three heads – the middle one being her own. A man masquerading as an eagle had talons curling over his shoes, while his companion sported a silhouette of a gondola as his headdress. A splendid Georgian couple dressed entirely in white satin with gold trimmings were destined to win one of the top awards.

Exotic characters with enormous turbans and bejewelled kaftans were plentiful. A girl dressed as a pink powder puff passed by with a youth portraying a blue 'cello. Small boys in Harlequin attire were darting in and out of the crowds. Harlequin, by the way, is the lovable, mischievous folk hero of Venice. Dresden shepherdess outfits seemed to be a favourite among little girls.

A crocodile, Norman knights, a family of dalmatians (the youngest spotted 'dog' being a toddler of about two), butterflies, rabbits, brilliantly-plumaged parrots, cats, clowns in violet and emerald wigs, angels and devils were other characters who particularly caught the eye.

In some instances it was ingenious make-up rather than spectacular costumes or masks that proved crowd-pullers. One clever example of trick make-up which really intrigued me was a girl with the centre of her face blacked out and a mock face traced on either cheek. In profile when she blinked it looked as if she was winking.

While people travel from all over the world to take part in the carnival, the lively uninhibited Venetians themselves contribute greatly to the fun. Young and old, rich and poor all wear costumes or masks of some description. Even babes in arms wear festive clothes. Dogs are dressed up too. I saw one in the guise of a gondolier with straw hat and striped jersey, and another masquerading as Red Riding Hood with little foxy face peering out between flaxen plaits. A special prize was awarded to a diminutive mongrel terrier wearing a red tricorn hat, white wig, lace cravat and brocade coat.Young girls who could not afford pretty dresses wore necklaces strung with brightly-wrapped sweets and had more of these stitched to gold paper bandeaux round their heads. I even saw a shabby old man who had fashioned a crude mask for himself from a page of the carnival programme.

On our way back to the hotel for lunch we had the good fortune to meet the remarkable Barone Emilio Targhetta d'Audiffret, whom Lory knew well. He was an eccentric middle-aged aristocrat who had been featured in international magazines because he made a point of wearing carnival costume all the year round. He personally designed and made all his splendid Georgian clothes at his exquisitely-furnished palazzo. When we met him he was wearing black and white striped satin and had a scarlet cloak over his arm. He was also carrying a fan which seemed a perfectly acceptable concession to dandyism in the elegant hand of Barone Emilio.

We returned to St. Mark's Square at dusk – this time costumed and masked ourselves. The Piazza was absolutely packed with revellers and golden arc lights had been added to the illuminations. Loudspeakers were relaying sparkling music by Vivaldi, Mozart and Rossini. Under the lantern-lit colonnades medieval merchants, cardinals in crimson and purple, and extragavant fantasies in clouds of multicoloured nets and gauzes tipped with feathers mingled like a timeless kaleidoscope.

Near *Florians* a cloaked figure in a pearl-covered mask posed motionless against a pillar. Harlequins and Columbines draped themselves round decorative wrought iron lamp posts to attract photographers. Black bats stood on carved parapets constantly changing poses and doing wondrous things with outstretched 'wings'. There were many drama and ballet students among the merrymakers.

Crash barriers had been erected outside *Florians* where the doormen were wearing black tricorn hats and red-lined cloaks, but somehow we managed to gain entry. On the strength of a cup of coffee each we were able to view the many magnificent costumes worn by rich patrons.

I particularly remember a beautiful girl clad as a Dresden shepherdess in turquoise silk, and a Chinese princess with a tall fan-shaped headdress of fresh flowers. Then there was a character I named *'The Spirit of Spring'* swathed in billowing pale green net from head to foot with white blossoms cascading from brow to waist. A male figure with an elaborately made-up face wore rainbow-hued floating silk draperies and scarlet leggings covered with spangles and preened and postured to the delight of photographers.

We went out into the Square again and were immediately swept into the very heart of the revelry. The most beguiling moment of all came when golden confetti cascaded down on our heads like snow-flakes and all the cares of the world seemed a million miles away. Then, carried along by the sheer movement of the crowds, we found ourselves on the edge of the Grand Canal awaiting a great piece of pageantry.

The last '*Doge'* was deposed by Napoleon, but for many centuries before this the head of state always used to come to St. Mark's Square to declare the carnival season open. Nowadays that tradition is enacted by a theatre group. We watched entranced as the Doge and his retinue arrived on board a splendid scarlet and gold barge and disembarked to a fanfare from trumpeters. To cries of 'Viva il Doge'! they proceeded ceremoniously into the Piazza. Churches on the other side of the Grand Canal were illuminated by arc lights in ever-changing colours and a line of swan-shaped fountains added to the spectacle.

For the next ten days Lory and I returned to St. Mark's Square every evening at dusk to join in the revelry. Between five o'clock and seven o'clock an orchestra in eighteenth century costume played popular melodies under the direction of a distinguished-looking silver-haired violinist. I shall never forget their exuberant rendering of *Brasile* and *Quando, quando, quando* while the huge crowds swayed enthusiastically to the rhythm. Then, after watching other entertainments which were compered by film star Valentina Cortesa, we would go into *Florians* for coffee.

Throughout the carnival season there was, of course, a great deal going on in other parts of the city as well. Theatres and musical venues staged entertainment by famous international performers and cinemas held a festival of film classics. Street theatre, puppet shows and art exhibitions were plentiful. Delicious recipes with witty carnival-flavoured names were served in restaurants. Many people wore their festive costumes by day as well as by night.

Every morning Lory and I would stroll round our favourite parts of the city. The quarter that always fascinated me most was the market by the Rialto Bridge where stalls nestled round the captivating little church of St. Giacometto and tasty tripe soup was served in tiny *trattorias.*

Lory introduced me to the lesser known 'Via Garibaldi' district on the outskirts of Venice close to the open lagoon where the inhabitants have always considered themselves a race apart from other Venetians. Lory loved its atmosphere and once made a film about life there.

After disembarking from the water bus a walk down a broad tree-lined avenue, dominated by a statue of Italy's great revolutionary hero, led us into the main trading thoroughfare where fresh produce was being unloaded from *sandali* the all-purpose working boats of Venice. Seafood is a speciality here and at the Trattoria Giorgione the proprietor let us sample his excellent shrimps with a glass of wine. At another eating-place we were treated to rice pies and coffee.

Reflecting the proud independence and dislike of modern innovations which are so characteristic of its residents, the Via Garibaldi is full of extremely ancient small shops and houses. There are numerous alleyways which are so narrow you cannot stretch out your arms sideways in them. The local pharmacy had frosted windows of elaborate design. No trace of sophisticated commercialism has been allowed to trespass in any shape or form. The 'Via Garibaldi' district is a unique township in its own right.

Much as I relished the perpetual excitement in and around St. Mark's Square when dusk fell, I would not have missed for anything the evening when Lory and I forsook the crowds and clamour and coffee at *Florians* to escape to a part of the city less familiar to tourists on the opposite shore of the *Grand Canal.*

Our destination was a concert at the Scuola di San Giovanni Evangelista and the first part of our journey was made by gondola. As I stepped on board I felt especially glad that I was in full carnival costume. On my feet were black velvet slippers with diamante buckles, in one hand I held a spangled scarlet satin mask on a stick and, my fan was suspended from my wrist by a loop of ribbon. The spirit of *'Venice Past'* embraced me in a way I had never experienced before.

This sense of elation remained with me when we disembarked at San Toma and continued on foot through dimly lit alleyways, across small deserted squares and over bridges bathed in misty moonlight. We passed tiny, shuttered workshops, unchanged for centuries where by day craftsmen still produced exquisite gold and silver work, wood carvings and furniture painted with garlands of flowers. It was in parts of the city like this that one saw captivating street names like *Alley of the Love of Friends, Alley of the Gondola Prow Polishers* and *Alley of the Paper Lantern Makers.*

Eventually we reached the walled courtyard of San Giovanni Evangelista. Climbing a broad staircase we entered a spacious apartment with accoustics that made it an admirable setting for musical occasions.

The star performer was Umberto de Breda, universally acknowledged to be the world's foremost exponent of gondoliers' songs. He was a most engaging personality and provided his own guitar accompaniment. Also on the programme, and eloquently demonstrating the world-embracing nature of carnival time entertainment, was a recital of music and dancing by a group of exiles from Kurdistan.

Later the same evening we went to the Malibran Theatre founded by the celebrated early nineteenth century singer whose name it bears. The proscenium arch is surmounted by her portrait and there is a superb painted ceiling. Fittingly (since Maria Malibran herself was of Spanish origin) we saw a breathtaking display by a troupe of dancers from Granada led by the ageless and charismatic Manuela Aquillar.

An exhibition of paintings by Tiepolo at the *Palazzo Rezzonico* gave me an opportunity to see the spectacular interior of the home where Robert Browning spent a happy old age in the care of his son Pen and wealthy American daughter-in-law. Pen had an insatiable passion for an extragavant life style, but he was a devoted son. *The Palazzo's* ballroom was particularly beautiful and lit by chandeliers lavishly embellished with flowers and fruit moulded in glass of many colours.

On Shrove Tuesday the Carnival ended. It was like closing a book on a sumptuous fairytale. That evening the crowds were thicker than ever in St. Mark's Square. We listened to the music for the last time and went as usual into *Florians*.

Then we returned to the hotel to watch the spectacular climax from a fourth floor balcony. We saw the Doge and his courtiers proceeding with great pomp in his scarlet and gold barge down to St. Mark's Square to declare the carnival was over. In his wake came a flotilla of gondolas painted jade, lilac, yellow and pink (they are customarily black of course).

A firework display provided a dazzling finale, the pyrotechnics being set off aboard a ship anchored out in the centre of the *Grand Canal.* As the last shimmering clusters of multi-coloured stars hovered on the night air before slowly descending into the darkness, church bells started tolling all over the city to mark the carnival's passing.

When I left Venice my souvenirs included a Harlequin doll I had bought on the Rialto Bridge, several masks, carnival posters, a quantity of blue chocolate and a box of *galani* biscuits. Lory's parting gifts to me were a copiously illustrated book on the history of the carnival and a volume of poems in Venetian dialect by Riccardo Selvatico. The opening line of a poem he wrote in praise of his beloved city is engraved in every gondola. It reads: 'In all the world there is no city more beautiful'.

CHAPTER FIVE

LIFE WITH JOHN

FROM EARLY CHILDHOOD John showed a lively way with the written word, keen powers of observation and a passion for travel. His hilarious gift for wickedly accurate mimicry, must have been inherited from his great-great grandfather Henry Nunn, theatre owner and amateur actor.

During the 1970's the Colchester Carnival route each summer lay past our house. We always marked the occasion with family parties, craning out of flag-garlanded front windows with fistfuls of coppers for profferred buckets and nets on long poles.

The passing pageantry included a magnificent Drum Horse named *Cicero* who starred in the Royal Tattoo. He made a deep impression on John. When my newspaper colleague, veteran journalist Bill Tucker, gave him a splendid picture of the majestic animal this led to interesting developments.

Our young scribe, who was nine at the time, wrote a series of stories about his equine hero which he also illustrated and gathered into a book called *The Adventures of Cicero & Co.* In professionally duplicated form and properly bound, copies were sold in aid of the *Save the Children Fund* under the auspices of the Colchester Committee headed by Janie Berry and Anne Rodgers. From the Fund's London HQ Neil Macleod wrote: 'I have greatly enjoyed reading it. The book is altogether a most enterprising bit of publishing.'

One copy was naturally sent to Princess Anne *(President of the Save the Children Fund)* and an extremely nice acknowledgement with a personal touch was received from Buckingham Palace and proudly framed. In addition to newspaper coverage John broadcast on Hospital Radio. In a programme appropriately introduced by a pop song called *Paperback Writers,* he was was interviewed by genial presenter Paul Diggens and then invited to read some of his stories. John performed with true professional aplomb and I still treasure a tape that was made live. When anyone I know is feeling a bit down I lend it to them because it is guaranteed to cheer them up!

As the introduction in the book stated: 'Cicero Windsorhoof is a rather homely horse compared with his namesake, but a very versatile character who can talk, has a wide circle of friends and owns a private bus-cum-dormobile named Caroline. A horse of many talents he is an excellent mechanic, carpenter, electrician, leader of a pop group and keen amateur detective.

Other characters include *Columbus Philiphoof, Red Rum Piggothoof,*

Leslie MacThistlehoof and *Sandra Posh-Hoof* (a snobbish mare). Their adventures are recounted with verve and humour and John makes lively use of the local scene.'

Buses with distinctive personalities were also featured in the fun including a rather wistful one *FPW* who could not get any lady bus friends because his exhaust pipe drooped.

At around the same time as *The Adventures of Cicero & Co.* appeared John put pen to paper in much more serious vein to the Mayor of Colchester (who was at that time Joyce Brooks). He called her attention to the bad state of pavements in Maldon Road and also suggested that a group of tumbledown buildings should be demolished to make way for an old people's home.

In a reply written on notepaper bearing the Mayoral Seal, Councillor Brooks invited her concerned junior citizen to the Town Hall to have tea and discuss the points he had raised. He came home glowing with pleasure. By a coincidence, many years later, a Retirement Home was, in fact, built on the derelict site John had mentioned in his letter.

When he was eleven he moved to the Philip Morant School which had such an excellent reputation that estate agents used it as a selling point when houses in that area were on the market. The School's four houses were named after famous people and, by sheer coincidence, John was placed in the one bearing Sue Ryder's name. He was in the 'A' stream throughout his school days excelling in English and hating maths.

He had little aptitude for ball games but gained his cross country running colours. In due course junior and senior prefect badges adorned his green blazer. In his first year he won a prize for endeavour and in his final year he was awarded the Peter Bouckley Memorial Prize for Art. 'There's a lot going on in his pictures' said the Head of the Art Department,

John was a pupil at Philip Morant during the headmastership of Bill Burton, a man of exceptional dedication whose forthright views on education were often quoted in the local newspaper. His staff were an able, enthusiastic team.

Nicknames for teachers usually indicate a certain degree of affectionate regard. At Philip Morant the deputy head was known as *Dubber*, Ryder's housemaster as *Jolly Roger* and the metalwork master as *Noddy*. An Australian maths master, who had been crippled in an accident, was known as *Hopalong Cassidy*. He had the knack of teaching his subject with a light touch. Using a phrase like 'decimal kangaroos', for example, was guaranteed to get his point across to even the dimmest of lads. He was an attractive bearded man with a swashbuckling air and when I wrote a seafaring story called *The Captain's Talisman* I based the main character on him.

Sports Day was always good fun. Ryder House pupils' kit was

orange and the biology master's dog always wore a rosette in this colour. The glamorous music mistress provided the afternoon's commentary in seductive tones. I remember being amused one year when a doting Mum told me she had washed a sack specially for her son to use in that particular race. In the event, however, somebody else got the laundered sack and her boy had to be content with a random rough one.

To John's delight the English Department laid great emphasis on creative writing so his verbal abilities were given full rein as this poem he wrote about two donkeys illustrates:

In the seclusion of Spring Lane
Two equines abide.
Four-legged lawn mowers
Ever seeking for foodstuffs.
The male is a rugged sort of fellow
Reminiscent of an unshaven sea captain.
A walking brillo pad with rough coat,
Enthusiastically consuming apples
And leaves like a vacuum cleaner.
Licking branches with blotting paper tongue,
He brushes away insects with a tail of unspun yarn,
Blinking through roast chestnut eyes.
The female is the captain's mistress,
A brown-furred, dark-eyed beauty
Looking somewhat Italian.
Her friendly muzzle
Lovingly caresses your hand
As if to acknowledge you.

He has always been fond of animals with whom – like his father – he enjoys a close rapport.

When John was twelve he was smitten with the dark charms of an Italian girl in his class and wrote his very first love letter. I would never have dreamed of reading it if it had not been open to full view when I dusted his room and I could not resist making a copy of it before he delivered it. It ran thus:

Dear M . . .

My reputation for being a passionate Polish lover boy with the Continental charm is not very good at present, science and technology seem to have temporarily taken me over. Being a Professor of Science and a lover boy at the same time is literally impossible. But really

I am full of humour and personality, my ability at disco dancing fair and real romance – excellent. I can sing several love songs very melodiously.

I continuously comment on your good looks, the words 'Pure Italian Beauty' *are perfectly true. To my mates, unfortunately, you are not so lovely. They jeer at me* 'Who loves that chocolate drop?' *That is not at all true in fact downright unkind.*

You may ask 'Why do you like me John?' *Well I like you because you are pleasant, have a good sense of humour and a kind heart. I can tell this by your warm, soft, gleaming., dark brown eyes.*

When I get my next opportunity to show you how nice I really am I shall be prepared to do it. To take you to the School Disco, to show my worth. Sample me M . . . , I am very pleasant really,

Sealed with a kiss X

from your ever loving John.

Incidentally in manhood he still prefers brunettes to blondes, but now they must have wild, wind-tossed hair and long legs that go on forever!

When John was in the Fifth Form one of his class-mates was a young 'smoothie' named Toby who held popular fancy dress parties at his home from time to time. On one occasion John went as a Roman charioteer, for another guests were asked to go as 'something beginning with P'. This time he masqueraded as a pillar box and wore a tube of red crêpe paper stuck all over with envelopes and used stamps. Predictably all the foreign ones had been nicked by the end of the evening but John enjoyed himself vastly. Needless to say a number of guests devised much ruder themes beginning with 'P'. A far cry from the jelly and balloon parties of early childhood!

Out of school hours significant long-term interests were being developed. When he was eleven I gave him my old Brownie box camera and he has been taking photographs ever since with progressively sophisticated equipment. Wherever he goes his camera goes too and he has an instinct for encountering dramatic and unusual subjects as well as lovingly capturing the beauties of nature.

The prodigious interest he has had in the transport industry ever since he was a very small boy cannot be traced to any other member of the family and, totally unconcerned by the ribbing it caused from many of his peers at school, he has pursued this subject with unabated enthusiasm into adult life. As a result he had now an encylopaedic knowledge of the international transport scene and a library to match. His work appears these days in various national magazines.

His deep attachment to and wide knowledge of London date from his first visit there when he was three. Throughout his growing up years we returned to the capital regularly to explore its many-sided personality. Highgate, Hampstead, Greenwich, Covent Garden, Chelsea, Richmond, Kew Gardens, Little Venice, Petticoat Lane, Soho, Limehouse and Wapping were all on our itinerary. We browsed around Harrods, had tea once at Fortnum Masons and fed squirrels in Regents Park. The London Transport Museum, The Victoria and Albert, and Pollock's Toy Museum were other favourite haunts.

Although he was a very loving parent and husband Marian never cared for the conventional type of English family holiday. We spent two extremely pleasant holidays with Polish friends from his war years who had settled in Yarmouth, and our supremely happy two month visit to Poland *en famille* is recounted at length in another chapter. But otherwise for the most part he never minded John and myself taking off on our own to various parts of the UK.

So every May half-term holiday during the 1970's and early 1980's I would spend a few days introducing John to some especially lovely part of England. In those days £100 would cover coach fares, modest bed and breakfast accommodation, eating out, local bus tickets and usually still leave enough to buy small souvenirs. We went to Bath, Brighton, Canterbury, Rye, Southampton and the New Forest, the Isle of Wight, the West Country, the Cotswolds and the Brontë Moors, and as a man he has returned with great pleasure to many of these places.

At all seasons, but especially during the summer months, I took John and various friends of his for country jaunts which they clearly enjoyed tremendously. The old wicker picnic basket that had seen so many outdoor meals under Devonshire skies when my grandparents' owned it, was our constant companion together with a camera to record joyful moments.

Our favourite destinations were in Suffolk. Sometimes we spread our table cloth by a deep pool in a riverside glade near Long Melford Hall. The corner of a ripening cornfield at the top of St. Edmund's Lane in Bures was another popular spot and later we would stroll down Cuckoo Hill to the playing field. If we went to Sudbury we would call in at the famous *Railway Pedlar's* model shop before continuing on to *The Croft.* A boat trip on the Stour was another treat.

On other occasions, much nearer home, we would head for Rowhedge and call on long-time family friend and poet George Pluckwell at his former smugglers' cottage. The most hospitable soul imaginable, George would give us tea and cake and enthral the boys with smuggling tales of Rowhedge long ago. Then we would stroll through the fields beside the Roman River to Fingringhoe and relax by a singularly picturesque willow-shaded pool. Just across the road salt-tanged marshland air and secretive woodland trails beckoned invitingly in the Nature Reserve.

Rambles like this kindled John's enduring love of East Anglia. Today he often heads his car northwards lured by Breckland forests and remote stretches of seashore.

After leaving school John (who by this time preferred to be called 'Pod' by all his mates) took a course in Business Studies at the Clacton annexe of the Colchester Institute. This was located on the seafront in the Grand Hotel, an impressive reminder of affluent Edwardian days. Because of its associations with Edward VII the restaurant there was named after Lily Langtry and catering students were able to practise their skills in a thoroughly professional way.

The Business Studies tutors had an excellent rapport with their students and the curriculum was both challenging and interesting. John was happy there and gained his BEC National Diploma. It was a good qualification to have under his belt, though the prospect of a 9–5 office job did not appeal to him at all.

Soon after he went to College he became a disc jockey at the weekly gigs held by the Students' Union at Clacton and his enthusiasm was boundless. After coming back to Colchester for supper he would set off on his bicycle (he had not yet acquired his car) with records strapped on the back and pedal down to Clacton. He had long been a hardy marathon cyclist anyway. After DJ-ing he would stay overnight at the home of his good friend Alex Ball. His services were much appreciated and at Christmas he was presented with a T-shirt and a record token. His final appearance was spinning discs at the Graduation Ball.

His Business Studies Diploma was framed and hung on the wall of his 'den', but he had firmly set his heart on becoming a professional DJ. After answering an advertisement and having an audition he assumed this rôle at *The Affair Club* which had a maximum capacity of about 300 and was one of Colchester's most popular social rendezvous.

Now sadly boarded up and forsaken-looking, *The Affair* was at that time a charming Georgian house with an elegant, graceful main staircase and chandeliers. There was a banqueting suite and overnight accommodation on the upper floor, food was served in a ground level restaurant and the Club was in a tastefully converted cellar with red brick arches, two bars and a good sized dance floor. It was run by a somewhat eccentric, larger-than-life character named Pip Marsh and his formidable sister, known as 'Big Jill', kept punters well under control. Pip's son Stafford was also involved in the business. He was an engaging self-effacing lad and one day John and I encountered him quite by chance while we were strolling past the marina at St. Katherine's Dock during one of our London excursions. He happened to be coming down the gangway of a trim little craft at the time but invited us on board and brewed a pot of tea. He said he shared this delightful waterborne home with his father and told us that before they purchased her she had been used on smuggling runs off the Scottish coast.

John still affectionately recalls his days at *The Affair* as 'great fun and a good laugh' and he forged several lasting friendships during that period. From his schooldays he much preferred being called *Pod* instead of John and this, of course, was eminently suitable for his DJ-ing identity. However, for the sake of continuity in my narrative as a whole, I will go on referring to him as John.

While gaining valuable all-round experience at *The Affair* he began saving up hard to buy a full range of disco equipment so that he could become a freelance DJ on his own account. He already had a car and was a long distance driver of considerable stamina.

Out of Club hours he did various other jobs to augment his funds. Lighting and sound equipment units and all the accompanying requirements, not to mention a constant updating of an extensive record collection, was a very expensive outlay and seeing how single-minded he was Marian and I gave him generous financial help to that he could launch his venture without further delay.

Because he was on the books of several London-based agents the majority of his "gigs' were in and around the Metropolis. Among the most interesting venues were the *Hispaniola*, a floating restaurant berthed alongside The Embankment, and a sister ship of the ill-fated *Marchioness* which was anchored near the Thames Barrier. Clubs, pubs, birthday parties and wedding receptions were also on his agenda.

Perhaps his most memorable engagement of all took place shortly before Christmas 1987 when he was booked to provide the disco for a party being held by a firm of leading accountants in the City. The location was the Connaught Rooms, one of London's top party venues.

All mobile DJ's have an assistant who is called a 'Roadie' and John's was his friend Peter. But only a few hours before it was time to set off for this major event Peter got a bad attack of 'flu. So it was at very short notice that I stepped into the breach as probably the oldest 'Roadie' around! After helping John stack all the equipment into the car I hastily packed my most glamorous dress into a suitcase and off we went.

The Connaught Rooms comprised a series of magnificently-appointed self-contained party suites with gilded mirrors and glittering chandeliers. After helping John unload and take all his equipment up in a lift to the Edinburgh Suite, I went along to the palatial ladies loo to change into my glitzy ensemble.

Meanwhile John skilfully set up all his gear on the stage in the

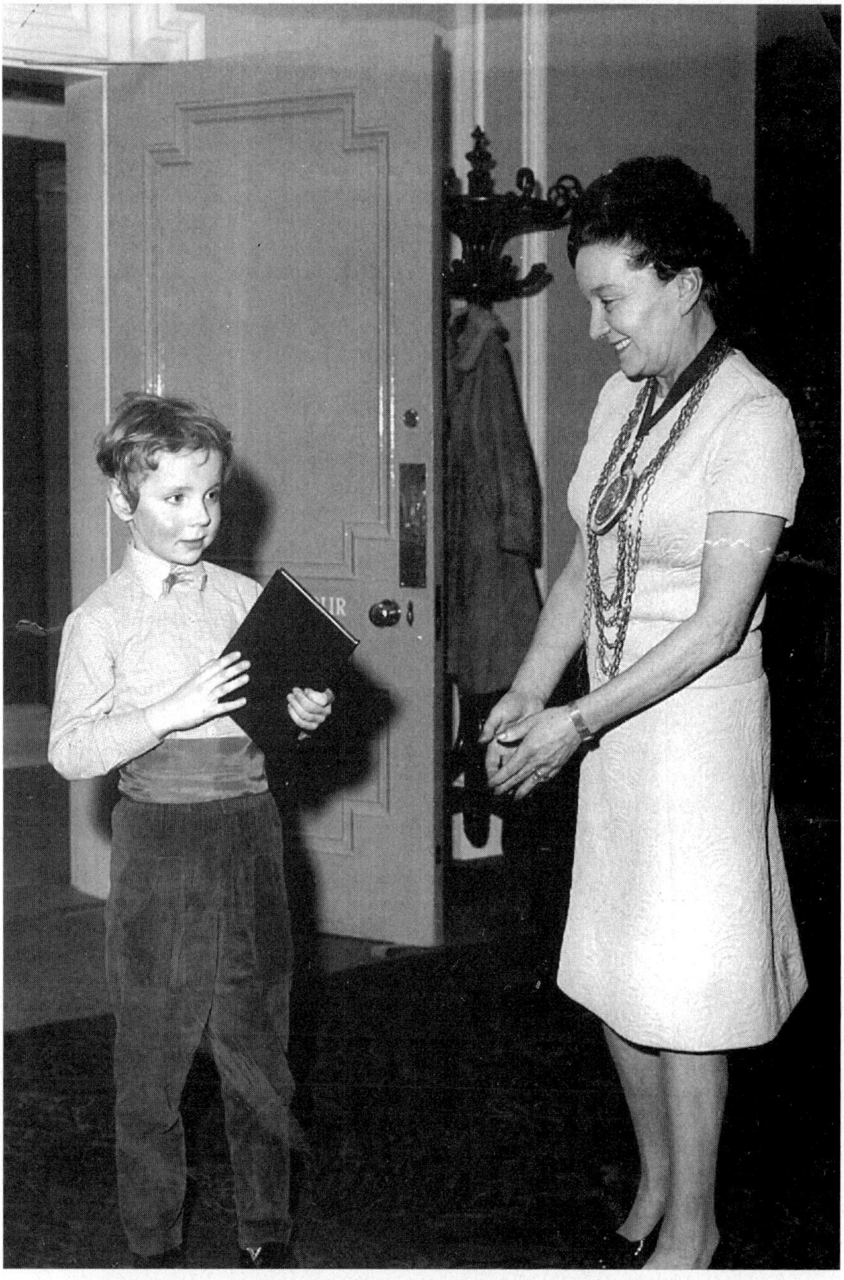

John with Ald. Nancy Smith at the launching party of Book One, December 1971, at Colchester Town Hall. (Essex County Newspapers)

A Sunday luncheon party held by the Roosters' Club at Jesus College, Cambridge. Dr. "Freddie" Brittain is sixth from the right in the front row, and I am immediately behind his left shoulder, in the second row, circa 1960.

My favourite photographs of Marian (left) and John.

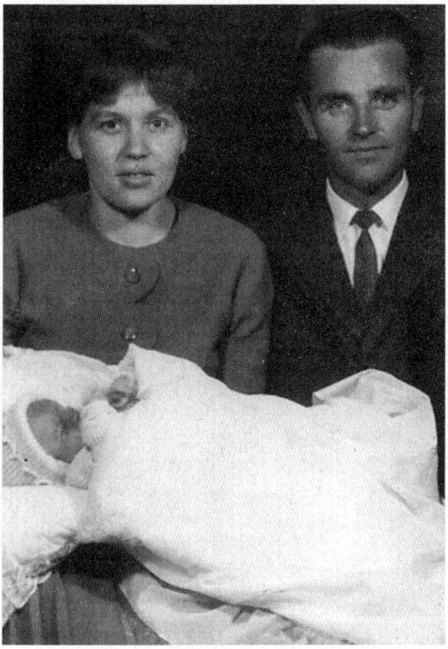

My Polish step-son Zygfryd and family, 1965.

My Polish step-daughter Izabela on her Wedding day, 1968.

On the shores of my beloved Mediterranean, 1957.

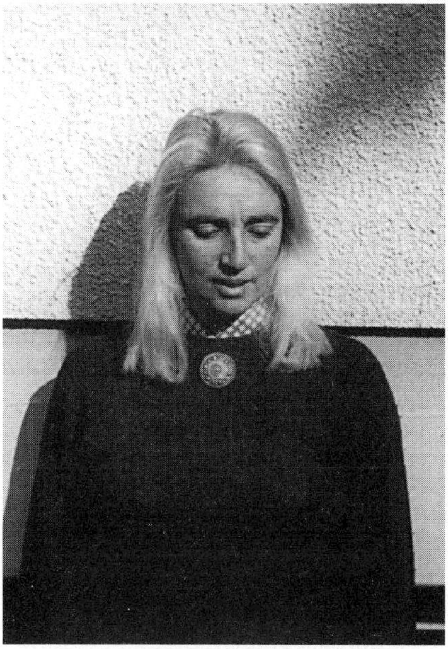

Lory. Gifted, witty, a true Veneziana.

Working at home, 1971.

Carnival in Venice. I pose in costume on a bridge, 1986.

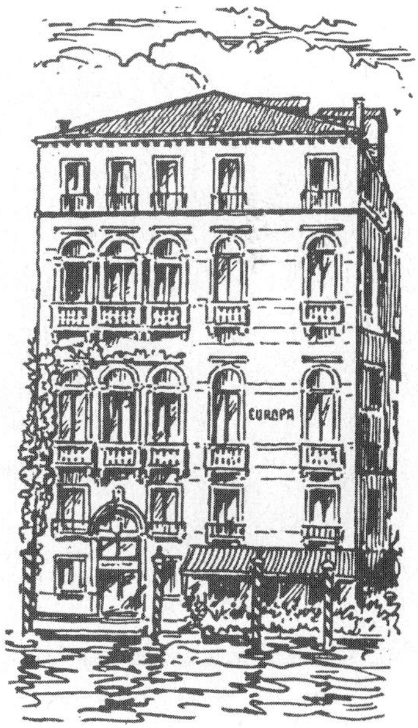

Hotel Europa and Regina Venezia.

Signing my Byron book at Hatchards, January 1988.
My late brother Peter, a gifted poet, is on my right. (Adrian Rushton)

In front of Newstead Abbey with Maureen Crisp (left)
and Megan Boyes, 1989.

The panel at "Going for a Song", May 1972. With me are Garth Cooper, Barbara Jones, Derek Lamberth, Mary Ellis and friend. (Essex County Newspapers)

After the show, Newstead. With Bill Studdiford (left), Ian Frost (next to me), Tina Gray, her husband and daughter.

In the costume for my acrobatic dance, 1944.

Giving a recital at Cambridge, 1959.

In Greyfriars garden at an Old Girl's Reunion. *(Mary Gurney)*

At the annual pre-Christmas lunch held by newspaper colleagues, December 1995. *(Barbara Butler)*

Edinburgh Suite and assembled his hundreds of carefully indexed records. He has always had a keen 'sense of occasion' and was not remotely overawed by the splendid surroundings.

There were elegantly-decorated individual round tables each seating eight guests and soon red-jacketed Italian waiters were moving from table to table with matchless expertise serving an excellent meal. After being welcomed by the hostess who had organised the event John and I were given a silver tray piled high with sandwiches and a generous pot of coffee.

After a sumptuous dinner the Managing Director made a speech, a retiring director received a presentation, and staff members gave a short 'cabaret' which was laced with assorted office jokes. Eventually the tables were removed, chairs ranged round the walls and the disco commenced.

John acquitted himself admirably. I sat on a chair beside the stage and wrote down requests received for particular records. When I was not doing that I simply watched people at play which is always highly entertaining and this night was no exception.

All the pretty girls were having a great time and the office wolves were in top form. Other males who had been the personification of starchy respectability when the soup was served became progressively more uninhibited as the heady combination of wine and music took over. In the background a group of 'wallflowers' smiled wistful forced smiles and pretended they were enjoying themselves.

But there was one figure in particular who aroused my interest. He was a dark personable man of about thirty who was being steered sedately round the floor by a succession of well-meaning matronly ladies and returned to his chair after each dance. I noticed that he did not invite any of the young girls to dance and none of them approached him. Discreetly I asked our hostess about him and she told me he was blind.

Well I suppose I fit the description of 'matronly' myself, but I was determined to help him join in the fun much more that he had so far. So I went over to him, asked him for a dance and made it my business to ensure that he had a thoroughly good time for the rest of the evening. Whether the numbers had a rock and roll beat or were more conventional *slows* (as they are called in the disco world), it was lovely to see his face light up as he relaxed, genuinely enjoying himself and chatting animatedly. I was so glad I had this opportunity of being more than a mere 'Roadie'.

When the party ended in the early hours of the morning the Managing Director declared himself delighted with John's performance and in addition to the £100 fee he got a £15 tip. We felt on the crest of a wave.

The following day I again acted as stand-in 'Roadie' when John provided the disco at another big Christmas party. The location this time was the Civic Centre at Aylesbury and the revellers were the directors and staff of a pipe manufacturing company and their families.

The hall had an enormous stage with various electric plugs at the back, but with his usual foresight John had brought plenty of spaghetti-like connecting leads and was able to set up all his equipment in advance while leaving plenty of room for the musical quartet who were to play golden oldies for the benefit of maturer guests before the disco took centre-stage.

Festive fare arrived in large metal containers like those used for school meals and John and I were included among the diners. I must confess that I thoroughly enjoyed tucking in to roast turkey while the quartet played melodies like *True Love* and *Night & Day* in the background. The drummer was also the vocalist. He was an extremely homely looking little man with a surprisingly pleasant singing voice.

After the meal the quartet continued to play for a short session of conventional ballroom dancing but soon the Younger Set grew restive and shouted 'We want the disco!'. For a moment I felt almost disloyal as, with a tinge of regret, I watched the four middle-aged musicians pack up their instruments and make their exit, but as the vibrant throbbing beat of John's opening number struck up I was back in the groove as a 'Roadie' again with my request list at the ready. Before long some youngsters came over and insisted I should join them on the dance floor. I did not need much persuading!

Peter recovered from 'flu in time to resume his 'Roadie' duties for other Christmastime engagements. But I shall always retain fond memories of those two nights when I felt about twenty again instead of sixty plus!

However, being a freelance DJ had its down-side too. The pay was excellent but naturally not regular. John has always been a 'night person' bright-eyed and bushy-tailed, as the saying goes, in the early hours of the morning. But Marian worried about his long late homeward drives and was always restive until he heard John's key turn in the front door and knew all was well. We had given him a *St. Christopher* medallion which he kept in the glove compartment of the car and I had great faith in this as well as in his driving abilities and the fact he never drank alcohol.

By now, of course, he had plenty of experience technically as well as in the purely DJ field and before long a suitable opening occurred for him much nearer home at *L'Aristo's Night Club* in Colchester.

I took an immediate liking to *L'Aristo's* when John showed me round. The stylish décor and general air of glamour and elegance was further enhanced by the rainbow mosaic effect of underfloor lighting in the dancing area. It adjoined a hotel which had been converted from an historic flour mill with exceptional flair and imagination and had been awarded an architectural accolade.

John inherited his practical skills from Marian and at this colourful riverside night spot had a significant opportunity to develop his knowledge of sound and light techniques. As his interest in this side of club work increased DJ-ing became very much a secondary activity, though he did spin records again on several carnival floats.

After more than three years at *L'Aristo's* (with which he was to retain cordial social ties), John was invited to join the technical team at the *Hippodrome* in the heart of the town. This was a listed building of considerable character which had originally been an Edwardian Music Hall. All the greatest stars of that era had graced its stage. Later it became a cinema and a bingo hall.

When it was converted into a night club in 1988 the splendid original dome, proscenium arch and richly decorated boxes had to be preserved and a satisfactory compromise was reached. A spectacular lighting system was introduced, powerful sound equipment installed on the stage and the auditorium transformed into a spacious dancing area. Lighting controls were sited in what had once been styled the 'Royal Box'.

What fascinated me most when John took me on a tour of the building was the old theatre gallery which had also been untouched by modern changes. The tiers of basic wooden seating were once crammed with threepenny ticket-holders boisterously applauding the saucy songs of Marie Lloyd, the touching antics of 'Little Tich' and the comic genius of Fred Karno and a young Charlie Chaplin. I could picture them vividly in my mind's eye.

What John enjoyed most during his years at the *Hippodrome* was stage managing facilities for live bands. Some of the musicians came from far afield and arrived in eye-catching forms of transport. He encountered many extremely off-beat, larger-than-life characters among them and found it an entertaining experience.

But eventually, as broad new horizons beckoned in the world beyond tinsel escapism, John outgrew the night club business. Nevertheless he still retains a compact recording studio and his advice on sound and light matters is often sought by folk he met during his disco years.

Today his feet are firmly set on a career path dominated by the three enduring interests that date back to his childhood . . . Writing, Photography and Transport. As a transport journalist and photographer he is finding true fulfilment and loves all the travelling involved. He also holds advanced driving qualifications which enable him to take the wheel of many different vehicles besides cars and has driven Charity Buses in his spare time.

Tall and slim, he is very Polish in looks and temperament, speaks some of the language and prizes his links with his father's homeland. He is noted for his remarkable memory and can even recall the colours, makes and registration numbers of his teachers' cars at school as well as those of the coaches he travelled on during childhood holidays.

Social issues are of great interest to him and he is a formidable debater, while his general knowledge makes him a useful man to have in a quiz team. He is a very keen member of Rotaract where his favourite projects concern the care of the environment.

I expect he will get married soon, but the unhappy marital experiences of two of his closest friends have made him cautious. He says his ideal girl is a long-legged brunette who looks equally good in a short-skirted business suit or a little black dress and has a low-pitched sultry voice. If she knows what goes on under a car bonnet and is handy with a spanner so much the better.

CHAPTER SIX

A GENEROUS LEGACY

NEWS REACHED ME on April, 16th, 1987, which was Maundy Thursday, that my beloved Auntie Audrey had died peacefully at Epsom Hospital. On her 87th birthday only two days previously she had written me a cheerful note saying *'I do not feel my age'.* Within a few hours of penning it her gardener of many years made his daily call on her and found her slumped in her favourite chair fatally ill. Her last thoughts were for the King Charles spaniel she adored and she died happy in the knowledge that her faithful little companion would be returned to the care of the people from whom she had bought her.

To John, Auntie had been in every sense of the word the equivalent of a grandmother. While he was growing up she sent him many delightful and imaginative playthings as well as books which he still treasures . . . especially the *Thomas the Tank Engine* stories. Marian was also very fond of her. She and I had always been kindred spirits who shared many common interests and I loved her very much.

During my childhood and adolescence I spent many holidays with Auntie and her genial husband, who was know to all the family as 'Churchie', at their charming house which was called *Monks Eleigh* in Chestnut Avenue, Ewell, Surrey. They named their home after a pretty hamlet in Suffolk that held romantic associations for them.

They had known each other since they were children. Most of their courting days were spent horse-riding with Eileen Grubb, who had stables at Fingringhoe, or bowling down to West Mersea in a pale blue Jowett. When I was invited to accompany them in this dashing car during the early 1930's I sat in the 'dickey' . . . a mode of transport I greatly relished. At that time the picturesque old Victory Pub still stood along the the Coast Road at Mersea.

After their marriage they moved to Surrey and 'Churchie' had an optician's business at Kingston-upon-Thames. Always keen animal lovers they had a succession of very appealing Cocker spaniels as well as *Mr. Chips* a stray mongrel who turned up in 'Churchie's' reception office one afternoon and found a comfortable berth for the rest of his days.

With Auntie and 'Churchie' I took long walks across Epsom Downs or on Box Hill and spent happy days at their caravan which commanded an idyllic view at Mickleham. We went to the Derby and that kindled my life-long interest in horse-racing.

'Churchie' died in 1968 following a severe stroke while doing an eye test in his consulting room, but Auntie continued to live at *Monks Eleigh.*

Life could have been lonely but with a dog to love, books to read, pictures to paint and a large garden where she virtually lived, slept and took all her meals during the summer months, Auntie was content. She slipped into old-age sweet-natured and young at heart.

Twice during her final years she was admitted to hospital for an 'assessment' but, as she told me heatedly, 'When I saw myself among a lot of old vegetables I was determined not to stay any longer'. *Carrying* instead of *using* the walking frame that had been issued to her, she demanded to be taken home. I am happy to say that, with strong back-up from the Social Services, she was able to stay at *Monks Eleigh* until the last few hours of her life.

When Marian, John and I moved from Yorkshire to Colchester in 1968 we were able to visit her frequently and we made it a special tradition to spend every August Bank Holiday weekend with her. We shared her delight in living *al fresco* in the garden, watching squirrels shinning up tree trunks as we lunched or had tea surrounded by mossy statuary and roses growing in profusion. John would mow the lawn and generally busy himself about the garden and take the dogs for walks.

My heart was full of all these happy recollections when, the day after Auntie Audrey's death, I travelled alone to *Monks Eleigh* where I spent three busy weeks. Making preparations for the funeral and visiting her solicitor were my first priorities, followed by a large-scale spring clean.

Auntie had lived in a state of considerable disarray for many years, though all the furnishings were top quality and included some extremely good antique pieces. One of her greatest delights during her later years was painting – a talent she had inherited from her father. She went to art classes held by Aubrey Sykes, who also lived in Chestnut Avenue, and exhibited and sold some of her work. Still life and flower studies were her principal subjects though my particular favourite, which now hangs in my own home, depicts a tranquil pool shaded by weeping willows.

I found the boxroom full of paintings both framed and unframed in company with her easel, palette and tubes of paint. After setting aside her best work for close relations, I thought it would be a good idea to display the remainder in the hallway and on the staircase so that mourners coming back to the house for tea after the funeral at Leatherhead Crematorium could choose a picture to carry away as a permanent memorial of a lively and lovable old lady. This decision proved very popular and also provided a colourful welcome to cheer sad hearts.

At the funeral, which took place on a warm, sunny afternoon. I quoted the Six Maxims of King George V which had hung on Auntie's bedroom wall for many years and admirably summed up her own philosophy about life.

Teach me to be obedient to the rules of the game.
Teach me to distinguish between sentiment and sentimentality admiring the one and despising the other.
Teach me neither to proffer nor to receive cheap praise.
Teach me to win if I may, If I may not win then, above all, teach me to be a good loser.
Teach me neither to cry for the moon nor over spilt milk.
If I am called upon to suffer let me be like a well-bred beast that goes away to suffer in silence.

After the funeral I put the house on the market. Being an attractive property in a singularly pretty road it did not remain long on the estate agent's books and was sold in a highly satisfactory cash transaction.

Next came the poignant task of sifting through the vast quantity of letters, photographs and small momentoes that had accumulated over many years. There were pictures of Auntie as a schoolgirl and as a medical student, some fine camera studies 'Churchie' had made of all their dogs, holiday snaps taken in their beloved Cotswolds, and recent shots John had taken of Auntie in *Monks Eleigh* garden.

I found a richly-embossed programme and menu marking 'Churchie's' installation as Worshipful Master of the *Virtue and Silence* Lodge at the White Lion Hotel, Hadleigh, on February 12th, 1930, when the Installing Master was Worshipful Brother A. J. Critten. I knew that Freemasonry had played an important rôle in his life.

For me the most touching discovery of all was a supremely tender love letter which Auntie had written to 'Churchie' in 1950 the night before she underwent an operation ('in case anything goes wrong'). Happily the envelope had never been opened because she made a complete recovery, so my eyes were the first to read it since she penned it. I was moved to tears. Auntie always had a wonderful way with words. I put everything of sentimental value in a suitcase to take away with me.

Finally I assembled the furniture, household goods, garden ornaments and tools for transportation to Colchester. Fingering through the *Yellow Pages* I picked a removal firm based nearby. The proprietor came to view the load that was to be packed into his pantechnicon and to assess the cost. As he looked around I noticed him peering closely at an antique barometer and he turned to me with an unexpected proposition. He said he would like to buy the barometer and asked me to quote a price.

I had been brought up to consider that there was something a trifle sordid about haggling (my views on this have changed since then), so I replied with the first three figure sum that came into my head. This prompted him to say that in exchange for the barometer he would offer his removal services free of charge. With a deplorable lack of business acumen I agreed. Since then, of course, I have learned that it was worth a good deal more than the price I quoted and would have fetched a handy sum in an auction room.

I was one of the two main beneficiaries under my Aunt's Will the other being an elderly cousin in Colchester to whom she was much attached. With a portion of my generous legacy I was able to embark on an exciting literary venture which Auntie Audrey would have heartily approved of and which brought me great artistic fulfilment and significant new friendships.

CHAPTER SEVEN

LORD BYRON & COMPANY

IT HAD LONG BEEN my ambition to make a personal contribution to the bicentenary celebrations of Byron's birth in 1988 by writing a book which covered lesser-known aspects of his parentage and early-life. I called it *A Timeless Fascination* with the sub-title *The Byron Story in Fresh Focus 200 Years On*. It was a challenging project that gave full rein to all my creative energies.

Ever since I was fifteen years old I had researched the Poet's life in depth both at home and abroad and had a wealth of material to draw on. The chapters I enjoyed writing most were about his travels in Greece and Turkey because I had seen for myself so many of the wild and beautiful places he described in *Childe Harold's Pilgrimage*. While in Greece I had worn a cameo brooch of Byron and even in the most remote mountain villages his likeness was immediately recognised as the English hero who helped to free their country from Turkish tyranny.

The book was aimed at a general readership and part of the 'blurb' on the back cover said: 'Into his first 24 years he had already packed adventures of the most picturesque kind in settings ranging from the Scottish Highlands to the mountains of Greece and from rural Nottinghamshire to the barbaric splendour of Ottoman Turkey'.

His brilliant, racy letters reveal his charm and humour as a friend, his cheerful hardiness as a traveller, his sympathy for the underdog and hatred of hypocrisy. The author has recaptured the flavour of Byron's life and times with a sure and vivid touch.'

During the Bicentenary Year I wanted to give money from the sales of the book to a cause that would have been close to Byron's heart if he were living today. After much thought I chose *'Action Research for the Crippled Child'*, because Byron himself had been born lame. This meant, of course, that my book could not be regarded as a straightforward commercial proposition by any publisher, though a reader at the *House of Robert Hale* did describe it as 'eminently readable'. So I assumed the rôle of publisher myself devising a classical lyre framed by a laurel wreath as the logo for my letterheads and book title.

In September, 1987, I took my manuscript to the Essex Telegraph Press Ltd. situated at that time in Childwell Alley behind Harrison's former furniture warehouse in Magdalen Street, Colchester. Their printing works specialised in text books and good quality brochures but, as far as I knew, they had never undertaken any work of a purely literary nature before.

It soon became clear that I had approached the right firm. The unusual nature of the assignment appealed to them. I said I wanted *A Timeless Fascination* to be produced in a thoroughly professional manner on high quality paper. It would be illustrated by early 19th century prints from my own collection of Byroniana including a rare picture of Gight Castle of which Byron's mother had been the last Laird. This latter was in the form of an old-fashioned glass plate negative which had been given to me by the Chief Librarian in Aberdeen.

A price was agreed upon (comparable to the cost of a modest car at that time) and *A Timeless Fascination* began to roll off the press. It was the prelude to one of the most exhilarating experiences of my life. Each week I called to read proofs and discuss various matters with genial Len Amos. Printer Eric Holmes told me that working on my book had made him more eager to get up in the mornings than ever before and added that every evening when he got home his wife asked him to tell her the latest instalment.

During the Autumn of 1987 Harrison's empty warehouse was extensively vandalised. One sharp shooter with a powerful catapult used to station himself out of sight on an upper floor at the rear of the building. From time to time pebbles or small shot of some kind landed in Essex Telegraph Press Ltd's. forecourt which could make comings and goings a trifle hazardous now and then, but I certainly didn't let this scare me.

At last the time came for me to design the book cover. I used George Harlow's celebrated drawing of Byron which featured in an early edition I had of *The Corsair* and I enclosed it in an oval gilt Regency-style frame. For the title lettering I chose Gothic print characters. Though a paper back, the book had a glossy cover which gave it a classy finish. I spent ages poring over a sample book to decide what colour this should be. Eventually I chose scarlet . . . not learning until much later that Byron always insisted on this colour for his own books.

By the end of November *A Timeless Fascination* was ready in a generous limited edition and delivered to my home. I was extremely pleased with the finished product and several booksellers were to compliment me on its elegant presentation.

Now began the enormous task of promoting it nationally and internationally through various media sources and by personal trips to towns that had especially strong Byron associations.

Without neglecting my loving duties as a wife and Mum I devoted as much time as possible for many months to getting my book known and talked about. Often I toiled far into the early hours but it was worth it and yielded results beyond my wildest expectations.

Shortly before Christmas, 1987, Ronald Norfolk, a director of Essex Telegraph Press Ltd., arrived on my doorstep with several bottles of wine and a handsome greetings card. I told him that I would set aside the wine as part of the consignment to be opened at the official launching of the book.

I very much wanted this event to take place on 22nd January, 1988, which was the actual bicentenary date of Byron's birth and I was equally keen that it should be held in appropriate surroundings.

At that time there was a branch of Hatchards in Colchester High Street under the management of Penny Bell who was as charming as her name. I called in to see her with a copy of *A Timeless Fascination* and asked if she would allow me to hold a signing session with wine and snacks in her shop on the Poet's birthday. To my absolute delight she readily agreed.

My husband fully shared my elation because Byron is widely read and greatly admired in Poland and I have a Polish edition of his works amongst my Byroniana. When we ushered in 1988 (as we did all New Years) with midnight drinks and embraces there was a special feeling of happy anticipation in the air.

Squally snow showers marked the morning of Friday, 22nd January, 1988, so I was very agreeably surprised by the number of people who attended the launching at Hatchards. My close friend Hilda Breckels presided over the refreshments and Bessie O'Halloran chairman of the local branch of *'Action Research for the Crippled Child'* was present. Press coverage ensured that I had a permanent record of the event.

Penny Bell had arranged for my books to be displayed in one of the shop windows fronted by a fine marble bust of Byron which I had bought many years previously at an antique shop in Lincoln. It was exciting to know that my book was also being sold that day at the venerable bookshop in Piccadilly where the first Mr. Hatchard opened his business in Regency times. Byron knew it well.

Toasts were drunk to the Poet's memory several times during the morning and on each occasion when glasses were raised I spoke briefly about Byron's courage, kindness, wit and passionate championship of the oppressed and observed that English literature would have been a good deal less colourful and exciting if he had never passed through the world.

I also had on show a number of simple timeless items that typify the spirit of rural Greece. They included a mule bell and a shepherd's pipe, both of which would have been very familiar sounds to Byron the traveller.

After an unforgettably happy morning I travelled over to Cambridge to rendezvous with another of my closest friends Gillian Edwards. We had a celebratory dinner at the *Garden House Hotel* and recalled Byron's links with the city when he was a student.

Nineteen eighty eight was to prove a charmed period in my life. *A Timeless Fascination* was well received and enjoyed brisk sales both in the UK and overseas. Orders from the United States and Greece were numerous. One copy even found its way to the University of Albania. There was a heady satisfaction in receiving orders from prestigious booksellers like Bissets of Aberdeen and Blackwell of Oxford.

The Westminster Abbey Bookshop said: 'It is very readable and should enjoy good sales'.

P. D. Hunter, Librarian of the Vaughan Library at Harrow School where Byron was a pupil, wrote: 'I enjoyed your lively narrative style which brings the story to life so interestingly'.

From Chicago-based poet Annette Budzisz came these heart warming words: 'I am writing to express my delight with your book. It was my companion during my recent travels in Turkey and Albania and will always remain a treasure in my library'.

English teacher Alison Davidson wrote: 'I want to tell you how much I enjoyed *A Timeless Fascination.* I shall be recommending it to those girls who are studying the Romantic period for A-Level Literature'.

Writing from Florida, leading Byron scholar Leslie Marchand applauded 'the Byronic enthusiasm of your account'.

I particularly treasure a letter from Melina Mercouri (whom I regard as one of the world's most fascinating women). She gave up making films like the delicious *Never On Sundays* to become Greek Minister of Culture and it was in this latter rôle that she wrote to me.

I have a suitcase full of appreciative letters from all over the world and to me there is something both humbling and uplifting to know that people took the trouble to put pen to paper to say how much they enjoyed something I had written.

Several contained engaging anecdotes. Like the one from a divorcée who was reading my book beside a swimming pool when the man who was to become her second husband introduced himself with the words 'I like your choice of reading'. A copy accompanied my friend Gwenda Watkins on a world cruise and by the end of the voyage *A Timeless Fascination* had been read by most of the other passengers on board as well.

Dynamic Philhellene Maureen Crisp invited me to become a member of the Newstead Abbey Byron Society which met regularly at Byron's idyllically beautiful ancestral home near Nottingham and with great pleasure I accepted. My involvement with this flourishing group of ardent Byronians has played a happy and important part in my life ever since. I shall always cherish the moment on my first visit as a member when I heard my book praised by the Society's Chairman Ken Purslow under Byron's own roof.

Through my membership of this Society I forged warm friendships with two very delightful and prodigiously knowledgeable Byronians. Lucy Edwards, M.B.E., was formerly in charge of the Byron Archives in Nottingham Library, and a learned, lovable personality venerated by Byron students from all over the world. Megan Boyes, a vivacious Welshwoman and lively letter-writer, was the author of painstakingly researched biographies on leading local figures in Byron'a life.

I was fascinated to meet the very remarkable Elma Dangerfield, the world's foremost champion of Byron's memory. A physically frail but mentally indestructible octogenarian of commanding presence, her home *Byron House* in Chelsea was filled with momentoes of the Poet.

After he had read my book, Geoffrey Bond, the well-known TV presenter and film-maker, invited me to a morning champagne party he was holding for a small group of leading Byronians at Burgage Manor in Southwell, a genteel and historic little town of most beguiling character not far from Newstead. Set among other handsome period houses round a fine green shaded by ancient chestnut trees, the Manor had been Byron's home during adolescence.

Rescuing it from years of neglect, Geoffrey had recently bought it as his family home and refurbished it throughout in exquisite taste and with an admirable sense of Regency elegance. Our comprehensive tour of the house included, of course, the bedroom where the young Byron had written his earliest poetry. While Geoffrey had made it above all things a family home and not in any sense of the word a museum, he had gathered around him plentiful Byron memorabilia and had a copy of Canova's bust of the Poet on a table in the entrance hall.

The guests at Burgage Manor that morning included an eminent London-based Irish osteopathic physician with an impressive string of qualifications after his name and a roguish gleam in his eyes. Later the same day I met him again at a gathering in Newstead Abbey when he gave me one of his professional cards saying, with a matchless display of Irish blarney, 'You know where to come if you want your back rubbed'.

The publication of *A Timeless Fascination* brought me charming gifts from several unexpected quarters. Although he had never met me an accomplished Colchester calligrapher and teacher of this art named Tom Hunter sent me an exquisitely written copy on vellum of Byron's poem *She Walks in Beauty* embellished with flowers and foliage. I was captivated – especially as he had no idea that this was my favourite Byron poem.

When I met Tom later I learned that, as a boy, he had lived in Nottingham and often roamed across the Newstead estate. We had both seen the *Book of Kells* in Dublin and talked about the extraordinary beauty of ancient monkish manuscripts. What, I asked Tom, happened in the rare event of a monastic scribe making an error? He told me that the monk drew a little devil by the mistake indicating whose fault it was.

Distinguished artist Molly Coubrough had lived at Newstead Abbey in childhood and I visited her at the beautiful house her father had built later in a secluded woodland setting nearby. While playing by the lakeside at Newstead as a little girl Molly had discovered amongst dense undergrowth the name panel of the boat *Maid of Athens* in which Byron had once had such fun with his beloved Newfoundland dog Boatswain. Following our meeting Molly painted for me two striking and unusual pictures of Byron's ancestral home. One was a delicate study of the Abbey front by moonlight and the other an entrancing view across the lake. She also drew a meticulously detailed map of the farms and other landmarks on the Newstead estate in the Poet's time.

After hearing one of my talks about Byron a member of the audience sent me a splendid bust of the Poet mounted on a black marble column. It had been in her family for many years.

After meeting Col. Andrew Brearley-Smith, director of Action Research for the Crippled Child, at his West Sussex Headquarters early in 1988 I kept in touch with him throughout the year and in November I was invited to the Charity's annual conference at the Queen Elizabeth Centre near Westminster Abbey.

The Charity's immediately identifiable collecting boxes were shaped like Paddington Bear, and Michael Bond creator of this appealing storybook character, was among the guests in company with other wellknown personalities like Jimmy Hill and Bernard Cribbins. As Patron of the Charity the Duchess of York was the guest of honour and I was introduced to her.

On 31st December, 1988, I sent a cheque for a very substantial four figure sum to the Charity's H.Q. I was not able to earmark it for any particular purpose, but if I could have done so I would have liked it to help finance equipment which would enable children without speech to communicate with the world around them.

Not long afterwards when I replenished my stock of books in the Newstead bookshop (housed in what was long ago the Prior's kitchen), I was photographed in front of the Abbey holding one of those king-sized mock-up replica cheques. With me were Maureen Crisp and Megan Boyes.

Several of the fascinating encounters which resulted from the publication of my book had strong connections with the theatre.

In the Summer of 1988 I saw actor, writer and singer John Watts give his virtuoso one-man recital as Byron in the Grand Drawing Room at Newstead Abbey. He had already presented his stunning bicentenary portrayal of the Poet at many venues but told me that nothing could compare with giving a performance in Byron's own home. He bore a definite resemblance to the Poet.

On a June afternoon, with no special lighting or music and few props other than an armchair and some papers, he transformed a small dais in front of a baronial stone fireplace beneath the Byron portrait by Thomas Phillips, into a world encompassing the Poet's whole life. His improvisation was brilliant. A rainbow-hued scarf, for example, was used with equal conviction as a babe in arms and as an Albanian warrior's turban. At the close of his performance John turned and saluted Byron's portrait.

That same memorable weekend I saw Derek Jacobi and Isla Blair give a Byron anthology with music at the Nottingham Playhouse. After the performance I was taken behind the scenes and introduced to Mr. Jacobi (he had not yet been knighted). I told him how greatly I had admired his performance in the title rôle of *I, Claudius*, one of my favourite plays.

Also in the audience at the Nottingham Playhouse that evening were Devon-born actor Ian Frost and American writer Bill Studdiford who formed a unique creative partnership with their immensely stylish Byron Trilogy. These three recitals they presented with considerable success on both sides of the Atlantic, as well as on board cruise ships, over a long period.

Ian was a consummate actor and, although not at all like Byron in appearance, he totally convinced audiences that he was through sheer artistry. He was brilliantly served by Bill's scripts which captured the essence of all that was Byron both as a man and a poet. Newstead Abbey was naturally one of their favourite venues during their summer European tours and I got to know them well. Their vitality and enthusiasm seemed boundless and in private, over after-the-show suppers, they were highly entertaining raconteurs.

I likened Ian and Bill to the strolling players of long ago. On their marathon tours both in the United States and in Europe they travelled from place to place in a modest car with costumes, scenery, props, lighting and sound equipment packed in the back. Before every show they set up everything themselves and assembled simple but very effective sets. It was a way of life which clearly suited both of them.

I have always admired young drama school graduates who, while seeking recognition and advancement, work in fringe theatre groups all over London, often on the upper floor of popular pubs. My Byron book led to a brief but very pleasant association with just such a group of youthful Thespians called the Redverse Theatre Company.

In April. 1990, I received an unexpected letter from Brierley Arnell the Company's founder and artistic director. She told me Redverse would be giving a four week run of the play *Bloody Poetry* (about Byron and Shelley in Switzerland and Italy) at the *Duke of Cambridge* in Kentish Town during July. Would I like to advertise *A Timeless Fascination* in their programme?

By this time sales of the book had been so good that I had no need to promote it in this way but, curious to catch an intimate glimpse of a fringe theatre group at work and sympathetically drawn to augmenting the Company's shoe-string production funds, I agreed. I noted with interest too that Redverse's Patron was the present Lord Byron, Robert 13th Baron, a barrister in London.

As I was due to go to London anyway within a few days of receiving Brierley's letter, I decided to call at the address she had given. While seeking directions in Camden High Street, I encountered another fringe theatre group the Etcetera Company who were rehearsing Goldoni's *Mistress of the Inn* in an upper room at the *Oxford Arms.* I was very impressed by the professional set-up they had achieved in such a confined space. Their publicity manager knew of Brierley and set my feet on the right path. Unfortunately she was not at home but, later, by 'phone we arranged to meet at an Indian vegetarian eating-house just off Oxford Street.

Apart from being very beautiful Brierley was extremely versatile. Besides acting she was an accomplished singer, pianist and cabaret artiste, made the company's costumes and was particularly keen to do work in the future among deaf actors. She told me how much she had enjoyed *A Timeless Fascination* and said that it was currently being studied by Dorian Lough who would be portraying Byron.

Shortly after *Bloody Poetry* opened in July I attended a performance with my good friend and ardent fellow theatre-goer Hilda Breckels. The *Duke of Cambridge* in a residential quarter of Kentish Town proved to be a decidedly attractive Edwardian pub. Upstairs the Redverse Company had created an admirable small-scale theatre with expert lighting and atmospheric background music. Tim Holloway's direction was thoughtful, spirited and imaginative and the period costumes were excellent. Amongst the cast several performances had a definite aura of future stardom about them.

And further agreeable 'spin offs' from the publication of my book have continued ever since in an on-going way.

Annual highlight among the Newstead Abbey Byron Society's many activities is the Birthday Banquet which is held every January on the Saturday nearest to the 22nd. Its venue is the elegant and evocative restaurant which now occupies the Abbey's south-west wing and is run by Maureen Crisp and Ken Purslow both leading Society members.

Much of the plentiful Byron memorabilia on view reflects the Society's strong ties with Greece and especially with Missolonghi the town where the Poet died. Each year the meal is preceded by a moving candle-lighting ceremony.

Members of other Byron Societies from all over the world are among the guests and the spirit of warm hospitality which filled Newstead during the Poet's residence there is particularly strong on this glittering occasion.

The year after *A Timeless Fascination* was published I attended my first Birthday Banquet wearing Regency costume. The Gothic casements of the lovely old mansion were aglow with welcome and peacocks were roosting on ancient walls close by.

Before going in to join the party I walked alone beside the Garden Lake in bright moonlight and the events in my book which had featured Byron's days at Newstead seemed to come to life all round me.

CHAPTER EIGHT

SPRINGTIME SHADOWS

IN JANUARY, 1993, Jadwiga, one of Marian's numerous cousins, and her daughter Marzena came to visit us in Colchester. It provided a very happy opening to the New Year and we had a wonderful time together. John and I already knew our guests as they had entertained us at their home when we were in Poland in 1976.

Since then Jadwiga and her husband Bolik had emigrated to the United States. Marzena was studying English in London and spoke the language very well. They brought a cassette of Polish Christmas carols for Marian, a bottle of vodka for John and a cut crystal bowl for me. Marzena and John found plenty to talk about while Jadwiga, Marian and I exchanged family news and reminiscences.

Among our topics was the visit of Jadwiga's elder sister Bogousha to Colchester some years previously. At the time Poland was still under Communist rule and her husband Vassek had not been allowed to accompany her. This rule seems to have applied to all married couples at that period to ensure that the partner who did go abroad would return home.

In her luggage Bogousha had a bottle of extremely potent *'Spiritus'* (much more fiery than vodka!) which she was anxious that I should sell for her. It was purchased by an adventurous newspaper colleague of mine who was noted for holding his liquor. When I inquired later what he thought of it he declared with some awe that it was 'dynamite'.

Once in England Bogousha was very keen to stay several months, get a job and earn some money. She did not speak any English so this presented something of a problem but, as luck would have it, a chance phone call to a Polish club in London brought the perfect solution.

A wealthy Turkish restaurateur with a Polish mistress was seeking someone to live in and care for their baby son so that she could help in his business. Bogousha was ideal for the job and I accompanied her to the house in North London where she stayed for several months as nanny to little Michael. She would no doubt have stayed longer if an urgent summons from her restive husband in Poland had not obliged her to return home. However, later on the generous Turk had treated her whole family to a holiday in Istanbul.

I subsequently learned that the pretty Polish girl who employed Bogousha was only one of several mistresses that the amorous Turk had in London. After they had borne him children he set each of them up in a comfortable establishment and everyone was happy.

These anecdotes and many others were recounted amid laughter and Marian was in high spirits. During their stay Marzena took some excellent indoor photographs, the last being of Marian, Jadwiga and myself in our hallway before John drove us down to the station to see mother and daughter off on a train to London. Marian's delight at their visit was reflected in his face and little did I realise that this was the last photograph that would ever be taken of him.

On 1st May he complained of pains in the chest and agreed to let me call a doctor. Then I knew that he must be feeling really unwell because usually he stubbornly refused to see any doctors. After examining him the GP wrote out a prescription for a course of tablets to alleviate a chest infection. Just as he was leaving I asked him on the spur of the moment, if he would also look at Marian's bad leg which I knew had recently been getting increasingly troublesome. Previously Marian had always been very reluctant to seek medical advice about the terribly mutilated limb. Apart from getting regular prescriptions for a powerful cleansing solution he had dressed the large open wound expertly from knee to ankle twice a day himself throughout our married life. His bandaging was immaculate for, during the war, he had assisted doctors in tending wounded comrades.

But on this May morning he readily allowed the doctor to look doing the unbandaging himself in his usual methodical way. When the dressings were removed the doctor said just one word 'Jesus!' and at once summoned a district nurse.

She came round and treated the ulcerated limb with some wonderfully healing balm derived from seaweed. The beneficial effect was immediate and at last Marian had no pain at all.

Regular calls were made by a district nurse (different ones but all equally fresh-faced and efficient) and on one occasion a senior nurse came along as well to see what she termed 'the famous leg'. They all expressed admiration for Marian's stoicism but also astonishment that he had never considered having the leg amputated. Nobody knew better than I did how determined he was to keep both his legs at any cost as long as he lived and how passionately he had waged a constant fight to do so ever since the day he was wounded in 1944.

For the next few days Marian was buoyed up by the absence of pain. He took the tablets prescribed, and spoke cheerfully of going to Poland again in the summer and I dared to hope that all would be well. But on 8th May he once more felt very ill and had breathing difficulties. Only one hour after being rushed to hospital his brave heart stopped beating. He was within three months of his 80th birthday. I had accompanied him in the ambulance but was not with him when he died because a medical team was working desperately to save him. The following day would have been our 29th wedding anniversary – a date which we always celebrated in some special way. I telephoned the news to Bogousha in Poland and to Marzena in London.

As a very young man before the war he had been noted for his great strength and even in old age there was an almost mystical electric energy about him. Despite the severe punishment his body had taken as an underground fighter I had come to regard him as indestructible. Up to a fortnight before he died we still made love in the fullest sense of the word.

Marian and I had never spoken at any length about dying because the subject always made him very emotional, but long ago I had secretly promised myself that if he died before I did I would take his ashes back to the village where he was born and place them in the cemetery where, he had told me, his mother Stanislawa lay in an unmarked grave. He was her only child and she died in her early twenties when he was three. Her husband Jan had been killed by the Cossacks.

Although Marian had lived in England since 1960 I knew that his roots remained profoundly and unchangeably in his native soil. The fervour which lit up his whole being when he set out on a holiday to Poland, the way he avidly followed Polish radio broadcasts twice daily and the intense joy with which he listened to his large record collection of Polish music were constant proof of this.

Of course patriots the world over love their country, but I do not believe any have a more passionate attachment to their homeland than the Poles. I remember how moved I was to learn during World War II that Polish pilots flew on missions with a bag of Polish soil in their cockpits.

Funeral arrangements were in the capable hands of Ernest Free, doyen of Colchester undertakers. Father James Hawes was to conduct the service and I discussed the proposed cremation with him explaining that I wanted to take Marian's ashes to Poland. He told me that nowadays cremation was permitted by the Catholic Church.

Marian was dressed in his best dark suit and his favourite shirt and tie (whenever we were going anywhere special he always asked me to choose which shirt and tie he should wear). In his lapel was the Warsaw crest brooch he had bought back from Poland the previous summer and in one hand was his rosary.

Also in the coffin was his favourite picture of the Pope which I had bought for him in Canterbury. The natural dignity which had been so characteristically his in life remained with him in death.

When I went to the funeral parlour I kissed him and placed a red rose in his hand. Then I sat beside him for a long time recalling our life together. He had been the cornerstone of my happiness. Being Slav he was often volatile and temperamental, but also incredibly kind, generous, compassionate and unashamedly sentimental. We made a good team and he inspired in me a fierce loyalty that never wavered. After all the turmoil and heartbreak of war and the rootless existence which had followed until we met, Marian cherished home life above all things and I loved creating it for him. The birth of our son John (*Janek* as Marian always called him) was our crowning joy. Our contentment was highlighted every New Year's Eve when we always stayed up until midnight to usher in the future with a drink and an especially loving embrace. I know some people were surprised that a couple from such different backgrounds could live so happily together . . . but that is the miracle of love.

At the cremation ceremony John and I drew great comfort from the presence and floral tributes of friends and relations for whom Marian felt a genuine regard. Polish music was played at the beginning and end of the service but the hymns were English ones.

John, of whom Marian was so proud, read the following tribute to his father:

My father died on the eve of his wedding anniversary – an occasion he and my mother always celebrated with special joy because their marriage was a strong and happy one. If all had been well last Sunday I would have driven them out into the heart of the East Anglian countryside they both loved so much. They first met when he came to England under the sponsorship of the Sue Ryder Foundation of which my mother was at that time Public Relations Officer.

My father was born in southern Poland and before World War II he owned a restaurant in Zamość. After the invasion of his country the Nazis confiscated his business and he joined the Polish underground army in which he encountered a great many dangers and hardships. He was a deeply religious man of very independent spirit and natural dignity. The courage and fortitude with which he bore a severe war wound for 50 years won the admiration of all who knew him.

He was also a very private person whose life revolved entirely around his family and his home. and who took great pride in his skills as a craftsman. He loved animals and had a truly magical way with them. His favourite childhood pet was a squirrel which he took to school in his pocket, and as a man he won a reputation for being able to tame and make friends with savage horses other people had declared unmanageable. Music was another of my father's greatest delights, particularly the music of his native land.

Later this summer my mother will take his ashes to the little village in Poland where he was born. Her pilgrimage will be a final gesture of deep and abiding love.

ETERNAL PEACE BELOVED FATHER (this he spoke in Polish)

When the coffin finally glided quietly from view and the curtains closed I did not say *'Goodbye'*. My Dear Love and I still had a long way to travel together when I set out on my pilgrimage.

After a small reception at the *Red Lion Hotel* we went home and started writing individual acknowledgments to the 150 messages of condolence we had received. Polish music played softly in the background as we did so.

During July, Sue Ryder (now, of course, Lady Ryder of Warsaw) arranged for a Mass to be said for Marian in her beautiful little Chapel of St. Christopher at Cavendish and to my great pleasure she was able to be there herself. Afterwards we stayed in the Chapel to talk quietly together on our own. She had recently been widowed herself, having nursed Group Captain Cheshire devotedly during the last agonising months of his life. Her eyes were still full of grief and loneliness. I told her how very sorry I had been not to be able to accept her invitation to attend her husband's memorial service at Westminster Cathedral. A long-standing speaking engagement had prevented me from doing so. We spoke also of her current missions of mercy. She told me that her work on the Continent was becoming increasingly difficult because the Governments of today did not give her the same support as she received during the 1960's.

The undertakers packed the urn containing Marian's ashes in a sturdy cardboard box wrapped immaculately in brown paper. Several people observed that it was 'quite heavy' and this caused me a temporary dilemma. Because of a tummy rupture (since corrected by surgery) I had been warned not to carry any suitcases or indeed any weighty items. Also John would not be able to accompany me to Poland for business reasons. But I had firmly set my heart on carrying Marian's ashes with me and not dispatching them in advance. So I prayed about it. The solution was to carry the precious parcel in the crook of my left arm and to pack all the other things I would need in a zip-up shopping bag to tuck under the other arm.

During the weeks preceding my departure I regularly lifted the box into the crook of my arm and walked round with it and it did not seem heavy at all. Toiletries, night clothes, lingerie, my best black dress and a raincoat fitted miraculously into the shopping bag and left just enough space to zip it across. This, with a capacious sling bag for documents and money, took care of all my travelling requirements and my rupture gave me no trouble at all.

Planning my journey did much to soften my grief during the summer months. I would be staying with Bogousha and her husband in Zamość, a picturesque old town near the Ukrainian border which I already knew well because we had stayed there during our holiday in

1976. I decided to fly out to Warsaw and then continue down to Zamość by train.

Although I have an extensive Polish vocabulary for all occasions I made a point of learning several important new phrases. For example, I felt I should be able to explain to security men that 'This box contains the ashes of my husband' and 'Here are the official documents from the funeral director'. I bought some red and white satin ribbon (the Polish national colours) with which to embellish the urn when I reached my final destination.

Many people had said 'It will be a very sad journey for you'. But nothing could have been further from the truth. It proved to be a marvellous experience beyond all my expectations and I would not have missed it for the world.

CHAPTER NINE

A HERO'S FAREWELL

I LEFT HEATHROW on the morning flight to Warsaw on Thursday, September, 2nd exactly a year to the day since Marian had returned from his last holiday in Poland. Flying conditions were perfect and as we climbed far beyond the sun-dappled clouds to the boundless brilliant blue horizons where eternity begins, I felt a deep sense of well-being.

Two and half hours later we touched down in the Polish capital. I had reserved a room in advance for one night at an hotel close to the Central Railway Station. After resting awhile I went to the Bureau de Change and drew out a substantial supply of Polish currency. Later I telephoned my step-daughter Izabela and invited her to dine with me in the 'Old Town'. In due course I drove out by taxi to call for her at her flat in a suburb of the city. She was waiting in the garden in her most elegant clothes and, after a warm embrace, we headed for our romantic destination. We have always enjoyed an affectionate *rapport.* I was also very glad to have her guidance in paying out the newly-acquired zlotych in my wallet.

The 'Old Town' is one of Europe's magical places and I love it because it has an atmosphere reminiscent of Venice. Taxis are only allowed to set passengers down on the fringe of this quarter, but a short walk up a narrow street brought us into the vast cobbled square with its lanterns, horse-drawn carriages and shops of great character selling books, antiques and objets d'art. Buildings with richly-decorated medieval façades and candle-lit casements further enhance the highly picturesque scene.

Tourists flock to visit it. The apparently authentic mellow old-world architecture was, in fact, faithfully recreated from old historical prints and maps on a bomb-devastated site after the war, and restaurants there offer first class traditional Polish dishes in surpassingly beguiling surroundings.

Izabela and I went to Bassilik's where, in addition to the delicious cuisine, there was live music. We stepped through a massive arched doorway bright with flowers into a flag-stoned hall and continued up-stairs into a richly-furnished apartment with candle-lit tables. Our main course was savoury meat-filled dumplings (a universally popular dish), and as we dined a violinist and an accordionist stood by our table and played my favourite Polish melodies which had close associations with Marian.

Afterwards we strolled through the 'Old Town' by the light of a full moon. The whole evening was a joyous experience and I was so happy to have Marian's daughter sharing it with me.

When I breakfasted the following morning I purposely chose a table overlooking the busy street. Trams and two-coach articulated trams were taking folk to work. Among private cars nippy little Polska Fiats predominated. A roadcleaner with revolving brushes was at work. A TNT Express courier van sped by and another advertising Electrolux. Then along came a sandwich service on wheels and an ice cream van painted with an overall pattern of well-filled cones with smiling faces.

It was a grey, wet day and my train to Zamośc did not leave until mid-afternoon, but I found plenty to occupy my time in and around the railway station. After leaving my precious parcel and my hold-all at a left luggage point I strolled off to explore the large shopping complex which is an integral part of the station site.

I enjoyed reading the advertisements and merchandise labels to test my Polish and the price tags gave me my first opportunity to evaluate the currency in relation to the man and woman in the street. I soon discovered that it cost 3,000zl. to use the ladies toilet and 4,000zl. to have a cup of tea. A frankfurter sandwich was 11,000zl. and a 1,600zl. note would just about buy a box of matches. One hundred and 500zl. notes are in circulation as change but on their own are not worth a farthing. The highest value note available was for one million zl.

Notable among advertisements were ones headed 'Tomorrow You Could Be A Millionaire'. They announced the days that national lotteries would be drawn.

Also prominently located along the walls were extensive displays of photographs from current shows at various theatres in the city.

On sale were adults' and childrens' clothes, shoes, jewellery, toys, cosmetics, books (including many by well known foreign authors), newspapers, china and glass, confectionery, cigarettes, greengroceries, arts and crafts and flowers. By more than one florists' stall old ladies were seated on the ground with large quantities of loose flowers which they were sorting and trimming and arranging in bunches. Refreshment stands were numerous.

The train to Zamośc arrived well on time. When I had purchased my ticket that morning I had been assured that it went straight through to my destination, so I stepped on board anticipating an uncomplicated five-hour journey. But this did not prove to be the case.

As I settled in a corner seat I noticed that a picture of Stephenson's *Rocket* hung on the wall facing me. A crowded corridor prevented me from viewing much of the passing scenery and I only caught an occasional glimpse of the various small stations we went through. The one large town we stopped at was Lublin where many passengers alighted. I knew that we were now fast approaching Marian's home territory and eagerly I went out to stand in the corridor and watch the countryside flashing by in the gathering dusk. Next stop Chelm, I thought, and then a straight run to Zamość . . . But journey's end was not as close as I expected.

At Chelm, which is near the Ukrainian border, my fellow travellers got off and eventually I did the same. I inquired whether the train standing at the opposite platform was bound for Zamość. No, I was told, it was going to Kiev. The train to Zamość divided in two at Chelm and I had inadvertently travelled in the section that went no further.

Being a seasoned traveller I was not worried. I went to the ticket office and asked the woman in charge when there would be another train to Zamość. 'Not for two hours', she replied, adding: 'and it would not be safe for Madame to travel on a late night train full of Russian workers. Would Madame like me to telephone to a taxi driver I know?'

'Is he an honourable man, a man of good character?' I inquired. She assured me he was and when, over the telephone, a price for the fare to Zamość had been agreed, I awaited his arrival with no qualms. He was a pleasant young man, married with a small son, and he told me he had once worked for a year in London on a building site. So, in a mixture of English and Polish, we conversed all the way to Zamość.

At their flat in a leafy suburb Bogousha and her husband Vassek greeted me with demonstrative affection and I placed Marian's ashes in her hands. Tenderly she set the parcel down on a side table in their living room. She and Marian had always been very close and had shared many perils together during the war.

Despite the late hour Vassek rang my dear stepson Zygfryd and he immediately came round to welcome me. The first part of my pilgrimage was over.

The next morning Vassek drove Bogousha and myself out to the hamlet of Dub (pronounced *Doob* as in wood) where Marian was born. Our mission was to speak with the parish priest Father Józef Tucki.

The route lay through countryside that can scarcely have changed at all since Marian knew it as a small boy. Thick forests of pines and silver birches bordered long stretches of the road interspersed with fields where horses and black-and-white cows were grazing.

There were single-storey wooden homesteads set in neat, colourful gardens where sunflowers grew in profusion. Railings and fences were festooned with bunches of maize drying in the sun. At frequent intervals along the wayside were shrines adorned in Maypole style with multi-coloured ribbons and crowned with flowers.

Many houses had shrines in front gardens and I saw one nailed to a tree on the forest fringe. Above all it was the timeless quality of the landscape which captivated me . . . sights, sounds and scents that would have been familiar to Marian when he roamed there in childhood.

Father Józef lived in a pretty pink-walled house next door to Dub church and a smart red car stood in his flower-bordered forecourt. A genial man he greeted us in his office informally dressed in an open neck shirt and casual trousers, and I learnt later that he was married and had several children. Celibacy is no longer a strict rule for the clergy in this devoutly Catholic country.

I produced the necessary documents and Bogousha explained the reason for our visit. Father Józef said a special service could be held in the church the following day (which was a Sunday) at 2.00 p.m. and I paid him a generous fee.

Our next call was at the humble cottage of the gravedigger who accompanied us further down the road to the cemetery. This was a good deal larger than I had expected but otherwise much as I had pictured it in my mind's eye. It was situated in an isolated position surrounded by open fields but sheltered by plentiful trees. At the end of the rough grass track which served as the main pathway was a small chapel with steps leading up to the entrance and to the right of this lay the oldest part of the cemetery now tangled undergrowth and bushes. This was, of course, my first visit to the place but it was there, Marian had once told me, that his mother was buried in an unmarked grave and so my gaze turned in that direction with special interest. How close to her, I wondered, would his own ashes lie?

The answer was immediately at hand as the gravedigger halted at an imposing grey stone tomb half way down the main track in the more recent part of the cemetery. The headstone with carved crucifix already bore two names and the flat slab covering a vault beneath bore the words *Rodzina Podgorski* (Family Podgorski). At last I was standing by my dear love's final resting place and I liked what I saw. By tomorrow afternoon, the gravedigger said, he would have opened up the small door in the brickwork at the front of the tomb.

Before leaving the cemetery I told Bogousha that I would love to look inside the chapel. The gravedigger overheard me and promptly unlocked it and showed us round. Repairs were in progress and I thought it was beautiful.

Many graves in Dub Cemetery were very modest wooden or metal crosses, but others were quite impressive like the Podgorski one and were adorned with candles in bowls. Bogousha told me these were called *snifki* (I spell this in phonetics) and were lit on special occasions. I said I would like to buy one to bring the next day.

On the way back to Zamość we called at several farmhouses where Bogousha had friends. It was, without doubt, one of the most fascinating mornings of my life.

After lunch I joined Vassek and Zygfryd in several glasses of vodka at the living room table and found my Polish conversation became increasingly fluent as a result. This was to prove a great asset as the afternoon progressed because many more relations called in for a chat. They all brought beautiful flowers which were ceremoniously placed round the table where Marian's ashes stood. By now I had unpacked the elegant bronze coloured urn and adorned it with red and white ribbon. The floral tributes included pink lilies, orange carnations, gladioli, pom pom chrysanthemums, asters and yellow silk roses. My own flowers were fresh red roses – Marian's favourite.

The family gathering delighted me and I felt thoroughly at ease with everyone. Bogousha's daughter Elsbiéta, whose wedding Marian, John and I had attended 17 years previously, now had three sons aged three, 10 and 13. The middle boy was a particularly engaging lad who expended a great deal of patience and energy blowing up an inflatable beach ball which quickly started to go down again because of a small hole. Elsbiéta's sister Grazynka and her husband Janeusz Sokolowski were there with their two sons aged nine and 11. Both boys were mad about *Robin Hood* and I told them I knew Nottingham and Sherwood Forest. I renewed my acquaintance with Bogousha's brother Kazimierz and his attractive schoolteacher wife Teresa with whom we had stayed *en famille* at Trawniki in 1976. Albina, the thin pinched elderly worrier in the family, but very kind, arrived with an armful of freshly cut flowers from her beloved garden. She lived in a charming green-painted wooden house with carved gables. A noticeable absentee from the company was Zygfryd's wife Helena who was universally disliked because of her predatory nature. The situation clearly saddened and embarrassed Zygfryd whose visits to Bogousha were always solo ones and his tired though still handsome face touched my heart.

We spoke about Marian's holiday in Poland the previous year and about the days just before his death. I passed round my favourite photograph of him and also a recent one of John which generated a lot of interest and approval and the comment that he bore a strong resemblance to his half-brother Zygfryd.

I was asked what Colchester was like and told them about its history from Roman times onwards. Many questions were put to me about our Royal Family and particularly the *'scandal'* regarding Charles and Diana which had received considerable coverage in Polish newspapers.

A late arrival and, by common consent, the most important visitor that Saturday afternoon was Pani (the Polish for Madame) Leokadia Sokolowska, aged 80, a distinguished matriarchal figure with whom I got on extremely well. This was my first ever meeting with her. Marian's father and her father had been brothers and she showed me a photograph of herself with my dear love when he was about 12. They had been playmates in childhood and he had often visited her home. Since I had previously had no idea that this photograph existed it was of intense interest to me. There was a certain poignancy about the picture for it depicted her as a strikingly pretty girl. Now the face of the white-haired old lady who sat beside me was sadly changed and not only by age. A tumour behind her left eye had caused it to bulge grotesquely. Yet this could not detract from the innate dignity of her presence.

While Bogousha served glasses of lemon tea, salami sandwiches and cakes, arrangements for the forthcoming ceremony at Dub were discussed at length. By now, I was fully aware that Marian was going to be given a *Hero's Farewell* by a large number of people and I rejoiced at the prospect. It was all going to be so excitingly different from what I had expected when I left England.

As I lay in bed that night thinking about all the kindness and generosity that had already been paid to Marian's memory I prepared a short speech to deliver in Polish at a suitable time the next day.

On the way out to Dub we encountered many cheerful-looking families taking Sunday afternoon excursions in farm carts drawn by horses or tractors. Their seats were bales of hay covered with rugs.

By the time we arrived at the church large crowds had already gathered to pay their last respects to Marian. I knew they were saluting him not only as a local man but also as a brave wartime partisan fighter and I felt very proud.

The charming exterior of the little wooden church reminded me of those meticulous models patient craftsman fashion entirely from matchsticks. Inside it was richly decorated with cream and gilt plasterwork. On one side of the High Altar hung an icon of the legendary *Black Madonna* and on the other a large effigy of the crucified Christ. Marian's ashes were placed on a table below the High Altar between two white candles and all the floral tributes were laid on the floor around it. Sharing the chancel were a number of small litters which had been brought to the church during recent harvest celebrations. They were garlanded with ribbons, flowers and sheaves of corn and I liked them being there.

The chief mourners apart from myself were Pani Leokadia and Zygfryd. We were given upholstered chairs while the rest of the congregation filled wooden benches behind us. The unaccompanied singing was beautiful. There were no hassocks to kneel on for the prayers, but like everyone else I knelt down on the bare tiled floor.

At the cemetery gates I gave Zygfryd his father's ashes and he led our procession to the graveside. More prayers were said and the urn was placed in the vault where I saw two coffins. The flat slab of the tomb was covered with our flowers and then twelve candles in terra-cotta bowls were placed along the front. I lit the first one and other members of the family followed suit. The gorgeous blossoms and the steady golden flames made a splendid sight in the afternoon sunshine. My pilgrimage was over. I had brought Marian back to his home village to rest among his own people.

Before leaving the tomb I purposely lingered there a moment by myself. Looking towards the old part of the cemetery where Marian's mother lay in a humble grave I whispered to her: 'Thank you for giving birth to the son who became my husband'.

Then I rejoined the family and we drove to a handsome farmhouse in the next village. This was the home of one of Pani Leokadia's five sons. In a spacious room with a hand-carved ceiling and a vast mural depicting a forest in autumn, a meal of banquet-like proportions for 50 mourners was awaiting us. Such an occasion in Poland is called a *Konsolazia*, and the food had been prepared by Pani Leokadia's daughters and granddaughters. It was a house Marian knew well and he had been there the previous summer.

I sat next to Pani Leokadia at the head of the table. The food was delicious and vodka flowed freely. Many toasts were proposed and the conversation sparkled. A perfect opening came for me to stand up and deliver the short speech I had learnt off by heart the night before:

'My dear family – old people and young people – I would like to thank you with all my heart for your beautiful flowers, your many remembrances of my darling Marian and your kindness to me. Very special thanks also to the Sokolowski Family for this splendid konsolazia. I give you all my great appreciation and my blessing . . . my dear family'.

My words were warmly received and I was very glad I had done it. After emotional goodbyes to my hosts, Bogousha, Vassek, and I drove back to Zamość. It was sunset and to me the darkening countryside seemed full of Marian's spirit. In my heart I felt an infinite peace and happiness.

I did not get to bed until very late that night. Kasimierz and Teresa, Grazynka and Janeusz, and Zygfryd and his family all invited me round to their homes for further refreshments with transport laid on to take me from house to house. Nevertheless I was up at 5.30 a.m. the next morning so that Zygfryd could drive me all the way up to Warsaw. Bogousha served a hearty breakfast before I left and gave me an eighteen-inch tall figure of a Polish Father Christmas which I had admired in her bedroom the night I arrived. Henceforward he will form the centrepiece of the display I mount in my front bay window every Christmas.

The long journey to the capital was an extremely interesting one which enabled me to see many further glimpses of provincial life. We had sufficient time when we reached Warsaw to call round at Izabela's for coffee and cakes. She gave me a necklace of real amber and agates. When she accompanied us to the airport she put some binoculars in her handbag saying she wanted to follow the course of my aeroplane until it was lost to view.

On the flight home I wrote the following verse which now stands in a frame beside my favourite photograph of Marian:

Nothing has changed
And yet everything has changed,
My Dear Love has gone to his rest.
Seasons will come and go,
Tide follow tide,
In my life's ebb and flow
He's at my side.

Apart from many photographs and records of Polish music I cherish several other tangible memories of Marian . . . the jaunty straw hat he was wearing when he returned from his last trip to Poland in 1992, a beautiful Russian gold ring he gave me, a silver coin bearing the head of medieval Queen Jadwiga which I regard as a lucky talisman, richly – embellished and lovingly – inscribed Valentine cards. Most poignant of all is a small much-worn red prayer book which he carried with him during many hard, sad years before coming to England and continued to keep by his bedside until the day he died.

CHAPTER TEN

AUTUMN GARDEN

REACHING THE AGE of seventy is a notable milestone in anybody's life, but it also marks the beginning of a decade when widowhood and the loss of other relations and long-time friends are most likely to occur. It is a time, I have found, when remaining friendships become doubly precious and nostalgia can be a sweet and enduring comfort.

It was nostalgia which inspired the old world garden I had laid out by professionals at the rear of my home during 1995. The patio which is bordered by jewel bright pansies, lavender and other traditional cottage garden flowers has a sundial, bird table and green decorative metal furniture with a parasol for sunny days. When the back wall was cleared of creeper we discovered there was a ledge half way up and this provided an ideal place for a statue of St. Francis which forms the focal point of the garden with stone fan-tailed doves on either side of him.

Among ornaments on and around the patio is a statue of a cherub from Auntie Audrey's garden in Surrey and a painted figurine of a squirrel because my husband loved those little creatures so much, Honeysuckle has been planted in memory of my father, for I still recall the evening scent of this beguiling flower in country lanes during childhood holidays in Devonshire.

Roses predominate in the main flowerbed and they have been specially chosen in memory of people who were dear to me. Red roses for my husband because they always had a special significance for us; white roses for my brother Peter (a very talented poet who died in April, 1995)* because of his pure, unworldly spirit; orange roses for my other brother John (who died in 1944) because of his vivid personality; yellow roses for Auntie Audrey because she was a warm and sweet lady, and pink roses for my mother who loved all gardens.

As for what flower might be planted in my memory – I wish for nothing grand or exotic but something symbolising cheerfulness of heart. Marigolds perhaps because they would recall my love of simple country gardens, or sunflowers because they would echo halcyon summer days I shared with Marian in Poland.

Nostalgia is also represented in my garden by the spicy fragrance of rosemary which is Sue Ryder's personal symbol on everything connected with her work, and by pots of geraniums to remind me of my travels round the Mediterranean.

When the plot was being cleared I asked the gardeners to spare the solitary five foot rose tree which stood in the jungle wilderness but

* A Memorial Collection of his work is in Colchester Central Library.

was so choked by weeds that it was barely alive. It was here when we moved in 27 years ago and in those days bore a wonderful crop of deep pink blossoms. When freed from its bonds and carefully nurtured it began to flourish abundantly again.

During its first season my new garden has been the scene of much laughter and good fellowship over cream teas by day and glasses of wine at dusk. Next summer I would also like to make it a venue for small-scale musical soirées and poetry readings. Whenever the weather is warm enough I always enjoy writing out there for my pen still remains very busy with articles, short stories and poetry.

Literary connections continue to play an important part in my life. As a member of the Newstead Abbey Byron Society I regularly make trips up to Nottinghamshire to take part in events at the Poet's magnificent ancestral home and am a keen contributor to the prestigious Newsletters.

Some years ago, through my late brother Peter, I was introduced to the Essex Poetry & Prose Society which has given me tremendous pleasure ever since. Distinguished poet Pauline Stainer is a founder-member and the chairman is Diana Mann a talented woman of great charm.

Meetings are held once a month in the drawing room of a gracious period house at Castle Hedingham called *Astles*. This is the home of Rose Kelk and Peggy Garge two extremely hospitable and delightful sisters. Our gatherings, which feature poetry readings or talks on literary personalities, are followed by a delicious homemade tea. Society members are gifted and stimulating company. I have given them talks on Byron, Charlotte Brontë and Thomas Moore among others and feel proud to have been made an honorary life member.

In September, 1995, I won a silver cup for the following humorous verses:

The Gipsy Violinist

I'm the hallmark of all cafés with a Continental flavour
Where the scampi and the goulash are not all the patrons savour.
It's my job to promote amongst the jaded clientele
An appetite for other spicy offerings as well.
In my braided red bolero and a shirt that's quite revealing
I sing my sad Slav love songs with explosive fire and feeling.
I cast a spell around the place directly I begin,
The epitome of passion with my gipsy violin.

With my ardour soaring fast between the borsch soup and the caviar
I sing of stormy wooings on the shores of wild Calabria.
To suit the meat and veg. I switch to quite another area
And tell of sly abductions in the mountains of Bulgaria.
To give your flame-ringed crêpe Suzette that extra bit of zest
I turn to Magyar courtships in the heart of Budapest,
With Tokay flowing freely and a czardas in full spin
I strike a tender tremolo upon my violin.

I wend my wistful, wailing way from table on to table
Becoming Cupid's right hand man as hard as I am able.
A whisper from my sighing strings yields magic transformations
And blasé, balding businessmen all leap to action stations.
While pimply youths with weedy frames all feel like Casanova
And skinny girls with mousey looks start blossoming all over.
It is our aim to fan the flame, me and my violin,
But don't you dare *to label it an instrument of sin!*

And when a girl is worth a look I flirt a bit – mock seriously
And indicate my mood by pizzicato-ing deliriously.
Then she's convinced I must have close relations in Seville,
But really I was born within a few miles of Bexhill.
There is not one *romantic touch in life that I can boast,*
I catch the last bus home to have a meal of beans on toast.
In a decaying boarding-house kept by an aged Finn
Who can't abide my singing or my gipsy violin.

I am often asked to give talks on 'My Life as a Writer' and this is something else I much enjoy. Now, as always throughout my life, I love meeting new people and particularly chatting individually with members of my audience afterwards, for often they have fascinating experiences to recount.

Now that I have finished this book I would like to get involved in contributing to the *Talking Newspaper for the Blind.*

I remain in close touch with friends abroad – especially Jennifer in Athens and Loredana in Venice with both of whom I have shared such exceptionally happy times.

My ties with Marian's family in Poland are still strong. Next time I visit them I hope to fulfil a longstanding ambition to see a unique herd of bison in their natural primeval forest habitat. The last bison roaming wild in Europe are only found on Polish soil.

More foreign travel features prominently in my future plans. I would love to be in Bethlehem at Christmas-time and also see a performance by the Bolshoi Ballet at their own theatre in Moscow.

With friends nearer home I make frequent excursions to London or out into the heart of my beloved East Anglian countryside to lunch at a rural pub.

Every December for many years a pre-Christmas lunch has been held by a group of my newspaper colleagues at some local upmarket eating-house noted for its cuisine. Masterminded by Barbara Butler and Mary Adams this has now become a firmly-established tradition no guest would dream of missing. Even in retirement I still receive an invitation and it is an event I look forward to tremendously.

Just before my 73rd birthday in October, 1995, I had to have a mastectomy – perhaps the form of surgery all women dread most. To anyone in this situation I would simply say 'never feel sorry for yourself, keep smiling and above all get on with living'.

While I was in hospital a visiting friend told me: 'You are the same tonic you have always been. I wish we could bottle you – or at least your joy in life!' Those words meant a great deal to me.

My own philosophy is admirably expressed by Winston Churchill, in his famous lines:

'Let us be contented with what has happened to us and thankful for all we have been spared. Let us accept the natural order in which we move. Let us reconcile ourselves to the mysterious rhythm of our destinies, such as they must be in this world of space and time. Let us treasure our joys, not bewail our sorrows. The glory of light cannot exist without its shadows. Life is whole and good and ill must be accepted together'.

PRAYER I WROTE ON MY 70TH BIRTHDAY OCTOBER 16TH, 1992

My dear Lord and lifelong friend I am writing this prayer of thanksgiving in a lovely church in the town where I was born.

I humbly offer my heartfelt thanks for being brought safely to my seventieth year. In fair days and dark days I have always been aware of your presence beside me sharing both my joys and my sorrows.

I thank you for giving me a cheerful disposition, a strong constitution and a boundless enthusiasm for Life.

I thank you for giving me a talent with words which has brought me such abundant creative fulfilment from my earliest years, an exciting career and sense of achievement.

I thank you for giving me a spirit of adventure which has enabled me to travel through some of the most beautiful and often remote places on earth – places where I have felt especially close to you because of the glories of Nature.

I thank you for encouraging me to step forward into the unknown along unfamiliar paths where new and enriching experiences have awaited me. With your hand in mine I have never been afraid of challenges and changes.

I thank you for the enduring friendships I have made both in my own country and throughout the world. I count these among the greatest blessings of my life.

I thank you for family ties which become increasingly precious with the passing of the years.

I give thanks for being married to a good and faithful man and for having a son of whom I am so proud.

Finally, dear Lord and lifelong friend, please grant that the years still left to me are full and productive ones and that my zest for Life will remain undiminished.

Amen.

This was written when a little girl asked me what Christmas was like when I was a child

A Carol of Childhood

Dear memories of Christmas past come flooding back to me;
Of childhood hearth adorned with holly from our garden tree –
So old and yet of wondrous yield each year with berries bright,
A frozen pond where robins skated to our great delight.
A swing we loved to ride upon through bracing winter air,
Herbs grown beside our kitchen door to spice our festive fare.
And in our hall a glittering pine with presents in its shade,
And nuts, shortbread and ginger wine upon a table laid,
With sugar-latticed lantern sweets and fruits of marzipan,
And figs and dates from Palestine where Christmas-time began.
While on our nursery window sill the Holy Stable stood
With gaily-painted figures and a cradle carved in wood.
Two smiling angels knelt each side with wings of silver spun
And lutes to play a lullaby to Mary and her Son.
Our eyes would scan the bedtime sky beyond our garden wall
To find among that twinkling throng the brightest star of all.

And music-making filled our home like larks upon the wing,
Each room and rafter, step and stair with gladness echoing.
While genial, much-loved Uncle Jack a tenor of great charm
Sang ballads in the parlour in a voice manly and warm.
And when the one-armed lamp-lighter had been along our street,
A brass band came a-carolling to make our joy complete.
Then wise and gifted Grandpa Nunn would set aside his rôles
Of pharmacist and councillor (he topped the Borough polls),
To masquerade as Santa Claus at family party-time
And book a theatre box for us to see a pantomime,
Where Grandmama would join us in her amber beads and lace
And chocolate creams in paper frills were given pride of place.
I wore my grand occasions dress – green velvet with a rose –
And soft bronze leather dancing pumps with pom-pons on the toes.
And what a thrill when dimming lights veiled my enraptured look
As gilded curtains opened like the covers of a book!

One frosty morn a straw-filled chest from Devon would arrive
Containing ham and clotted cream and honey from the hive,
A fresh plump fowl, a rich fruit cake and glacé plums and pears;
Grandparents in the West Country this custom kept for years.
Our eager hands would delve into the crisp gold packaging
And find a porcelain dish, a toy, a necklace or a ring,
A Noah's Ark tin of biscuits or a puppet on a string.
No High Street store with 'Fairy Grotto' or a 'Magic Cove'
Could match the hidden treats within that annual treasure trove.
Age has not dimmed those childhood scenes and happily tonight
I sit recalling Christmas past by Memory's candlelight.

Illustrations

Illustrations are from mainly private sources,
but grateful acknowledgements are due to:–
Essex County Newspapers Ltd.,
Nottingham Evening Post
and
Adrian Rushton